In the Middle

Writing, Reading, and Learning
with Adolescents

In the Middle

Writing, Reading, and Learning with Adolescents

Nancie Atwell

BOYNTON/COOK PUBLISHERS
HEINEMANN
PORTSMOUTH, NH

Boynton/Cook Publishers
A Division of
Heinemann Educational Books, Inc.
70 Court Street, Portsmouth, NH 03801

First paperback edition 1987
First hardcover edition 1989

Library of Congress Cataloging-in-Publication Data

Atwell, Nancie.
  In the middle.

  Bibliography: p
  1. Language arts (Secondary) — United States.
2. English language — Study and teaching (Secondary) —
United States. 3. English language — United States —
Composition and exercises. I. Title.
LB1631.A72   1986   428'.007'12   86-24408
ISBN 0-86709-163-0 (Paperback)
ISBN 0-86709-164-9 (Hardcover)

Photographs by Robert Mitchell

Printed in the United States of America

89   90   10   9   8   7

for Toby,
and for Anne

Acknowledgments

In the Middle is a book about teaching and learning, mine and my students'. I am grateful to many teachers for what I've learned about writing and reading.

I am grateful to the past and present writing teachers of Boothbay Region Elementary School: Connie Bataller, Patty Bell-Rines, Pam Brackett, Alan Burgess, Judy Burgess, Judy Calhoun, Ruth Davison, Alice Fossett, Cindy Greenleaf, Lee Hall, Pam Hall, Jo Haney, Priscilla Lewis, Connie MacCarthy, Debbie Matthews, Donna Maxim, Anne Niles, Joyce Parent, Nancy Tindal, Kathie Trafzer Sherman, Debbie Vermillion, Gloria Walter, Nancy Wheeler, and Jane Williams. I am particularly grateful to Susan Stires for what she knows and how she knows it — and for listening. Susan never once objected to those afternoons I invited her for a drink, then pulled out my latest draft. With these thoughtful and committed colleagues I learned most of what I know about our students.

I am grateful to other teachers:

- to Susan Sowers for inspiring what happened at my school;
- to Dixie Goswami for making me believe I had something to say and that I could say it;
- to Denise David and Thomas Newkirk for helpful response to early drafts;
- to Lucy Calkins for her insights into the art of teaching;
- to Donald Murray for inventing writing process teaching and for his generosity in sharing what he knows — often before he knows he knows it; and
- to Donald Graves for all the good talk about writing, reading, teaching, and kids; for showing me how to move out from behind the big desk; and for encouraging this book and a whole nation of writing teachers.

I am especially grateful to my friend and colleague Mary Ellen Giacobbe, from whom we all learned how to listen, wait, and nudge. Her voice can be heard throughout this book.

And I am grateful every day for my best teachers: all the writers and readers of 8A, 8B, and 8C. This book would not be if not for you. Thank you for one of the happiest and most productive times of my life.

I also wish to acknowledge the role played by Robert Dyer, Boothbay Region Elementary School Principal, and Ronald Corkum, former Superintendent of Schools. Because they allowed teachers to learn from our students and each other, we were able to create a model for teacher inquiry that benefited schools and children far beyond the Boothbay peninsula.

I'm thankful, too, to Lois Jones of the Maine Department of Educational and Cultural Services for her assistance as administrator of the old E.S.E.A. Title IV-C, our original funding agency; to my typist Geraldine Bell for making sense of the messiest of manuscripts; and to Robert Mitchell for his photographs that show workshops in action.

I was very lucky to have Peter Stillman as my editor. This book was long overdue and I will always be grateful for his encouragement and patience — and for my collection of some of the funniest correspondence any editor wrote to any author.

Finally, I am luckiest to have Toby McLeod. He is the most literate person I know. From him I learned how to read literature, how to love it, and how to share that passion with others.

Foreword

At 7:30 p.m. on Monday, February 21, 1983, twelve professors from the English and Education Departments at the University of New Hampshire met to examine the writing of one middle school teacher's students. They had heard about the writing of these children and wanted to see for themselves. The teacher was Nancie Atwell from the small town of Boothbay Harbor, Maine. I was fortunate enough to be one of those professors who sat in a circle randomly perusing the mass of student folders from a large box on the floor.

I remember looking across the circle at Don Murray, who shook his head as if to say, "Can you believe this?" The variety of student voices, range of genres, uses of writing, and experimentations were of a quality few of us had ever seen before. Tom Newkirk said, "I'd like to have some of these students in freshman composition." In a typical folder I'd see a male scrawl several sentences long in September grow into major pieces of confident prose by February. *Esquire* magazine heard about the work of Nancie Atwell and chose her as one of the fifty men and women under forty "Who Are Changing America" featured in its December 1984 issue.

Here at last is the book that tells the story of how Nancie Atwell changed from a teacher who gave pet writing assignments thirteen years ago to a teacher who learns from her students in order to challenge them still more. Students rebel, approaches don't work, misunderstandings occur, yet Nancie learns and we learn with her as we share in the victories of student texts published here in this book.

For some time the nation has been preoccupied with student improvement in writing and reading. National reports speak of student failure, slipping scores, or at best, "no change." Some improvement is seen in the elementary years but by the middle school and senior high school years problems are particularly acute. Teachers have less time with their students, and the accumulation of school failure causes still greater problems in student attitude. The recent report card from the National Assessment of Educational Progress (1986) reminds us that although student skills are adequate, there remain major problems in text coherence, and the ability of students to use information to persuade is severely lacking. Worse, there are few classrooms to which we can point and say with assurance, "There's good writing." Still more rare, "There's a book that shows how teachers in the upper years can help students improve their literacy." *In the Middle* is just that book.

The book is filled with the details of conducting conferences in reading and writing, mini-lessons, working with various genres, the uses of time, grading and proofreading. Useful stuff, but still not the heart of the book. The power of the book is in the details of engagement between a teacher who has brought the full meaning of literacy into the lives of students — gangling, emotion-filled adolescents who confess they are too busy to read and lie about the numbers of books they've read in the past. Readers will see students deal with the deaths of parents, divorce, write letters to the editor, and struggle with what it means to be an emerging adult. Through dialogue journals Nancie Atwell writes some 2000 entries to students extending them into new books, articles, or poems, all within the context of growing up. Her students gossip in journals to each other about the poetry and books they read. They speak, read, and write to live.

Readers looking for methods or step-by-step approaches to a sure-fire literacy program will be disappointed. Atwell has no method. Rather, she provides a full-immersion approach to reading and writing, an immersion not unlike the acquisition of a new language, where only the new language can be spoken. There is relevant, literate talk in this room; there are no canned lessons, assigned topics, workbooks, language arts textbooks, or the following of prescribed curriculum guides.

Immersion is possible because Nancie Atwell herself is immersed in her own literate engagement with the world. Readers who try to bypass a re-engagement in their own reading and writing will say, "Atwell's approach doesn't work." They'll be right, of course; it won't work for them. I was impressed by the numbers of books Nancie carries in her head as she refers students to new authors. She knows the students and the books that will help them as she provides new opportunities for learning because of the literacy that crosses her dining room table. In this book the dining room table becomes the symbol for her own literacy. She has spent thousands of hours around that dining room table reading, writing, and sharing books with her husband, Toby.

Back in May of 1984 Nancie Atwell demonstrated with middle school students before a gallery of teachers at the International Reading Association convention in Atlanta, Georgia. I remember her words as she emerged from the demonstration. "Gosh," she said, "This stuff works anywhere." That was the first time she'd tried her approaches with students outside of Booth-bay Harbor. What happened was no accident. She brought the same open, intense, literate engagement to her student conferences. Soon the students from Atlanta were sharing their stories, writing, and telling about how they composed. Through this book we can find as she did that informed, caring literacy works anywhere.

For professionals who wish to bring that same intensity to their own reading and writing, and then to the classrooms, this book will be an adventure in learning. There's plenty of common sense here. I remember being struck by her simple decision to have students read in school. She reasoned that if they read in school they'd read outside of school. When I taught I always assigned reading for homework. Her students are known for their travel to book stores in other towns in search of good books to read. Not surprisingly, they read an average of 35 books a year. Again, the intensity. She shows how adolescents need to write and read books in order to grow at a precarious time in their lives. I think she answers the greatest question for teachers and students today: "Why would anyone want to read and write?"

Teachers will meet their own adolescents on these pages and be able to help them. There is enough detail in classroom description and student text to do that. Because *In the Middle* was written from the inside by a teacher who understands the perplexities of erratic development, we are able to apply her recommendations for planning, mini-lessons in reading and writing, response to texts, grading, and organizing a classroom. We can make these translations not because of methodologies, but because these practicalities are joined with the principles of literate development within the lives of real students.

Donald H. Graves

Reference:

Langer, J. A. (with A. Applebee and I. Mullis) 1986. The writing report card: Writing achievement in American schools. Princeton, NJ: Educational Testing Service.

Contents

In the Middle

*Writing, Reading, and Learning
with Adolescents*

SECTION I
Beginnings

Readers in their workshop

CHAPTER 1

Learning How to Teach

". . . the logic by which we teach is not always the logic by which children learn."
Glenda Bissex

I confess. I started out as a creationist. The first days of every school year I created; for the next thirty-six weeks I maintained my creation. My curriculum. From behind my big desk I set it in motion, managed and maintained it all year long. I wanted to be a great teacher — systematic, purposeful, in control. I wanted great results from my great practices. And I wanted to convince other teachers that this creation was superior stuff. So I studied my curriculum, conducting research designed to show its wonders. I didn't learn in my classroom. I tended and taught my creation.

These days, I learn in my classroom. What happens there has changed; it continually changes. I've become an evolutionist, and the curriculum unfolds now as my kids and I learn together. My aims stay constant — I want us to go deep inside language, using it to know and shape and play with our worlds — but my practices evolve as eighth graders and I go deeper. This going deeper is research, and these days my research shows me the wonders of my kids, not my methods. But it has also brought me full circle. What I learn with these students, collaborating with them as a writer and reader who wonders about writing and reading, makes me a better teacher — not great maybe, but at least grounded in the logic of learning, and growing.

This book describes what I've learned so far about teaching junior high writing and reading. It shows what we do in the classroom and why we do it. It tells stories about my teaching and my kids' learning, stories set in the middle school years in the middle of literacy.

The word *story* can be traced to the Greek word *eidenai*, which means "to know." As a reader, I look to stories to help me understand and give meaning to my life. As a writer, I tell stories so I may understand, teaching myself and trying to teach others through the actions and reactions of those "people on the page," Donald Murray's "little scenes in which people reveal both themselves and the subject" (1982, p. 40). This book tells stories because it's the best way I know to reveal myself, my students, and my subject:

helping adolescents put written language at the crux of their emotional, social, and intellectual worlds. Framing these is my own story, the evolution that brought me out from behind my big desk and allowed my students to find their ways inside writing and reading.

In the Middle begins here, with my story, because I think how I ended up where I have is the best invitation I can extend to other secondary English teachers to come out from behind their own big desks. I didn't intuit or luck into this place, and I didn't arrive overnight. I paved the way through writing and reading about writing, through uncovering and questioning my assumptions, through observing kids and trying to make sense of my observations, through dumb mistakes, uncertain experiments, and, underneath it all, the desire to do my best by my kids.

A lot of the time, doing my best hurt. It meant looking hard at what I was doing and asking kids to do. It meant learning — and admitting — that I was wrong. And, most painful of all, it meant letting go of my cherished creation.

I learn in my classroom these days because I abandoned that creation. I had to. When I stopped focusing on me and my methods and started observing students and their learning, I saw a gap yawning between us — between what I did as language teacher and what they did as language learners. I saw that my creation manipulated kids so they bore sole responsibility for narrowing the gap, and my students either found ways to make sense of and peace with the logic of my teaching, or they failed the course. In truth, it was I who needed to move, to strike out for some common ground. I learn in my classroom these days because I moved, because the classroom became a reading and writing workshop, a new territory my students and I could inhabit together.

I'm beginning with the story of how this workshop came to be because its genesis sets the stage for the chapters that follow. All the particular methods of writing and reading workshop grow from my particular experience; I'm hoping other teachers, in sharing my experience, will grow right along with me. Above all, I'm hoping the story of my evolution points to one crucial and heartening message: if I've ended up here, anyone can. So I'll start ten years ago, when the gap was at its widest, with an eighth grader who taught me that I didn't know enough.

Jeff

In 1975 I became the junior high English department at Boothbay Harbor Grammar School. My husband and I moved to Maine from New York State, where I'd taught at a middle school in Tonawanda, just outside Buffalo. We moved because of Maine.

That summer we wended our way up the coast, then down the twelve-mile peninsula to Boothbay. We were looking for a small, beautiful place to vacation; instead, we found a small, beautiful place we wanted to live. It really is small. The combined population of all the communities nestled along the peninsula comes to just over four thousand. And it really is beautiful. The sea is everywhere — coves and harbors, salt pond marshes and mud flats, tidal rivers and fresh water lakes — and it's everywhere surrounded by masses of pines and firs and birches.

The last day of our vacation we drove one last time around Southport Island, feeling sick about heading back to Buffalo. Toby parked at Hendricks Head beach and we sat staring at our Triple-A maps—and the lighthouse and the breakers and each other. I asked, "What do you suppose you could do if you wanted to live here? You know, as a job?" Toby said, "Well, you're a teacher."

I was a teacher. There was an opening. I got the job. We put a new tail-pipe on our old Valiant, rented a truck, loaded our furniture, tranquilized our dog, and returned to Boothbay Harbor on Labor Day weekend. I was twenty-three years old, and I'd been teaching just over a year.

The first time I saw my new classroom was the day before I was to teach in it. The junior high building was a two-story brick bunker separated from the grammar school proper — a classic, clapboard schoolhouse—by ledge, playground, and tradition. I walked up the bunker's dark stairwell and found my room — its linoleum floor half gone, bare light-bulbs hanging from a falling tile ceiling, and all the walls green and peeling. One wall, plywood and portable, divided into halves what had once been a normal-sized classroom. Terry, the science-social studies department, taught next door. The next day, when our students arrived, I discovered every word said in either room was perfectly audible in the other.

The principal handed me the junior high language arts curriculum, which turned out to be a copy of my schedule: so many class periods each day of my two subjects, reading and English. Then he scurried back across the blacktop to the safety of K–6 and white clapboard. I took a good look around.

No books sat on my dusty shelves. No papers filled the rattle-trap file cabinet. But there were twenty-seven desks to somehow squeeze into place. The next morning, when the first class of twenty-seven eighth graders chose their seats, one of them was Jeff. He was hard to miss.

Jeff was big, almost sixteen. His parents traveled because of their work, and they'd withdrawn him from school on and off over the years to take him with them. Because he hadn't grown up with his classmates and had missed so much school, Jeff talked to almost no one and was almost always alone. He stood out academically too. His reading and writing abilities were the lowest I've ever encountered.

Jeff could barely read the primary level texts the reading coordinator provided. He couldn't distinguish some letters from others — *m* from *n* or *d* from *b*. He could spell his name, the names of his brothers and sisters, and maybe two dozen simple words. I spoke to his previous years' teachers and heard six versions of the same report: they'd done what they could for Jeff in the limited time they'd had him, tried to provide appropriate remedial work, and either kept him back or, because he was just too big, promoted him to the next grade. In a conference with his mother, she told me Jeff was learning disabled and nothing could be done for him.

By the end of September I'd banished memories of my pretty Tonawanda classroom and its suburban kids. I started to learn about life in rural

Maine from my new students, whose families mostly made a hard living from the sea — small boat building, fishing, Boothbay's seasonal tourists. And I faced up to life in the bunker. I covered the peeling paint with Argus sensitivity posters. I demanded money for books. I cadged paper and folders for writing. And I took up the challenge of doing something for Jeff.

At recess time, Jeff stayed in most days to talk to me or Terry, whichever of us didn't have playground duty. I liked him. He knew about things I didn't — boats and sailing and the Southwest. But I did know something about books on those subjects. *Dove, Kon-Tiki, Ram, Survive the Savage Sea*, and *The Teachings of Don Juan* became the texts for Jeff's remedial reading course, while the other kids suffered the new literature anthology. I wanted to inundate Jeff with reading experience by endowing all his reading experiences with huge measures of personal meaning. All that fall and winter during reading class I gave him time and books, and he struggled to read. All that fall and winter he took my breath away again and again as I watched him break through to meaning and teach himself to read — as he moved his finger and lips, tracing each word, then abandoned pointing and voicing when they got in the way of his sheer pleasure in the stories. And all that fall and winter, as I denied this same kind of personal meaning in my English course, Jeff absolutely baffled me when it came time to write.

I did have a writing program, one developed with Tonawanda colleagues and Charles Cooper, then at the University of Buffalo. In theory and practice the program drew heavily on James Moffett's hierarchy of discourse (1976); its basic tenet was that students learn to write by working systematically through an assigned sequence of modes — drama to narrative to idea writing — with extensive pre- and post-writing activities. Cooper and some of us had co-authored an article in *English Journal* describing the methodology — my first professional publication. I was wedded to this program.

I had a writing assignment for each week of the school year, my own composition treasure trove. Students role-played, then wrote monologues. Or they talked in small groups, then wrote dialogues. Or they read selections from an anthology, then wrote fictional narratives. Then I wrote all over their drafts and they "revised." On Friday I collected all the compositions. On Saturday I avoided the room where they lay awaiting me. On Sunday I wrote all over them, recorrected too many of the same mistakes, then started pumping myself up for Monday morning's pre-writing activity. Whatever that activity, the resulting compositions always broke neatly into three divisions. There were six "gifted" writers who made my task their own and did something wonderful with it, fifteen kids who did the assignment more or less adequately, and six whose papers I chalked up to poor effort or low ability.

This writing program fit my assumptions about junior high students and writing instruction. I assigned topics because I believed that most of my kids were so intimidated by expressing themselves on paper they wouldn't write without a prompt, and also because I believed that my structures and strictures were necessary for kids to write well. When it came right down to it, though, I assigned topics because I believed that my ideas were more credible and important than any my kids might possibly entertain. And from my perspective — that big desk at the front of the classroom — it looked as if real writing were going on out there. Then I came up against Jeff.

One of the assignments involved uncovering memories of personal experiences, chaining these on paper, talking about them, choosing one, and writing. All my eighth graders worked through the prescribed pre-writing procedures. Except Jeff. He spent the period whispering to himself as he drew a picture of a boy kneeling on a beach in front of a pitched tent. At the end of class he folded up his drawing and took it home. The next day Jeff came to school with a finished first draft — an account of his baby brother's death on a Mexican beach. In fact, it was a finished piece. Although I wrote questions all over it that pushed him to reflect and elaborate, Jeff just copied it over, one excruciating letter at a time.

This became his pattern. At school Jeff drew a becalmed sailboat; at home he wrote a *Dove*-like short story. He sketched a desert scene during the day and that night wrote about peyote, witch doctors, and Don Juan. I developed a pattern too. My voice regularly sounded on the other side of the plywood wall, "Jeff, stop drawing and *get to work.*"

I coped by resorting to the only teaching strategy I knew. I made assumptions. Then I tested them. When they didn't hold water, I made new assumptions.

For example, Jeff's drafts weren't badly misspelled, so I asked him about their relative accuracy. He said, "My sister helps me when I get stuck." I decided he wasn't writing in class because asking for help in front of the other kids would embarrass him. I told him not to worry about spelling on first drafts, that he and I could work on correctness later on. Jeff agreed not to worry. Then he drew all through the next day's writing class.

I thought Jeff was distracted by the noisy classroom. I assumed he didn't want the other kids to see how slowly he wrote. I blamed his lack of self-confidence. I guessed he was frustrated by the absence of an art program. My theories and remedies accumulated, and Jeff continued to draw in class and write at home. I never asked him why. After suffering my remonstrations for almost half a school year, Jeff ran out of patience. One morning when he stayed in during recess he let me have it: "Listen, Ms. Atwell. This is the way I do it, the way I write. As long as I get it done, what do you care?" He was so vehement I backed off, finally conceding his right to use whatever method worked for him — just as long as I got my requisite number of finished products to file away in his folder.

By the end of the year Jeff's writing folder was as fat as many of the others. And although he still drew in his spare time, he seldom drew during the last months' writing classes. Suddenly, he wrote. Maybe something in Jeff had changed. Maybe persevering in the face of his teacher's stony disapproval finally became too much for him. Whatever the reason, I didn't ask. I just held my breath each Monday that spring and hoped he'd get down to the task I'd set.

Then Jeff moved on to high school. New kids moved in. And I taught my curriculum all over again.

Two years after Jeff, I had reason to be grateful for his perseverance. A friend sent me a volume of papers presented at a conference at S.U.N.Y.

Buffalo; among them was Donald Graves's "The Child, the Writing Process, and the Role of the Professional" (1975) in which Graves described his early observations of seven-year-old writers. One, John, wrote extremely slowly, spoke aloud as he wrote, proofread at the single word level, and rehearsed his writing through drawing. That is, he drew a picture in order to plan his writing. Graves went on to suggest that teachers look for and accommodate young writers' natural patterns of behavior.

Graves's words rang loud in my head for days. Seven-year-old John called up too many images of sixteen-year-old Jeff, images I wanted to forget. Instead, I remembered — how I'd done my level best to overlook and overcome all evidence that my helpful structures had served Jeff as constraints. And in Jeff's case, the evidence was blatant — all that talking to himself and all those drawings. I remembered the other students who'd sat in front of my big desk, writers of whom I knew little beyond the degree to which they carried out my Monday morning assignments.

I was lucky Jeff had insisted I let him go his own way. But I'd missed the chance to understand what I was seeing and support what he was doing, to talk with him about his drawing and writing, to learn from him how to help him. And even if I'd had the background of Graves's early research, what would I have looked for and asked about? I didn't know.

What I did know was this: kids can't be the only learners in a classroom. I also had to learn. Common sense, good intentions, wide reading, and the world's best writing programs aren't enough. As Graves observed in the conclusion of his 1975 report:

> It is entirely possible to read about children, review research and text-books about writing, "teach" them, yet still be completely unaware of their processes of learning and writing. Unless we actually structure our environments to free ourselves for effective observation and participation in all phases of the writing process, we are doomed to repeat the same teaching mistakes again and again.

I didn't want to be doomed to blunder forever at my kids' expense. Two years after Jeff, I was teaching in a brand-new, consolidated elementary school. My room had carpeting, books and book shelves, fluorescent lights, wall-to-wall Argus posters, and plenty of room for desks to be arranged however I chose. I had a new, supportive principal. I even had colleagues; in the new school I was one of three junior high English teachers. Yet I felt doomed. How could I learn about writing? How could I learn to look, and how could I make sense of what I saw? How could I learn anything at all in Boothbay Harbor, Maine?

On the Verge of Learning: Bread Loaf

The next summer I left Maine for seven weeks to try to begin to learn. The Bread Loaf School of English Program in Writing was in its second year. Paul Cubeta, Bread Loaf's director, had secured full-tuition grants for English teachers from rural schools, and I qualified. My qualifying essay was the story of Jeff and me.

I chose Bread Loaf because I thought its catalogue promised resources Boothbay Harbor couldn't offer, but when I got there, Dixie Goswami, my teacher, persisted in inviting me to become *my own resource*, to learn about writing firsthand by becoming a writer and researcher. All that summer I wrote, looked at how I wrote, and thought about what my discoveries meant for my kids as writers. It was a summer of contradictions.

I saw that the choices I made as a writer — deciding how, when, what, and for whom I'd write — weren't options available to the writers in my classroom. But I also saw an unbridgeable gap between my students and me. As an adult writer, I knew my intentions and ways to act on them. As an English teacher, I knew only the safety of my assumptions about students: their need for my pre-writing structures and post-writing strictures.

When Bread Loaf ended and school started again, I went right back to my program. But this time around I tried to open up the structures and strictures. I gave kids more options and made my assignments more flexible — now they had a choice of four role-play situations and could write the required monologue as any one of six fictional characters. And this time around I started writing with my students, taking on the tasks I gave them. It was a daunting experience.

My assigned poetry was formulaic and cute. My assigned narratives never went beyond first draft; I wrote them at the breakfast table the day they were due. My assigned essays consisted of well-organized and earnest cliches. But the worst was the assigned daily journal write. Every English class started with an enforced ten-minute "free" write, and I either had nothing to say or so much that ten minutes was far too brief a stretch.

All the while I was writing this awful stuff I was conducting research. I wanted to show the beneficial effects on their writing when students viewed their teacher as a writer. But I wasn't writing; I was performing. I did my real writing at home, mostly poetry and letters for me and for people I cared about. I wasn't even conducting research; I was method-testing, trying to prove the integrity of my creation. In January I called off my research project and buried my writing portfolio in the back of a file drawer.

I'm a good rationalizer, and I rationalized hard that winter. What I needed were even more creative, more open topics. I needed thrilling pre-writing activities. I needed better students — kids who could consistently make my assignments their own, who didn't "revise" by recopying and changing three words, who came to me prepared by their teachers to write well. I needed better colleagues.

This last was my favorite rationalization. I assumed the classic stance of secondary English teachers everywhere: if you elementary teachers had taught properly, I wouldn't have to work so hard. On our language arts curriculum committee I made an officious case for more creative writing in the elementary grades. The chief beneficiary of all this creative writing would, of course, be me. If someone else moved these kids to show some imagination and take some initiative before junior high, all I'd have to do when they came to me was frost the cake. So I passed around copies of my best creative writing recipes and held forth about THE composing process, that lockstep sequence I orchestrated every Monday through Friday. And I was generally, justifiably ignored.

Not one of my colleagues — and some had Masters degrees plus forty hours — had ever attended a course or workshop concerned with the teaching of writing. In that respect, their undergraduate and graduate training was typical: in an informal survey of 36 New England universities, Graves (1978) found 169 courses dealing with instruction in reading and only two courses in teaching writing. Teachers needed information about writing, but the information I shared and the way I shared it didn't help them. Boothbay's K–7 students continued to not write. Their teachers continued to follow — or not — a language arts curriculum consisting of grade-level skills lists patched together from textbooks and other schools' curriculum guides. And I continued privately, and not so privately, to lay blame.

In the early spring of 1980, we started a new round of curriculum development. Eight of us from grades K–8 volunteered to serve on a language arts committee whose task was to produce a new curriculum guide. Gloria Walter, our chair, suggested that we begin by posing questions the committee could investigate. So we posed questions, settling finally on the query: How Do Human Beings Acquire Language? An obviously overambitious question, it at least put us on a new track. I couldn't lecture or condescend (although I did feel pretty confident that the answer would point toward a writing program rather like my own). We couldn't exchange gimmicks, borrow philosophies, or draw up skills sequences. Instead, the committee began looking for resources that could help us find answers. Remembering Jeff, I sought out Donald Graves. He responded by sending us Susan Sowers.

Graves, Sowers, and Lucy Calkins were then nearing the end of their second year as researchers-in-residence at Atkinson Academy, a public elementary school in rural New Hampshire. Under a grant from the National Institute of Education, they spent these two years following sixteen first and third grade writers and their teachers (Graves, 1983). They observed students in their classrooms *in the process* of writing in order to discover how children develop as writers and how schools can help.

Susan came to our curriculum committee with copies of reports from their project. She also brought her authority as a teacher and researcher, a wealth of knowledge — and patience. What she had to say was not what I wanted to hear. According to Susan, children in the Graves team's study learned to write by exercising all the options available to real-world authors, including daily time for writing, conferences with teachers and peers, pacing set by each individual writer, and opportunities to publish their writing. Most significantly, these students decided what they would write. Because the topics were their own, children made an investment in their writing. They drafted and revised and edited; they cared about content and correctness. They wrote on a range of topics and in a variety of modes wider than their teachers had dreamed of assigning. And their teachers had come out from behind their own big desks to write with, observe, and learn from young writers.

Atkinson Academy sounded a lot like Camelot. As Susan extolled its merits, I rolled my eyes and ground my teeth. I wanted to leave our meeting nearly as much as I wanted *her* to leave. As it worked out, however, I kept Susan at school that day much later than she intended to stay, arguing.

"But Susan, what if I have my class come up with a chain of memories, talk about them, choose one, and write it?"

"Well, that sounds very nice," she answered. "But that's really an exercise."

"Okay . . . but what if I give them a choice of four really funny dramatic monologues, and they get to role-play these, then choose one to write up?"

"Ummm, I guess I'd call that an exercise, too."

"Wait, wait. I haven't told you my best . . ."

It was an exercise. They were all exercises.

For the next week I explained to anyone who would listen how Susan's findings couldn't possibly apply to me and my eighth graders, how all my classroom experience and secondary English teacher expertise argued against the certain anarchy Susan had advocated. I railed at the art teacher: "Sarah, can you imagine what would happen if someone said kids should come into the artroom, check out the materials you've got here, and come up with their own projects?" I raged in the local service station: "Mr. Andrews, what if someone said customers should come into your garage, borrow your tools, and repair their own cars?" Sarah and Mr. Andrews and everyone just shook their heads.

But all that week, on my free periods and in the evening, I waged a silent, losing battle with Susan Sowers as I read and reread the manuscripts she had left behind. Eventually I saw through my defenses to the truth. I didn't know how to share responsibility with my students, and I wasn't too sure I wanted to. I liked the vantage of my big desk. I liked setting topic and pace and mode, orchestrating THE process, being in charge. Wasn't that my job? If responsibility for their writing shifted to my students, what would I do?

And what might Jeff have done as a student in this other kind of classroom?

What I did, finally, was talk to my kids. One day in March I gathered my courage and closed my door. I told my English classes about this elementary school in New Hampshire where children came up with their own topics and wrote for all kinds of real audiences, where writers got response from their friends and the teacher *while* they were writing. Then I asked, "Could you do this? Would you like to?"

Yes. Some said it tentatively, some resoundingly, but they all said yes. Together we had made an amazing discovery: they did have ideas for writing. Even more amazing, given the nonsense I'd had them writing for the past six months, they had good ideas. We found out in-school writing could provide a natural way to solve problems and see the world. This wasn't Camelot; it was genuine and it was happening in my own eighth grade classroom.

Brooke wrote a short story about the slaughter of baby seals. Doug wrote about duck hunting and Greg told about deep-sea fishing. Shani described the night she heard the news that her brother had died in an automobile accident. Evie wrote letters of inquiry to private high schools, and Ernie wrote a parody of Stephen King. One of my Sarahs told about her experiences learning to drive a junked Oldsmobile in her parents' driveway; the other Sarah took her reader-friends on a bus trip through Harlem that had shaken her small-town complacency. Eben's short story about the aftermath of a nuclear holocaust went through three drafts to become a letter to the editor of the *Portland Press Herald* objecting to the reinstitution of selective service registration. Melissa's letter to the Society for Animal Protective Legislation was forwarded as evidence to a Congressional sub-Committee. Lauren's letter to the local YMCA resulted in expanded gym hours for junior high kids. Erin's letter to Louis L'Amour questioning the credibility of one of his plots brought a long letter from L'Amour explaining his historic source.

Ted wrote an angry essay about time's effect on his life, Kim wrote a loving essay about her mother's effect on her life, and Joey wrote an essay about himself as a writer. When a Maine dairy announced a Down East story-writing contest, a group of eighth graders decided to enter. They listened to Marshall Dodge's "Bert and I" albums over and over again, making notes about dialect and story structure, and they wrote draft after draft. Roy won the contest and a $250 scholarship; five of his classmates were runners-up.

There weren't six top writers in each class anymore. Every student could seek help in conferences, spend sustained time on single pieces of writing, and discover that writing well isn't a gift. Their commitment to their topics made them work hard; their hard work made good writing happen.

After the novelty of self-selected topics faded, the writing didn't always come easily. In April some students begged, "Just tell me what to write. Anything. I'll write it." But I held firm. Those days had ended. Instead I questioned, modeled, and insisted, "Write about what you care about. What *do* you care about? What do you know? What do you know about that I don't know?"

After the novelty of no lesson plans wore off, the teaching didn't always come easily, either. But in spite of blocked writers, my uncertainty about what to say in conferences, big administrative questions about grading, record-keeping and classroom management, I couldn't wait to go to school in the morning to see what my kids would do next.

I saw them taking chances, trying new subjects, styles, and formats. I saw them taking responsibility, sometimes judging a single draft sufficient, other times deciding the sixth draft represented their best meaning. I saw them taking care, editing and proofreading so their real readers would attend to their meanings, not their mistakes. I saw them taking time, writing and planning their writing outside of school as well as in. I watched as my English classroom became a writer's workshop. Suddenly, the pieces fit.

Here, Goswami's teacher-as-researcher posture worked because the context created real writing and real questions about real learning. Here, I could relate as a writer to my students because we were all acting on our intentions as writers; insights from my own writing experiences, my real letters, poems, and stories, helped me help them. Here, isolated in a small school at the end of a long peninsula, I could learn how to discover and support young writers' ways of learning. Here was a context Graves might have had in mind when he advised teachers to "free ourselves for effective observation and participation in all phases of the writing process." Now that I was freed from the constraints of my big desk, my kids would become my teachers.

One of my eighth grade teachers that spring was Sheilah, a perfectly ordinary student. On the following page is her final of three drafts of a story about her cat. Written in May, "Friskey" is a perfectly ordinary piece of eighth grade writing.

How Sheilah got to her final draft, however, isn't a perfectly ordinary story. She took time, planning on her own what she'd write and how she'd write it. She conferred with her mother and friends and remembered ways other writers had written, techniques she liked and wanted to try. She had intentions, and she had a sense of herself as a writer. In a conference with me about "Friskey," Sheilah talked like an author.

ATWELL: Sheilah, can you tell me how you came up with the idea for this story?

SHEILA: Well, on a day we were sitting in a circle, you know, sharing our stories, someone read a really good, sad story about a pet they lost. I think it was Matt. He made me think of what happened to different pets I've had. I remembered this story the most, and I thought it would be one I could tell really well, you know, make it sad.

A: Can you remember how you got started?

S: Umm ... I thought about Friskey for a couple of days, about how I would write it, and then I talked with my mother, and she thought it sounded good. So when I went to write, I had some ideas about what I'd try to do.

A: I see that right from your first draft you began this story with a conversation between you and your brother. Would you be willing to delete that dialogue and begin here: "It was my tenth birthday . . ."

S: No, that has to be there.

A: Why?

S: Well, once in a group we talked about how you could use dialogue to make a story more interesting — somebody did it, and it worked really well. I wanted to make the story more interesting for my reader, you know, bring him right in, and I also wanted to keep him from right away knowing what was going on in the story.

A: Did you share this draft with anybody else?

S: Yeah, with Lori. I read it to her a couple of times and took down notes on what she said.

A: Yeah, I notice she wanted you to change the introduction. Here it says "more feelings."

S: But I didn't want to do that, because of what I already told you. I wanted the feelings to come later, as a kind of surprise.

A: She also responded by saying, "not so many saids." Why did you take her advice here, and change some of the "saids" to words like "yelled" and "laughed"?

S: Well, she was right. I just hadn't heard it until I read my piece out loud, and then it sounded funny, so I changed it.

A: I see here, after "stiff," you crossed out "as a board." Can you remember why you didn't want to say Friskey was as stiff as a board?

S: When I read it over, it sounded really stupid. It was supposed to be a sad story, and that made it sound funny.

Frisbey

"Please, just give me a hint," I begged.
"You can wait," Mike said.
"Come on Mike," I said.
"Nope," Mike answered.

It was my tenth birthday and my brother knew what I was getting from my mom. It didn't seem like he was going to tell me either.

A big grin spread across his face. I knew he was up to something.
"Well..." he said, "you're getting a kitten."

"I am!?" I exclaimed. I had never had my own pet before. I was very happy.

"Hey, you ruined my surprise!" I yelled.
"You asked," Mike said.
"Well, I didn't expect you to tell me!" I said.
"You know now," my brother said and laughed.

The next day was my birthday and my mother had a big box for me. I knew what it was so I was planning to act surprised. But when I opened the box I was surprised. It was the cutest little black kitten I'd ever seen! It had these big, green eyes and this little pink nose. I named him Friskey.

It wasn't more than three months I had him when he disappeared. I searched everywhere for him. Then the third day came; I looked again. I went to his favorite place, which was under the deck. I saw this big, black ball of fur and big, green eyes staring at me.

"Friskey!" I yelled. I was so happy and relieved to see him! I wondered why he didn't move. Then I realized it: Friskey was dead. He was stiff and his big black eyes had a lifeless stare. I couldn't believe Friskey's life with me was over. I hoped it was a happy one.

A: Sort of like Tom and Jerry, right?

S: Yeah.

A: And then on your third draft, you got rid of this whole section where Friskey clawed at your hand. Can you tell me why?

S: I didn't like the way it sounded. It didn't fit, you know, if I told about him clawing my hand, when I wanted to show how much I liked him.

A: I guess I'd describe your conclusion as a surprise ending. Can you tell me how you decided to end the story this way — withholding the information that Friskey was dead until the last minute?

S: Well, I thought Friskey was alive at first, and I wanted to make other people feel that with me, to feel it the way it happened to me. I didn't know he was dead until just then, and I wanted a reader's feelings to change like mine did when it happened.

A: Are you happy with this story?

S: Yeah, I think I did a pretty good job of doing what I wanted to.

The classroom allowed Sheilah to find out what she wanted to do; I allowed it. My role in that classroom is so changed Sheilah barely mentions me in telling how "Friskey" came to be. But I'm there, learning about the circumstances that help Sheilah find her way. A big desk at the front of the classroom is not one one these circumstances.

When Susan Sowers described her findings that day in March, I'd traced and retraced two words on the cover of my notebook: *naive* and *permissive*. I'd thought, "Here's a sure road to undisciplined writing and general chaos." But I learned this wasn't true. Freedom of choice doesn't undercut structure. Instead, kids become accountable for developing and refining their own structures. Everyone sits at a big desk, and everyone plans what will happen there. And one of my roles is to move among those desks, helping my kids discover and act on their options, expecting that every writer has something to say and acknowledging that saying it can be a tough job.

Learning in Earnest: The Boothbay Writing Project

Getting here has been a tough job. One afternoon last spring, five years after Susan Sowers came to Boothbay Harbor, Tracy and her friend Kristen were talking about what they'd like to be when they grew up. As I walked past their desks, Tracy stopped me and said, "You know, Ms. Atwell, I think I'd like to be an English teacher."

This doesn't happen a lot, not with junior high kids anyway. So I asked why.

"Well, it's so easy," she answered.

"Easy? Tracy, do you know . . ."

But she stopped me again, blushing. "No, I mean, I see what you do," she explained. "It's all just writing and reading and talking about them. I wouldn't mind doing that for a living."

I love it that Tracy doesn't (or, at least, didn't then) view English teachers as lecturers, assignment-givers, test-makers, paper-correctors, or ditto-designers. English teachers make their living doing the good stuff —

writing, reading, and talking about them. But the underpinnings of this job Tracy fancies don't show — all the hard thinking that led me to abandon lectures, assignments, tests, and dittos as ways of teaching, and all the hard work of discovering how writing, reading, and talking about them could become practical ways of teaching. I didn't get here alone.

Much of what happens in my writing workshop is informed by the work of Donald Graves, Donald Murray, Lucy Calkins, Susan Sowers, and, especially, Mary Ellen Giacobbe. And much of what happens is informed by the work of my colleagues, the teachers who became the Boothbay Writing Project.

In the early summer of 1980, still reeling from the miracle of the final months of that school year, I submitted a proposal to the old Title IV-C, requesting funding for a local in-service program on the teaching of writing. The time was ripe for Boothbay's K–7 children to write — and this time not for my benefit, but so they too might find their voices and exercise the power and freedom that I'd learned young writers could enjoy. And by then I knew exactly what I didn't want to do by way of helping develop a K–8 writing curriculum for our school.

I didn't want to dictate methods to my colleagues. Nor did I want to engage in any more swapping, borrowing, or secondhand philosophizing, all in the name of saving labor. Nor did I want to depend for the most part on outside experts' counsel to change our ways; except for me and Gloria Walter, whose seventh graders briefly experimented with self-selected topics, Susan Sowers' visit had been a fizzle.

Instead, we needed to find a way to break with the fine old tradition that had governed our previous curriculum efforts, the one that bore the motto, "Let's not re-invent the wheel." To do that, I needed to climb down from my secondary English teacher high horse and find a way to learn with my colleagues just as I was learning with my kids. When Title IV-C awarded us funding in August, 1980, Dixie Goswami helped us develop a process for learning together.

First, we gave ourselves time. We couldn't expect to come to serious understandings of writing in a few, quick-fix committee meetings. So we devoted two years to writing process, meeting for a week each August, two or three times each month after school, and on regular half-day release times for project teachers, paying our subs from the grant.

Next, we gave ourselves authority. Only those teachers interested in writing and its teaching joined the project, and we alone implemented the curriculum we developed. To his great credit, Bob Dyer, our principal, didn't mandate full-staff participation. I talked to all the teachers at my school about the proposed project and, starting with my three closest friends, fourteen teachers of grades K–8 eventually joined me that first year. By the end of the second year we numbered twenty-two. Today, a half dozen or so teachers at my school continue to go their own ways. To ask that they do otherwise would be to revert to one of the worst of the fine old traditions: across-the-board curriculum adoption. Our authority as teachers of writing can't be adopted by others on an administrator's command; it comes from the knowledge we've gained through diverse personal experience.

Finally, we gave ourselves opportunities for diverse personal experiences of writing. We read writing research, especially the ground-breaking reports by Graves, Calkins, and Sowers from the Atkinson study. We started attending professional conferences. When we had particular questions we sought consultants who had answers; Mary Ellen Giacobbe, then a first grade teacher at Atkinson, spent an invaluable Saturday with us talking about writing conferences.

To these data we added our own information. Borrowing ethnographic methods from the Graves project and Glenda Bissex's case study of her son's writing and reading (1980), we conducted year-long case studies of one or two of the writers in each of our classrooms. We also kept logs of observation, notebooks in which we recorded what our student writers said and did, along with our questions and speculations. We conducted self-research, looking long and hard at ourselves as writers, at our own writing processes and our histories as writers learning to write. We compiled portfolios of our writing on topics of our own choosing. And we met to share our writing and talk about the implications of all these activities for our teaching. Finally, I arranged with the state department of education for writing project teachers to receive recertification credit for their studies.

The process worked. It worked because it was so complex. Layer upon layer of experience accumulated to form a body of shared knowledge and expertise. No one handed us a program from on high; in intense and personally meaningful collaboration, we invented our own wheel. Together we learned from ourselves, each other, and our students.

I've described our process in more detail elsewhere (Atwell, 1982; 1985). Its end product, writing workshop, is one of the subjects of this book. Today, writing workshop at Boothbay Elementary is less a program than a way of life. The wheel we invented daily revolves with the energy generated in our twenty classrooms. Our new curriculum isn't a neat formulation of grade level skills and methods. It's messy, as thinking often is; as we learn more it changes, as thoughts often do. Always, though, a fixed framework of shared beliefs undergirds this messy enterprise, seven principles that constantly inform our teaching and our students' learning:

1. *Writers need regular chunks of time* — time to think, write, confer, read, change their minds, and write some more. Writers need time they can count on, so even when they aren't writing, they're anticipating the time they will be. Writers need time to write well.
2. *Writers need their own topics.* Right from the first day of kindergarten students should use writing as a way to think about and give shape to their own ideas and concerns.
3. *Writers need response.* Helpful response comes during — not after — the composing. It comes from the writer's peers and from the teacher, who consistently models the kinds of restatements and questions that help writers reflect on the content of their writing.
4. *Writers learn mechanics in context,* from teachers who address errors as they occur within individual pieces of writing, where these rules and forms will have meaning.

5. *Children need to know adults who write.* We need to write, share our writing with our students, and demonstrate what experienced writers do in the process of composing, letting our students see our own drafts in all their messiness and tentativeness.

6. *Writers need to read.* They need access to a wide-ranging variety of texts, prose and poetry, fiction and non-fiction.

7. *Writing teachers need to take responsibility for their knowledge and teaching.* We must seek out professional resources that reflect the far-reaching conclusions of recent research into children's writing. And we must become writers and researchers, observing and learning from our own and our students' writing.

Some of the specific practices of writing workshop evolved in response to student needs: helping writers discover topics and helping blocked writers become unblocked; learning how to talk to writers in sensible, sensitive ways and giving them ways of conferring with each other; figuring out effective means of helping kids control format and mechanics; making room for audiences other than the teacher by developing ways young writers could go public; and organizing our classrooms so they allowed the time writers need to write well, accommodated all the activities in which writers engage, and offered all the materials writers use.

Some writing workshop practices evolved in response to our needs as teachers and the needs of the school system: keeping track of each writer's activity, accomplishments, problems, pacing, and growth; knowing what, how, and when to teach about process, genre, technique, and conventions; and putting grades on report cards that reflect what we ask of the writers in our classrooms.

In the Middle describes solutions to these writing workshop questions, but solutions grounded in the particular experience of junior high school teaching. In many ways eighth graders' writing workshop looks the same as first graders'; in other ways, because of the nature of junior high kids, it has a look all its own. I'm convinced that writing workshop is as appropriate at junior high as at every other level, and I'm certain it's more appropriate than what typically happens in junior high English classes.

A workshop approach benefits adolescents by affording them the responsibility and autonomy they're ready to begin assuming as they approach adulthood. The workshop uniquely accommodates junior high students' social, physical, and intellectual needs; it provides a structure that keeps them on track, and an authoritative adult model with whom they can discover the sense of reading and writing. The nature of adolescence and the ways a workshop approach helps adolescents grow and learn is another of the subjects of this book. And there is one other subject. Reading workshop is the most recent phase in my evolution as a junior high English teacher.

Beyond Writing: The Dining Room Table

I see our school's three sections of eighth graders twice each day, once for a course officially known as English (now writing workshop) and once again for reading. Whether reading is taught as a separate course or considered as one component of an English curriculum, there seem to be two ways a junior high reading program can go: either skills-and-drills (SRA kits are big here) or watered-down lit crit of a type found in too many high school English classes (see Ginn, Scott, Foresman, or just about any grade-level literature anthology and teacher's guide). Until two years ago, I played the lit crit game.

For a long time, the same groups of students who sat at their own big desks each day in writing workshop returned to my room each day when it came time for reading to find me barricaded behind my big desk. Writing was something students did, and literature was something I did to students: pass out class sets of the anthology or novel, introduce vocabulary, lecture, assign, test, spoonfeed, forcefeed. I made all the choices, took all the responsibility, and found all the meanings. Tom Newkirk accurately characterized writing workshop as a "writing ghetto" — the one period each day when students made their own choices, took responsibility for their own learning, and found their own meanings.

Admitting to problems with my writing curriculum had hurt, but owning up to problems with my reading curriculum promised pure heartache. Where writing had been relatively virgin turf, literature was my field. I'd become an English teacher in order to teach literature, and for years that's just what I'd done. I'd taught my eighth grade reading curriculum, not my eighth grade readers.

Three things happened.

First, on the heels of research showing that sustained silent reading programs boosted students' reading comprehension — something I should have learned but hadn't from Jeff's experience as an independent reader — I began letting my kids read their own books one day each week, and they began driving me crazy. Daily at least one student would ask, "Ms. Atwell, are we having reading today?"

I didn't want to hear this. We had reading every day — or at least that was my impression. I felt little pinpricks of conscience whenever someone voiced a desire for more SSR. But there were too many wonderful anthology selections to cover and too many activities to orchestrate to waste valuable class time dallying with students' uninformed tastes in texts. So I continued to cling to each week's four days of curriculum and one day of reading.

Next, some Bread Loaf friends came to Maine for a weekend, and during dinner one night Toby discovered that one of our guests actually read and, better yet, appreciated his favorite author. Long after the table had been cleared, the dishes washed and dried, and everyone else had taken a long walk down to the beach and back, Nancy Martin and Toby sat at our dining room table gossiping by candlelight about Anthony Powell's *Dance to the Music of Time*. This didn't help me appreciate Anthony Powell, but it did open my eyes to the wonders of our dining room table.

It is a literate environment. Around it, people talk in all the ways literate people discourse. We don't need assignments, lesson plans, lists, teacher's manuals, or handbooks. We need only another literate person. And our talk isn't sterile or grudging or perfunctory. It's filled with jokes, arguments, exchanges of bits of information, descriptions of what we loved and hated and why. The way Toby and Nancy chatted, the way Toby and I chat most evenings at that table, were ways my kids and I could chat, entering literature together. Somehow, I had to get that table into my classroom and invite my eighth graders to pull up their chairs.

Finally, I did something I should have known to do long before. I matched my own reading process against the reading process I enforced in my classroom. It was not a very close fit. For example, I usually decide what I'll read, but my students seldom decided for themselves. And when my reading isn't up to me — when the application has to be correctly filled out, or I want to serve an edible dinner — I at least decide *how* I'll read. My students never decided. They read at the pace I set, often fragmented bits and pieces of text at a time, looking for the answers I wanted to the questions I posed.

I read a lot, and I have routines — times I count on being able to read, like before I fall asleep at night, or in the morning when Toby's in the tub. Too many of my students seldom read, and other than Friday's silent reading class, I did nothing to encourage or accommodate the habit of reading for pleasure.

Most significantly, there was that dining room table. I talk about books, authors, reading, and writing as a natural extension of my life as a reader. My students had little opportunity — and, I assumed, less inclination — for congenial talk about literature.

While writing workshop had long ago come to reflect what writers do and need, the reading program had continued to reflect my English teacher assumptions about my eighth grade readers. What I did as an adult reader had little to do with what I asked of my kids, which, in truth, was very little. They were passive recipients of literature I selected and interpretations I devised. Four days every week I dosed them with my English teacher notions of good literature, and on Fridays they became readers.

Two Septembers ago, I began a very slow, painful dismantling of the wall around the writing ghetto. I started by adding another day of independent reading to each week's schedule. In January, I added another; the following September another; until finally the literature curriculum languished in my file cabinet and my kids became readers full-time. I was learning about teaching reading and, once again, eighth graders were my teachers.

My kids taught me about adolescent literature, a genre that barely existed twenty years ago when I was an eighth grader. They introduced me to contemporary authors of juvenile fiction who write as well for adolescents as my favorite contemporary authors — Atwood, Tyler, Godwin, Updike — write for me.

They taught me to fill my classroom with books — novels, and also short stories, biographies, autobiographies, and poetry. They showed me that if I gave them the chance they would devour books. The first year, when I scheduled reading workshop three days each week, my students read an average of twenty-four full-length works. Last year, with four or five workshop days each week, they averaged thirty-five titles each. I never had enough books.

My students taught me that the context of their own books is ripe for good, rich, dining room table talk about literature. We went deeper than I'd thought possible into traditional teacher's manual issues of theme, genre, technique, character. And we went beyond these to new issues — reading process, professional authors' processes, relationships between reading and writing, between one text or author and others, between literature and real life. This was reader-to-reader dialogue, a far cry from empty lesson plan questions and sterile book report answers.

My students taught me that they loved to read. They showed me that in-school reading, like in-school writing, could actually do something for them; that the ability to read for pleasure and personal meaning, like writing ability, is not a gift or a talent. It comes with the freedom to choose, and with time to exercise that freedom. Finally, I learned that freedom to choose and time to read in school are not luxuries. They are not complements to a good literature curriculum. They are the wellspring of student literacy and literary appreciation.

Just as I'd had to learn about teaching eighth grade writers, I had to relearn my role as their reading teacher, working to find solutions to many of the same questions of methodology that had come up in writing workshop. Some of my new practices evolved in response to readers' needs: helping kids find books they wanted to read and helping non-readers become readers; learning how to talk to readers in sensible, sensitive ways and giving readers ways of conferring with each other; making room for audiences for reading other than the teacher; and organizing my classroom so it allows the time readers need to read well, accommodates the activities in which readers engage, and offers all the materials readers use.

Some reading workshop practices evolved in response to my needs and the needs of the system: keeping track of each reader's activity, accomplishments, problems, pacing and growth; knowing what, how, and when to teach about process, genre, technique, and conventions; and putting grades on report cards that reflect what I ask of the readers in my classroom.

The third section of *In the Middle* describes my solutions to reading workshop questions. In discussing reading separately from writing, I know I've created an artificial division; I know now that writers write reading, and that readers read writing. I also know, as a teacher of both subjects, that I could bite off only so many changes at one time. Writing and reading workshops are presented here in the chronology in which I came to understand them because I think this may help other junior high English teachers grow into similar understandings, gradually getting a handle on the theory and practice of workshop teaching and learning.

This book represents what I've come to understand about teaching writing and reading at this point in my evolution; I also know that my students and I will continue to learn and change. This causes me some difficulty when I try to put a name to what we do together in our writing and reading workshops. "Curriculum" just doesn't fit anymore. A curriculum puts limits on learning, kids' and teachers', spelling out what may be covered as orchestrated from behind a big desk. I can't call what we do "creative writing" or "literature." Creative writing implies exercises, all those precious assignments that distance kids from natural, purposeful writing; and literature suggests book lists, all those genteel "classics" that distance kids from natural, purposeful reading.

A couple of summers ago at Bread Loaf, Shirley Brice Heath suggested I call it "life's ways of reading and writing," because eighth graders and I write and read in school for all the reasons literate people anywhere engage in literate acts. This label works pretty well. I can think of one other possibility.

Every day in our writing and reading workshops, my students and I try out and test our beliefs about written language, and every year we come to share certain beliefs about language, its learning, and its teaching. What we do, day in and year out, is our *theory in action*. When my kids and I enter language together, collaborate as theorists, and act on those theories in the classroom, we forge and inhabit a common ground where the logic of their learning and my teaching can finally converge and become one.

Writers in their workshop

CHAPTER 2

Making the Best of Adolescence

"You don't have to suffer to be a poet. Adolescence is enough suffering for anyone."

John Ciardi

Short Hair

With hot tears streaming down her cheeks
she stood before her image,
scrutinizing herself
to see the damage of her hair.

Relishing the thought that it would grow back
she reasoned with herself:
it will!

"How do you like your new haircut?"
a voice cut in.

In a trembling voice,
"I love it,"
came out.

"Let's see it,"
came the delighted response.

Quickly washing away her tears
in the cracked basin,
she rushed down the narrow staircase
and almost stumbled into a child of one.

She walked into the room
not sure of herself.

"I love it, honey,"
said her mom.

I love it; I love it,
echoed in her ears.

"She loves it,"
she thought.
"*She* loves it."
SABRINA LEWIS

When I read Sabrina's poem, I remembered my own short hair. Until seventh grade I'd worn it long. My mother, like Sabrina's, had scheduled a haircut; my haircut, too, had broken my heart. It was a pixie cut, and I didn't have a pixie face. It took my mother almost an hour to convince me to come down from my room and show my father the transformation, and when I did it was with my own hot tears streaming. None of their compliments helped. Clearly, my social life was over. Everyone at school was going to recognize that I'd had a haircut and comment on the change. It was going to draw notice, and I didn't want to draw notice. I wanted to be the same unremarkable me I'd seen in yesterday's mirror. I cried all night over the worst thing that had ever happened to me.

Surviving adolescence is no small matter; neither is surviving adolescents. It's a hard age to be and teach. The worst things that ever happened to anybody happen every day. But some of the best things can happen, too, and they're more likely to happen when junior high teachers understand the nature of junior high kids and teach in ways that help students grow.

This chapter considers the nature of these adolescents, the nature of instruction they typically receive in U.S. junior high and middle schools, and the nature of good junior high teaching. In general, what our adolescent students get from us by way of schooling isn't very good. Our main concern as teachers seems to be to skirt all the messiness — and exuberance — of these years, mostly by regimenting our kids' behavior: tracked groupings, busy work and seat work, few opportunities for students to initiate activity or work together, and fewer opportunities for any demonstration of affect in our classrooms. Our policies tell junior high kids that their active participation is too risky an enterprise. It's safer to keep them passive and under control, thereby avoiding the certain discovery that our students' tastes and values are, alarmingly, not our own.

We won't get the best from our junior high students until we stop blaming adolescents for their adolescent behavior and begin to invite their distinctive brand of junior high best. I think we make the best of adolescence when we recognize and act on three principles — the three themes of this chapter.

First, teachers of junior high have to accept the reality of junior high students. Confusion, bravado, restlessness, a preoccupation with peers, and the questioning of authority are not manifestations of poor attitude; they are the hallmarks of this particular time of life. By nature adolescents are volatile and social, and our teaching can take advantage of this, helping kids find meaningful ways to channel their energies and social needs instead of trying to legislate against them.

Next, we have to recognize that adolescence is as special and important a time in students' intellectual development as any other phase in a child's life. They might not be quite so charming in their attempts to learn as their little brothers and sisters, but adolescents, too, need to be seen as individuals and responded to as people who want to know.

Finally, we have to organize our junior high teaching in ways that will help our kids begin to understand and participate in adult reality. This means more independent activity, more say in what happens in the classroom, and more responsibility for their own learning. It also means teachers who model the importance and usefulness in our own lives of the subjects we teach, demonstrating our own processes as learners and our personal knowledge of our fields, inviting students inside academia by showing that inside is a worthwhile and interesting place to be.

I've illustrated these themes throughout with poetry written by eighth graders. When my students use writing as a way to capture their feelings, trying to give shape to their inner experience, poetry is the mode to which they most often turn. The philosopher Susanne Langer calls a poem "a glimpse into a lifetime of feeling"; their poetry is my best window on adolescents' hearts and minds.

The Garden

It's a garden of roses —
Throwing their buds toward the sun,
Growing up, growing stronger,
Climbing up the supportive wall.
A little bud blooms
Throwing off its old petals
And leaving the wall.

It's a garden of thorns —
Slowly overtaking the delicate rose.
And as the rose climbs . . .
So climb the thorns.
Every so often
A thorn grows
Too close to the rose
Causing a tear . . .
A ruined petal.

It's a garden of roses —
It's a garden of thorns.

AMANDA CRAFTS

Adolescence

Adults are the supportive wall in Amanda's garden. One of the best things junior high teachers can do for students is acknowledge that the thorns of adolescence are real and cause real pain. I'm not a counselor — I have no desire to be one — but I can affirm that growing up is hard, and I can try to help it become a more productive undertaking. I begin to help when I look at my students as teachers who will instruct me about their lives.

I'll spend the rest of my years in junior high classrooms learning about the lives of junior high kids. I don't think there's a more unpredictable or interesting age. Twelve-, thirteen-, and fourteen-year-olds, in the middle of everything, are especially in the middle of changes — emotional, physical, psychological, and intellectual. Their sense of themselves, the world, and the relationship between the two is challenged every day by their own needs and by the demands of new roles.

Because they respond to these changes in such varied ways, I've stopped trying to anticipate my eighth graders' entering behavior. All I can predict with any certainty about any class is the widest imaginable range of abilities, problems, attitudes, and levels of maturity. My kids are boys who play tag at recess, and boys who grow moustaches. They're girls who slip and call me Mom in class, and girls who come to school wearing more eye shadow than I'd thought humanly possible and holler "Yo, Nancie!" when they see me in town on Saturday. Their looks constantly deceive me.

My kids pretty much look like adults. Many are as tall as I am; some are taller. When an eighth grade girl lets me try on her new shoes, they're often too big. When the shoe does fit — when it's even a style I'd buy for myself — I forget for a minute that although my students' worlds and my world intersect, they are different. I have to keep relearning the ways adolescents are like me, and the ways they aren't.

Last year I thought my eighth graders would drive me crazy over the Jim Morrison question. It goes like this: Do you think Jim Morrison is really dead? Morrison wrote lyrics and sang lead for the rock group The Doors. He is, in fact, dead. I still have my old Doors albums from high school, and I still play them once in a while. I listen to "Light My Fire" and think, "Great song." Perfectly bright kids listened to "Light My Fire" and whispered, "Mystical Jim is alive, biding his time." They were less interested in music or truth than they were caught in the grip of communal intrigue. Somehow Jim had escaped the grave — the fervor of their belief would make it so.

The American Poet

He is not dead;
he still lives on
to let us hear his
poet's song.

His songs are different
from any kind;
they make me think
and puzzle my mind.

But his songs brought him
wealth and fame.
From then on,
life wasn't the same.

Concerts were cancelled;
his life fell apart
Psychics foretold an early death,
Causing rumors to start.

> Then one day they said he died,
> which I don't think is true!
> He left the city, for the hills,
> and from the world — withdrew.
>
> HILARY SMITH

At the same time Hilary wrote this poem she was reading Pat Conroy's *The Water Is Wide* and couldn't get over the lack of sophistication of his Yamacraw Island students: "They didn't even know who the President of the U.S. was!"

Eighth graders shuttle back and forth between naïveté and worldliness. They shuttle back and forth between everything. They are self-confident and self-doubting; they are responsible and irresponsible. They never know — and I never know — what they'll be when.

One day last June when the temperature outside was in the nineties, it was even hotter in my classroom. Jody asked me if we couldn't go outdoors for reading workshop before we all fainted. I said fine, but first tell me what the procedures will be. So Jody's class proposed and agreed on rules: anyone who has to go to the bathroom go now, once we get outside sit together, read and don't watch the little kids' recess. They neglected "Don't throw acorns."

About five minutes into our retreat from the heat, acorns started flying. I had to round up the shooters, glare at their "but we didn't have a rule about acorns" excuses, and keep them by my side for the rest of the period. They hadn't planned to misbehave; their seriousness of purpose had flown the moment they discovered all those missiles on the forest floor. A poem Tim had written exaggerating his study hall teacher's very, very specific rules rang even truer.

Study Halls

Mr. Maxim always says,
"Now, in this study hall there is
        NO
sleeping,
      spitting,
           swearing,
                  staring.
      NO
singing,
      slapping,
           shouting,
                  scaring.
      NO
saluting,
      scaling,
           scowling,
                  howling.

       NO

escaping,

     gaping,

          taping,

               hesitating,

(and, of course, no constipating).

       NO

talking,

     taming,

          taxing,

               teaching.

       NO

tearing,

     telegraphing,

          telephoning,

               telling.

       NO

testing,

     trimming,

          tenting,

               bad-tempering.

       NO

tonguing,

     teething,

          tipping,

               time-watching.

       NO

tying,

     throwing,

          tracking,

               trashing . . .

   and

       NO

     talking.

Is that understood?"

"Yes."

"I said NO talking. Is that understood?"

(Pause.)

"Good. Now get to work."

                       TIM McGRATH

    Ken Maxim knows his kids. When it's time for study hall, where the point is managing a large group of adolescents, Ken isn't subtle. Physically and emotionally, adolescence can be a pretty unsubtle time of life. Physically, junior high students are antsy. They tap pens, jerk their legs and feet, squirm, gaze around the room and into space. Even when the teaching mode decrees that kids remain stationary — in rows, facing front, and silent — ripples of constant motion break the surface of the classroom. They cannot sit still.

Emotionally, junior high students experience wide swings of mood and deep extremes. When they like something they love it; when they dislike something they hate it. And the loves and hates are transient — best friends speak only to each other or don't speak to each other at all, romances last two days, obsessions are fiercely defended until they give way to new obsessions.

For a week last winter one wall of my classroom became a battleground. Someone put up a Michael Jackson poster. The next day, Bean erected a mammoth, homemade sign: IRON MAIDEN. Then more Michael Jackson posters went up. Then Teresa's Adam Ant poster. Then Jake's Ozzy Osbourne. There were shouting matches about whose music was best. Bean asked me if I liked Iron Maiden. I said no, and he stopped talking to me. And as hot and quickly as the controversy flared, it died. The posters stayed on the wall, but it was as if they weren't there anymore. The next week I looked to see stuffed animals, Smurfs, and Cabbage Patch dolls propped on desktops.

Although their interests can shift with amazing speed, adolescents' raging enthusiasms achieve incredible ends when the ends are kids' own. I've seen eighth graders work harder than I thought possible on claims they staked for themselves — all the hours Kelli spent writing and rewriting her novel, Jonathan spent customizing his go-cart, Tracy spent sewing her Gunne Sax suit. Boothbay Elementary celebrated eighth graders' graduation with a special ceremony the past two years because eighth graders proposed, planned, and produced it. They developed their own end-of-the-year slide show, made speeches, wrote and performed skits, and gave awards. They followed their graduation ceremony with a graduation dance. For weeks they held meetings, called bands, and dealt with agents. They made individual tickets, elaborate decorations, and rules. The afternoon of the dance they set tables with flowers and cloths, stood on ladders twisting streamers, and blew up hundreds of balloons. They came to the dance dressed to the teeth, looking more than ever like adults. They danced until 11:30. Then, despite their clean-up committee plans, they all went home, leaving the principal and me to clean up.

Eighth graders also decided they wanted an eighth grade yearbook; they take similar initiative every year and produce their own, calling meetings, selling ads, setting deadlines, writing copy, and scheduling photograph sessions. And every year, when the yearbook comes back from the publisher, they complain — about their pictures, and any mistakes they can find, and anything that isn't exactly as they'd dreamed it.

Sometimes all this loving and hating can get brutal. Adolescents see themselves and others through new, critical eyes. They measure themselves against the way they think they should be, and they seldom measure up; suddenly the world doesn't measure up either. My students can be sharptongued, even cruel, in their judgments of the world, but often their criticisms of others begin with dissatisfaction with self — an unpopular eighth grader torments an unpopular third grader on the school bus; John laughs at the paucity of Brendan's vocabulary, then misuses three words in one sentence; one chubby boy makes a loud proclamation about another chubby boy's baby fat. When I bring my camera to school, Jake puts up the hood on his sweatshirt and keeps it up all day. He also points out to me that my hairstyle makes me look like his grandmother.

Until a few years ago, I would have taken this to heart. If the comment were brutal enough — in my first year teaching, a boy told me he had decided to make me cry in class — I would cry (but not in class). And if the comment were a compliment — "Ms. Atwell, you're the best teacher in this school" — I'd take that to heart too. Now, even if it's in writing I don't take it to heart. Junior high kids aren't insincere. They're trying to fit in, but the ground keeps shifting. With every mood swing, their whole world changes. They can be ecstatic for no reason; they can fall into the deepest depressions for no reason. They can feel connected to the whole world and utterly alone.

My students write a lot of poetry about this syndrome. Their poems, describing a terrible, unbidden feeling of isolation, illustrate one more way they are not like me. When I'm depressed, I can usually analyze the cause: something's wrong, and I can put a name to it. With adolescents, depression lowers like a cloud bank out of a clear sky. One girl called it, "that feeling of nothing. All of a sudden something's wrong, but I don't know what."

The Merry-Go-Round

Never before in an upside-down way
Did anyone explain to me
What to do when all the happiness
     goes
     and stays
     away.

When the merry-go-round inside my mind
Starts its trip around,
The horses they gallop
     looking for something
     that cannot be found.

The people astride their saddles
Fall off and tumble away.
The horses they kick
And start to battle.

Sometimes it seems the horses go round
And round, and round, and round.
They won't go away —
     just stay
     stuck on the ground.

Never before in an upside-down way
Did anyone explain to me

What to do when all the happiness
goes
and stays
away.

JUSTINE DYMOND

Alone and Beneath

She just sits there, looking outside —
No reason to run, or to hide.
Sitting, her head turns just to one side.
She sits before the window, looking
Outside.

She looks out and sees the bright, reddish sky.
She sees something little fly by.
She sits there as if something has died.
She is the only one who can see the
Sky.

There's no one there that she can hold.
She feels something gone, something she sold.
No one's there, so it can't be told.
There's no one left that she can
Hold.

She's gone somewhere; she's gone beneath.
She's out of breath; she cannot breathe.
She's the victim of a heartless thief.
Now she's gone, down,
Beneath.

Now she's gone, and there's nothing to hear.
She's all alone; no one's her peer.
Her face turns white, and down comes a tear.
But no one's there, her to
Hear.

DEDE REED

This stirring up of new, dark feelings is balanced by the awakening of new intellectual powers. Adolescents begin to go deeper into ideas — political, moral, and artistic. They're powerfully attracted to metaphorical language and levels of meaning. They glimpse shades of gray amidst all the black and white that surrounded their pre-adolescence. They begin to see patterns and significances in what were once just events, as in the way Billy chose to describe a winter night's campout, and in Randy's new perspective on the family cat.

Field of Light

It was twelve o'clock in the night
and I was in the field of light —
snow on the ground,
moon in the sky,
and oh, how I wondered why.
Why does the moonlight play on the snow
in such a quiet place, so . . . ?
And then the dawn, a spark of light.
Oh, what a night
in the field of light.

BILL SNOW

Catstalk

He lies on my bed
as cool as can be.
While he licks his paws
he purrs,
purrs,
purrs —

then raises himself,
takes flight,
and sort of floats down the stairs.
He is so light,
so graceful,
and yet —

he's deadly
as he sits by the door
meowing to go out
so he can stalk the land.

RANDY SHEPARD

One lovely aspect of this deepening awareness is adolescents' humor. Junior high students, especially eighth graders, discover that they can be witty. They can quip and ad lib. They understand puns and double *entendres*. They get Woody Allen's *non sequiturs*. They write parodies that cut right to the heart of the original. They imitate and caricature, and their imitations and caricatures are dead on. I admit it: one big reason I teach English at the junior high level is that junior high kids can be so funny.

One spring morning I arrived at school early to try to teach myself to use the new computer. I was too late. A message from one of my students was taped to the keyboard.

In Loving Memory

Dearly beloved, we are gathered here today
in Boothbay Region Elementary School's library
to mourn the apparent loss of a dear, dear friend
who met an unfortunate, untimely end.
He was known as TRS 80.
None will feel the loss more than we.

We can only hope and pray
time will ease the pain of this day.
We'll miss his comments, so cheerful and steady,
especially "Syntax error?" and "Ready?"

So on this day
in the middle of May
we mourn the loss of our matey,
TRS 80.

Eulogies for dead computers aren't commonly prescribed in junior high
English curriculum guides. Neither is parent-teacher correspondence. Because
my kids can play with language, so can I. Last May, Tom's "father" and I
exchanged letters.

```
      TO:MS. ATWELL
(with good will and good tast)



    Dear MS. ATWELL,
I am very pleased with my sun's writing
ability!
      PLEASE !.keep up the good work!
                     S. Appleonio
      P.S. THANKS


this is a  sample of his  writing
      THIS IS MY NAME DR.X
      .Tom Apollonio.
      Txtxxxxxxxxxxxxxx
      111111111111111
      mmmmmmmmmmmmmm
      NNNNNNNNNNNNNNN
      mmmmmmmmmmrrmommm
      This is the
      aLphbet;!.,!!!!!
      -098765432"#$%_&
      '()*oqwertyuiop½
      asdfghjkl;¢zxcvb
      nm,./QWERTYUIOP½
      ASDFGHJKL:@ZXCVB
      NM,.?

      THIS IS MY
      GRADE       8D

I live here =
#Lʌ31Eastern
ave.  B.B.
Harbor, ME.
U.S.A.
EARTH
                     fill in for me ( )
I am (8)years 2 (?)
```

```
        XXXXX
    OLd.
    I CAN WRITE@ ?
    X x-*&5%$$099,00


        Y  A
          Y  A
              Y  A
          Y  A
        Y  A
```

BOOTHBAY   TELEPHONE 207-633-5097   BOOTHBAY HARBOR

Boothbay Region Elementary School

Boothbay Harbor, Maine 04538
ROBERT DYER, Principal

Deer Mr. S. Appleonio,

   You're letter ment a grate deel too me I am also vary impressed with Toms riting ability he writes lik me : good.

   It is a plesure two be his teecher. I cant weight to git my hands on Taylor.

Sinsearly,
Ms. Atewell

I'm looking forward to the day Taylor, Tom's little brother, sits at a big desk in my classroom. I'm about to move into my twelfth year of teaching — I'm no dewy-eyed novice — and I'm looking forward to the fall. I know I'll be surprised, perplexed, and interested; I know I'll learn. And I know, finally, that what I can take to heart about eighth graders is how they wear their hearts on their sleeves. They can be highly emotional — elated, confused, angry, afraid — but their high emotions are usually short-lived. Water flows over the dam in torrents in my classroom because I'm learning what to take seriously and seriously respond to, and what to wait out.

"This is boring." "This is stupid." "Why do we have to do this?" It's a test, one I've learned to take and respond to seriously. Adolescents question our adult authority because they're trying to figure out adult reality. They want answers. They expect the teacher to be a model — to make them work and be good but, more importantly, to make adult sense of the subject at hand. It took me a long time to discover that my adult authority didn't lie in my big desk, red pen, acid tongue, detention slips, seating charts, lesson plans, grade book, or any of the other trappings of the junior high school status quo.

The Junior High School Status Quo

When I listen hard to my junior high students, their message to me is, "We're willing to learn. We like to find out about things we didn't know before. But make it make sense. Let us learn together. And be involved and excited so we can be involved and excited." When I listen to educators talk about junior high, I hear a different message. I'm told that my role is to keep the lid on, consolidate "basic skills" covered in the elementary grades, and prepare my students for high school, regardless of the logic or appropriateness of the high school program in question.

If I look at my classroom as a holding tank, a place where kids pass their days reviewing and getting ready, all learning stops — theirs and mine, too. We mark time waiting for somebody's idea of the real thing. It's like the line I used to get from graduating eighth graders: "Gee, Ms. Atwell. We're gonna miss you. Maybe some day you'll be smart enough to teach at the high school."

Our junior — and senior — high classrooms too often function as holding tanks. We separate the big fish and the little fish into their homogeneous groupings, and we provide the minimum environment required for survival. The tanks are drably furnished, the effect is flat, and the inhabitants have little say about what they'll do while they while away six years of their lives. The American secondary school status quo presents a bleak picture, revealing little evidence of the collaboration, involvement, and excitement in acquiring knowledge that our students crave — that all humans crave.

We have access to a more sharply focused version of that picture, thanks to *A Place Called School*, John Goodlad's remarkable study of U.S. public schools and classrooms (1984), and we know a lot more about the junior high classroom specifically. For example, we know that junior high students value their school friendships and social relationships far more than their school subjects and teachers. We know that junior high students, whose independence and self-reliance we might well encourage and nurture, actually have much less say in how their education will proceed than elementary school students. And we know that tracking is widespread by the seventh grade, despite repeated findings that homogeneous groupings don't lead to increased learning but rather to teachers' — and learners' — acceptance of poor performance.

I'm concerned in this section with the nature of instruction adolescents typically receive in U.S. junior high schools; how our classroom ambience, instructional approaches, and ability groupings do not meet adolescents' needs; and how this is no accident. Our junior high schools are structured to deny, or at least delay the satisfaction of our junior high students' needs, physical, intellectual, and social.

In looking at adolescents' social needs and the social status quo, Goodlad turned up findings that are markedly similar to numbers of other studies of American adolescents. Junior high teachers won't be surprised: school is our students' social milieu. When asked, "What is the one best thing about this school?" well over a third of the junior high kids in Goodlad's study responded "my friends," 15 percent named sports activities, and 10 percent referred to good student attitudes, for a combined total of 62 percent. In other words, almost two-thirds most appreciated school as an occasion to meet and mix with other seventh and eighth graders. In fact, at 8 percent "nothing" outranked "classes I am taking" (7 percent) and "teachers" (5 percent) as the "one best thing about this school" (p. 77). Finally, when asked how they perceived the most popular students in their schools, 60 percent of junior high students identified good-looking or athletic peers, and only 14 percent named "smart students" (p. 76). As Goodlad concludes, " 'School work' is not all school for adolescents . . . [it is] quite sufficient to be considered good-looking, popular, and one of the gang."

As teachers, it's easy for us to respond to all this the way we usually do: to remark on how incredibly shallow junior high kids are, harrumph about the mythical good old days when students were serious about their studies, and impose even tighter regulations against students fraternizing in our classrooms. But I'm willing to bet that in respect to kids' peer group preoccupations, school *most* closely resembles the "life in the real world" we're preparing them for; that is, ask any group of working adults, "What is the one best thing about this job?" and at least a third will respond "my friends."

Junior high students look in school for what really matters in life; they don't look at school as a place *to get ready for* what really matters in life. Social relationships matter in life, and in spite of our view of adolescents' social needs as "dissonance in conducting school and classroom business," adolescents nonetheless become "variously adept" at working out those needs in our schools and classrooms (Goodlad, p. 80). In large part they come to our schools and classrooms *in order* to work out social needs.

My eighth graders who live in Boothbay's most remote reaches generally have miserable school vacations; they're happy when the school bus reappears. When they arrive at school they'll be variously adept at renewing their social lives — catching minutes with friends between classes, sitting together at lunch time, passing forbidden notes, scheduling rendezvous in the library or restrooms, maybe talking during art or phys ed, and definitely talking during writing and reading workshops, conferring with each other and me.

A few years ago some former eighth graders made the mistake as ninth graders of believing that conferring about writing in progress continued to be something that really mattered in life. When they attempted to read their pieces to each other during the half hour their teacher had given them to complete an assigned essay, she was aghast: "There'll be none of that in here. This isn't the eighth grade, and cheating will not be tolerated." So students became variously adept at passing a new kind of forbidden note, a draft to which they wanted a friend to write a response.

The status quo regards collaboration as cheating and learning as a solitary, competitive enterprise. Even though junior high students spend most of their school day sitting with groups of twenty-five peers, they will spend most of their time in those groups working alone, either completing a seat assignment or listening to the teacher lecture or give instructions. Goodlad observed that American students spend at least 70 percent of their class time listening to teacher-to-student talk. These are not conferences; it's not even conversation. As Goodlad points out, we talking teachers "are not responding to students, in large part because students are not initiating anything" (p. 229).

The ubiquitous listening-as-learning mode, complemented by varieties of seat and busy work, wasn't arrived at haphazardly. Losing control looms as our greatest fear; rather than risk overstimulation we consciously choose not to stimulate. Better to limit the possibilities and keep a neutral tone than to risk a display of adolescents' strong feelings — like the shared laughter, overt enthusiasm, and angry outbursts Goodlad rarely observed in secondary classrooms. Better to limit the possibilities and keep them quiet and facing front than to risk big, adolescent bodies in motion — or a situation where a Jody could be inspired by acorns.

Last June, at the end of a day spent observing my eighth graders' writing workshops, a visiting ninth grade teacher remarked on how refreshing it was to visit an elementary school classroom. Since I thought of my eighth grade as a secondary classroom, I asked her what she meant. She replied, "Oh, you know — all this activity and independence. My kids could never handle it."

In general, we don't ask our secondary level kids to handle it. One result is increasing conformity as students progress through the grades, rather than the increasing independence adolescents might reasonably be expected to assume as they approach adulthood. While fifty-five percent of elementary school students in the Goodlad study felt they did not participate in any way in choosing what they did in class, *two-thirds* of secondary students reported having no say (p. 109). When Goodlad looked closely at who made what decisions in junior high classrooms, he found that 90 percent of the observed classes were dominated by teachers "with respect to seating, grouping, content, materials, use of space, time utilization, and learning activities" (p. 229). What's left for students to decide? Which educational goals or ends can students legitimately call their own? When are junior high students' needs — social, personal, or intellectual — addressed in their junior high classrooms?

In fact, our academic curricula take little account of adolescents' concerns or values; the curriculum, a closed system, shuts the classroom door on any ends that kids might call their own. When adolescents do find channels in school for their raging enthusiasms, the resulting projects generally take place outside the regular academic program — like the go-cart Jonathan built in shop class and the Gunne Sax dress Tracy sewed in home ec. It comes as no surprise that the subjects best liked by the junior and senior high students in Goodlad's study were the arts, vocational education, and physical education (p. 116). Students chose as favorites classes where they routinely collaborate with other students and the teacher, where they have some degree of ownership of the educational product, and where they can be active — where whole-group listening and busy work are minor components of the educational process. This is a finding we teachers of academic subjects can't afford to dismiss. Goodlad's question wasn't "Which course is easiest, most fun, most frivolous?" He asked students, "Which do you like best?"

Learning is more likely to happen when students like what they are being asked to do. Learning is also more likely to happen when they can actively engage as learners, and when they are not engaged alone but are grouped so that as they engage together they may learn from each other.

When students are tracked according to ability levels, the possibilities for collaborative learning are severely diminished. Yet huge numbers of U.S. school districts view the junior high as a convenient occasion for identifying and sequestering "fast" (we think they'll go to college) and "slow" (we think they won't) learners. The groupings that we establish at the beginning of seventh grade often proceed through the senior year — for those in the "slow" track who make it to their senior year, that is. Although low-tracked students obviously get the worst of it, both groups lose out.

Kids tracked into the junior high's top groups now see their classmates as competitors; measuring themselves against fast-learning friends they often worry that they're not smart enough to warrant inclusion and panic over grades. Kids tracked into the bottom groups are plenty smart enough to look around them the first week of school and catch on: "I'm in the dumb group, I'll be here forever, and I know what's expected of me." They also catch on to who's in the top groups when old friends from other sections describe their courses and homework — inevitably, activities more interesting, challenging, and worthwhile. Those students placed in lower homogeneous sections most need interesting, challenging, worthwhile instruction. They most need school to enlighten and make sense. They most need individual coaching. And they mostly get remedial work, low-level texts and low-level ideas, and teachers faced with a crazy situation: a whole class of kids who could benefit from one-to-one help, but mostly need to be disciplined and managed.

Worse than inappropriate, tracking denies lower-placed students' basic right to equality of educational opportunity. When Goodlad looked closely at tracked groupings, he found that the crucial difference between high and low groups constituted a "marked inequality in access to knowledge"; that ability tracking creates an "instructionally disadvantaged" subclass of students in our schools (p. 152) as we set a different course content, encourage different behaviors and attitudes, and relate and respond differently as teachers.

When secondary teachers deal with higher tracked kids, we're more organized, clear, and enthusiastic. In turn, high-track students perceive teachers as "more concerned about them and less punitive toward them," see their classmates as more friendly than do lower tracked students, and seldom feel left out of class activities. Low track students report the lowest levels of peer esteem and the highest levels of discord in the classroom; they view other students as unfriendly and feel left out of class activities; and they see their teachers as more punitive and less concerned about them than do other students. In short, students in the low tracks are "the least likely to experience the types of instruction most highly associated with achievement" (p. 155).

Most significantly, Goodlad found that instruction of heterogeneous groupings, classes that include students achieving at all levels, did not sink to the lower levels associated with lower students. Rather, classes containing a heterogeneous mixture of students "were *more like high than low track classes* (italics mine) in regard to what students were studying, how teachers were teaching, and how teachers and students were interacting in the classroom" (p. 159).

Our justifications for tracking remain fairly constant in schools across the country. Whatever terms we couch it in, the bottom line is usually the contention that we're meeting each individual student's academic needs by grouping homogeneously. We continue to believe this in spite of the body of research which shows that tracking doesn't produce gains in students' achievement (Borg, 1966; Borg *et al*, 1970; Alexander *et al*, 1978; Rosenbaum, 1976). We choose to believe this, I'm afraid, because it makes the junior high status quo easier to maintain — one lecture and dittoed seatwork assignment for one group, another lecture and dittoed seatwork assignment for another. However much we might talk about "providing for individual differences," tracking at best exists for the benefit of teachers and the listening/busy work mode. At worst, tracking allows us to blame students for our failure to teach them well — all those low-tracked adolescents of whom we ask and expect less and less.

In most junior high language arts programs, the status quo combination of ability groupings, passivity, and solitary effort takes its own peculiar forms. "English" becomes a content course. It involves listening to teachers talk about English, writing an occasional theme about the English teacher's ideas, reading assigned literature texts, memorizing vocabulary definitions, correcting errors of usage and punctuation in English handbooks, and drilling assorted "facts" about static, inaccurate versions of English grammar (not to be confused with the complex systems linguists invent, refine, and re-invent). Students in the lower tracks get a watered-down version of this content, consisting of "skills" (generally the very same, very deadly skills, such as names of parts of speech, year after year) and "fundamentals" (workbooks, low-level readers, and few actual stories or whole pieces of real literature).

Goodlad found this same content in junior high English classrooms throughout the U.S. in every kind of community. This consistency may account for another of his findings: the subject rated "interesting" by the fewest number of students at both junior and senior high levels is English (p. 120).

It doesn't have to be this way. When the content of a junior high English course is ideas — thinking and learning through writing, reading, and talking — and when students in the course pursue their own ideas in the company of friends and their teacher, the junior high English classroom has the potential to become an interesting place. This place is a workshop, a way of teaching and learning uniquely suited to junior high students of every ability. Workshops accommodate adolescents' needs, invite their independence, challenge them to grow — and transform the junior high school status quo.

Making the Best

When Susan Sowers told me about Atkinson Academy's writing classes, a workshop struck me as exactly the wrong approach to take in an eighth grade English class. In fact, it struck me as dangerous: all those big, unpredictable kids suddenly let loose to set their own agendas, moving around my classroom, talking with their friends, writing about adolescent ideas and concerns. Given even the limited knowledge of junior high students I'd gleaned by then from the perspective of my big desk, the prospect of twenty-seven eighth graders engaged in a workshop made the junior high status quo look pretty good.

Now, as I constantly learn more about eighth graders, I continue to learn about the ways a workshop approach is exactly right for them. I'm learning that the behaviors I anticipated with such dismay are exactly those in which active learners engage. I'm also learning that because they do engage, there's little danger. My students are busy going about the business of the workshop — writing, reading, and talking about writing and reading. As we let junior high writers and readers assume control, they assume responsibility, too, for the hard work of considering and shaping their ideas.

A workshop is student-centered in the sense that individuals' rigorous pursuit of their own ideas is the course content; in this student-centered environment, Murray says, "the student has no excuse for getting off the hook. He has the opportunity, the terrible freedom to learn" (1982, p. 133). A workshop grants me a terrible freedom, too. As the workshop leader I can't hide up front. I have the opportunity now to learn how to support and extend my students' learning.

At the beginning of this chapter I described its themes in terms of three principles teachers and schools might take into account in making the best of our adolescent students. In classrooms organized as workshops, junior high teachers transcend the junior high status quo and act on these principles. We recognize and accommodate the realities of adolescence. We see our students as individuals and teach to the needs and intentions of each. And we begin to involve them as participants in adult reality.

In considering the realities of adolescence, if we know that social relationships come first, it simply makes good sense to bring those relationships into the classroom and put them to work. In a workshop, social needs find a legitimate forum in students' conferences about their writing and reading. Here kids talk about their ideas and kids are the initiators of talk. And here genuine conversation occurs, not just between students but between students and me, as well. One-to-one and in small groups, writers and readers socialize about the world of written language and teach each other what they know. This kind of on-the-job talk belongs in the classroom.

Writing workshop conferences are different from the student talk I used to try to sponsor. For years I read all the articles in *English Journal* about procedures for assigning "peer response groups" and I exhausted all the available alternatives: picking names out of a hat, counting off, asking kids to establish their own permanent groupings, then dealing with constant requests to switch groups as friendships bloomed or fell apart. The *EJ* articles missed the point. The issue isn't how to assign and manage peer response: it's how collaboration can move an individual forward in the context of what the individual is trying to do.

Within the structure of a writing workshop, students decide who can give the kind of help they need as they need it: if Luanne knows about leads, call on her; if Mike knows about motorcycle helmet laws, call on him; if the teacher knows about methods for writing dialogue, call on her. In the writing workshop, small groups form and disband in the minutes it takes for a writer to call on one or more other writers, move to a conference corner, share a piece or discuss a problem, and go back to work with a new perspective on the writing.

Jonathan spent almost the whole school year considering he might write a poem but sticking with prose, mostly narratives and correspondence. In writing workshop one morning in April, his friend Ernie asked Jonathan to listen and respond to his poem "The Boothbay Blues," a satire about the many exciting things to do when the summer people go home and the town closes down for the season. Looking for help with his conclusion, Ernie showed Jonathan how he'd composed "Boothbay Blues" in lines and stanzas, something he'd learned about in an earlier conference with me.

The next day, Jonathan came to class with a draft of his first poem — except it was a paragraph. During the status-of-the-class conference, where I call the roll and record writers' plans, Jon said, "I'm gonna confer with Ernie today because he knows what a poem is supposed to look like." Then he and Ernie went off to a conference corner and divided Jonathan's paragraph into lines and stanzas:

Frogs

As the sun quietly departs
beneath the trees,
a misty haze settles,
encasing the silent pond in a semi-
transparent blanket.
Many tiny sets of eyes
float in the water,
watching,
watching.

As twilight comes,
one set of eyes
rises, then a green
head appears.

Then another,
then another,
then one sings out into the night.
Then another,
then another.

Finally the whole pond rings out
with the chorus of the frogs,
frogs,
frogs.

JONATHAN HOLBROOK

Because I know how junior high students can talk to each other, I've learned to set the tone for workshop talk. Peer conferences won't work unless writers can trust that their peers won't shoot them down, so I show my kids how to confer, talking to them just as I'd like them to talk with each other. When I'm judgmental, sarcastic, directive, or gushing, I'm demonstrating that this is how they might respond. When a response is brutal, or a best friend's empty flattery, I confer on the conferring: "How will that response help the writer?" And in order to maintain a volume level that won't interfere with other writers' thinking, I give them places to go to talk with each other, conference corners apart from quiet areas for writing.

The workshop is filled with places to go. A reality of adolescence is that junior high students need to move; so do real writers and readers. My students move purposefully among the areas of the room where they find what real writers and readers need: books of every kind, materials for writing, resources and references, permanent writing folders, places to publish, address files, bulletin boards, response, solitude. When I organize my classroom as a workshop, the resulting physical arrangement calls for motion; in turn, the organization of the workshop structures that motion and keeps it purposeful. With all these kids moving around the room I have fewer discipline problems than in the old everybody-face-front days — less fidgeting, less restlessness, less boredom. And they have greater independence — more say in what they'll do, more self-regulation, and more involvement.

The workshop demands involvement because it exists to serve students' own purposes. All the strong feelings and raging enthusiasms of adolescence get directed toward ends that are meaningful because students chose them. When they can choose, junior high students will write for all the reasons literate people everywhere engage as writers: to recreate happy times, work through sad times, discover what they know about a subject and learn more, convey and request information, apply for jobs, parody, petition, play, argue, apologize, advise, make money. When they can choose, junior high students will read for all the reasons literate people everywhere engage as readers: to live other lives and learn about their own, to see how other writers have written and to acquire other writers' knowledge, to escape, think, travel, ponder, laugh, cry. The writing and reading workshop is a literate environment; by definition it is a place to become involved in writing and reading. And once they're involved, junior high students can become genuinely excited about finding out things they didn't know before, thinking about new ideas in new ways. Often, they just need a "nudge" — Mary Ellen Giacobbe's word for the gentle guidance that takes learners beyond where they are to where they might be.

In reading workshop conferences, I've learned to nudge toward novels that give shape to kids' feelings and portray adolescents' emerging intelligence and understandings — *A Summer to Die*, *The Outsiders*, *Gentlehands*, *And You Give Me a Pain*, *Elaine*, Lipsyte's *Summer* series. I also nudge toward books that address the world of ideas — *1984*, *Hiroshima*, *Z for Zachariah*, *I Am the Cheese*, *To Kill a Mockingbird*, *Autumn Street*.

In writing workshop conferences, I've learned to pose questions that ask kids to reflect on personal experience. Dostoevski wrote, "One sacred memory from childhood is perhaps the best education," and I nudge writers to uncover and bring meaning to their own sacred memories of friendship and family. I also nudge students to explore ideas and consider those social, political, and ethical issues that encircle personal experience, topics I used to think were the science and social studies teachers' domain. When they have avenues for considering the shape of the world around them, junior high students will take on that world in their writing, confronting such issues as acid rain, lab experiments on animals, selective service registration, the lack of local zoning laws that allows a Burger King to displace a meadow, the wisdom of nuclear energy, and the threat of nuclear annihilation.

Nothing Lasts Forever

Sooner or later the world will end.
Nothing will be there to take or to lend.
No mail to come; no mail to send.
The whole world is coming to an end.

The people come and the people go.
There'll be no friends; there'll be no foes.
No one feels happy; no one feels woe.
Sooner or later the people will go.

There'll be no feelings to hurt or to hide.
Something's wrong: the laughter's died.
No more love; no tears cried.
There'll be no anger to have or to hide.

Sooner or later the world will be gone.
There'll be no sun to have a dawn.
There'll be no stars to inspire a song.
Nothing will be there; the world will be gone.

DEDE REED

Day by Day

Day by day,
year by year,
I run from my life,
living in fear.

Day by day,
year by year,
someone dies;
there is a tear.
A button is pushed;
lives are gone.
The world is dead;
there is no dawn.
It's the beginning
of the end.
No gardens to tend,
no dresses to mend.

Day by day,
year by year,
there is a hope;
the skies will clear.
The grass is greener;
hope is winning.
It's the start
of a new beginning.

Day by day,
year by year,
a bird sings;
the start is near.
Life has to come
to reign once more —
    to go to work
    or go
        to war.
                    JENNIPHER JONES

These are individuals' genuine concerns, and the help I can offer eighth graders in writing and reading conferences is truly individualized instruction — nothing like the brand of "individualization" promised by language arts kits where everyone works through the same set of materials but on a slightly different schedule. In the workshop I mostly teach individuals, moving within the group to stop and confer with one writer or reader at a time. Because kids are writing on topics they've chosen and reading books they've selected, my teaching and their learning are about as individualized as they can get. And so is evaluation. Because kids are acting on their own intentions, rather than my whole-class intention, I have to look for individual changes and self-improvement. There's simply no basis for comparing one student against others; the context demands I grade each student's growth over time, an important spur to learning for its own sake.

And students do grow and learn. Every day for two weeks Tim came into reading workshop waving his copy of Jay Bennett's mystery *The Dangling Witness*, saying in an awed voice, "This is a good book. I mean, this is a *really good* book." Every day for two weeks Andy came into writing workshop waving the drafts of his piece about a typical baseball practice, saying in an awed voice, "This is a funny piece. I can't believe what a funny piece this is." One good book, one successful piece of writing, are enough to convince junior high students of the challenges and satisfactions of written language. They want to find more good books, they want to write well again, and over the weeks or months of a workshop, they come to believe they can do both.

To persuade our adolescent students of their academic potential, we, too, must believe they can succeed, demonstrating an expectation that every student has an academic potential. Student-regulated activity, individualized instruction, and heterogeneous groupings are strong demonstrations — and more. Non-tracked workshops work. Instead of accommodating one ability level and one level of instructional activity, heterogenous workshops represent the whole range of junior high abilities, attitudes, and intentions. There are twenty-eight teachers in a workshop. Everyone learns from everybody, and our less able students may learn most and best of all.

Less able students need more able models; they need to be surrounded by other learners whose ideas will spark and charge the environment; and they generally need more individual coaching. No matter how high my expectations, if I have a class of twenty-five low-tracked writers and readers, I'm hard put to be a model sufficient to inspire the whole group or to provide the individual response each student needs. But if I have a handful of low ability students in every class, they can catch fire with enthusiasms generated by other kids and I can give them the extra time they need as I circulate among my students and confer. As Goodlad concluded, I can provide conditions favorable for everyone's learning because everyone has access to the same knowledge, and my low ability students can take an active part in interesting and complex activities.

Identified as special education students, Sean and Leah could be mainstreamed for English instruction because my eighth grade English course is a writing workshop. They brought their individual interests and ability levels to the workshop, and I brought my expectation that they would write. Leah wrote a play, narratives, and letters, entered two essay contests, and composed pages and pages of poetry. Leah's favorite of her poems, the one she decided to publish in the eighth grade yearbook, described one of her favorite places.

The Island

Seaweed, shells along the rocks.
The cool breeze blew across my face.
I sat there on the island,
looking across at from where I had come.
Surrounded by trees,
all alone.
As I sat on some grass by the water
I pictured myself
living here on the island
in a beautiful house.
The currents got stronger
and the sun was going down
all yellow and orange
as I went back across
to from where I had come.

Sean compiled a book of poetry. His favorite poem described his least favorite place, a small, stark room off the main office where he sat out an in-school suspension.

Green Walls

Green walls here,
green walls there,
green walls everywhere.
Would it,
could it,
ever stop . . .
the green walls of the office?
I sit and work three days long.
Help me, please, would you, please?
Finally someone comes through the door.
It's a teacher — she sits down and says,
"Could I get you anything?"
I have a problem,

here, there, and everywhere.
Please, get me out of here!
It's driving me up the
green walls.

Sean and Leah learned about poetry by reading it, hearing it read by me and their friends, and writing their own. Leah, in turn, nudged her friend Julie to try her hand at poetry and responded to each of Julie's drafts. When students are surrounded by poetry, they'll write poetry. When students aren't measured against each other, they'll feel free to take risks and give and accept help. When students aren't tracked, we teachers will be free to expect and encourage each student's best, and our less able kids will have the chance to see themselves as capable.

Barry sees himself as capable. He's another special ed student mainstreamed for English. When he came to the group share meeting that ended one afternoon's writing workshop, it was with the language, information, and expectations of a writer. Before he read his piece to the class, Barry told them what he needed: "This is my second draft about going squirrel hunting up to Back Narrows, but it ain't got no context. I'm looking for places to embed the context." Until the bell rang, Barry taught us what he knew about squirrel hunting, and we listened for places where we wanted to know more.

As exasperated as I get with the bells that regulate my time with my kids, I know it's essential that Barry and the others in his section pack up and travel to other classrooms and other teachers. Departmentalization in junior high is valid not just because adolescents need to move, but because they need a variety of adults with whom to interact, a range of personalities and perspectives from which they can learn and choose to align themselves. And they need teachers who know their subjects. Goodlad found that teachers of the subjects for which kids expressed greatest liking and interest tended to be those who viewed themselves as adequately prepared (p. 185). I know — and love — language. Junior high students are at an age when they still know they don't know everything. They're more likely to learn in cooperation with knowledgeable teachers convinced of the value of their subjects and enthusiastic about sharing what they know.

My brother, a genealogist and historian, was hooked in the seventh grade by Miss Campbell, his social studies teacher. She belonged to all kinds of historical societies and professional groups, conducted her own research, showed kids how she went about studying local history, and engaged them in local research of their own. She hooked Glenn for life.

Nicholas Gage, former *New York Times* correspondent, is also the author of *Eleni*, the story of his mother's execution by communist guerillas for planning the escape of her children from their Greek village in 1948. Gage was hooked by his seventh grade English teacher, Miss Hurd. She listened to the young immigrant struggle to tell his mother's story, then helped him find the English words to write it. Gage's composition won an award from the Freedoms Foundation; more importantly, he discovered that his writing gave him the power to make up for his mother's sacrifice and avenge her death. Miss Hurd empowered Gage — and hooked him for life.

David Halberstam, the author and Pulitzer Prize winning journalist, John Bushnell, chief of mission in the American Embassy in Buenos Aires, and Ralph Nader, the consumer advocate, were all in the same seventh grade social studies class and were all hooked by the same teacher, Miss Thompson. Halberstam wrote, "She taught with genuine passion . . . encouraging young people at a delicate moment to think that they could be anything they wanted" (1984). Miss Thompson opened her classroom door to a world rich with intriguing possibilities.

Adolescents are ripe to be hooked. With good teaching, this is an age when kids who are going to, become interested and excited. When teachers demonstrate interest and excitement in our fields, we invite students to believe that learning is valuable. We answer the question, "Why do we have to do this?" with our own conviction and passion, modeling the power we derive from our knowledge and experience. We invite our students to join us in a compelling and worthwhile version of adult reality. In my writing and reading workshops I've cast off the trappings of the junior high English teacher status quo. I put my true authority on the line from the very first day of school: "I'm a writer and a reader. Writing and reading and teaching them to you are my life."

I write with my students. I show them my drafts. I ask for their responses in writing conferences. I tell them writing is a new habit, one that's changing my life. I tear my hair over my writing, but I keep on writing because I can't stop.

I read with my students. I show them what I'm reading and I talk about and lend my books. I tell them reading is an old habit, one that shaped my life and gives it so much meaning I don't know if I could go on living if I suddenly couldn't read. I even write about my reading:

Bibliophile

I can't control them.
I can't seem to intercede.
My eyes have a mind all their own.
With me or without me, they read.

They need to fix
On print at all times:
Cereal boxes at the breakfast table,
Junk magazines on the checkout line.

But mostly my eyes
Are craving good stories —
Stories about my life and times,
Found in others' loves and worries —

Stories that take me inside myself,
Stories that take me away,
Luring me into other worlds
Where, whenever I can, I stay

And stay
Until it's distressingly late

(Until my eyes need that other world
Where they rest and anticipate)

Fixing and fixing and fixing again
On someone's words and ways,
Making those words belong to me too,
Reeling in wonder and rage and dismay.

I couldn't live if I couldn't read.
It's nothing less: I'm hooked.
I know it sounds like a sales pitch
(YOUR ENGLISH TEACHER LOVES BOOKS)
But your English teacher loves books.

I'm demonstrating the truth. I love these things so much I can't imagine that my students won't love them, too. From the first day of school I expect they'll participate in written language as real writers and readers do — as I do — and I promise what we do together will make sense and bring satisfaction. These days my reputation as a teacher depends on the importance I place on writing and reading, how my passion informs my teaching, and how I invite kids to share that passion.

The first day of school last September I started the year by surveying my kids about their reading. I said, "This is for my information. I'm really interested in the truth. So please don't try to impress me or depress me. For this research to be valid and useful, I need you to be serious and honest." In one section of the survey I asked students to estimate how many books they'd read over the past twelve months. The final average was surprisingly high: twenty books. In June I readministered the survey, then gave back the September surveys and asked kids to conduct some research of their own, describing and analyzing any changes they found. What they did, in each class, was burst out laughing.

"What's so funny?" I asked.

"We lied," they answered.

In September, three-quarters of my students exaggerated the number of books they'd read. Their dishonesty blew the validity of that particular piece of research but turned up something ever more interesting. I asked why they'd lied, and all their answers were some variation on, "Because we'd heard about Ms. Atwell. We came in here knowing you expected us to be readers."

My teaching has to make good on my expectations. While trusting that all my kids will become involved, I also have to invite their involvement just as generously and sensibly as I can. My best invitation is the writing and reading workshop. Here, adolescents' social relationships can serve scholarly ends. Kids can be active, talking and moving as part of their activity as engaged writers and readers. They can capture and channel their ideas, feelings, and enthusiasms, have more say in their own learning, and assume greater independence. Here, I can teach by example, in conversation, and in context. I can nudge, challenging my kids to grow. I can watch their faces shine like beacons when they and a new idea connect. I can help make school make sense.

Junior high teachers make the best of our students when we accept and build on the realities of junior high kids. We can't wish away, discipline away, or program away a time of life. Nor can we afford to devote our days to reviewing past lessons or introducing "skills" to be tapped in some nebulous and assumed future. We're there to help our junior high kids open a window on adulthood, on what really matters in life; we help by opening our curricula to junior high preoccupations, perspectives, and growing pains.

In *School and Society*, first published in 1899, John Dewey wrote, "From the standpoint of the child, the great waste in school comes from his inability to utilize the experiences he gets outside of school in any complete and free way; while, on the other hand, he is unable to apply in daily life what he is learning at school."

When a junior high school begins to reflect the nature of its kids, the great waste in our schools wanes, and great purpose waxes. School can be good for something. School and life can come to terms in practical, rigorous ways. We make the best of adolescence when we make the junior high classroom the best context we can for the mercurial minds at work and play there.

SECTION II
Writing Workshop

Keith borrows a resource book from the materials center.

CHAPTER 3

Getting Ready

"Be regular and ordinary in your life like a bourgeoise so that you may be violent and original in your work."
Gustave Flaubert

One spring day Donald Graves and Mary Ellen Giacobbe drove up from New Hampshire to visit Boothbay Elementary's writing workshops. Our kids had been hearing about Don and Mary Ellen for a long time, so their visit was a special occasion schoolwide. Bert happened to be passing through the front lobby when they arrived that morning. He took the stairs to the junior high wing three at a time, then whipped down our corridor like some eighth grade Paul Revere, shouting as he passed each room, "The world's most famous writing teachers are here! The world's most famous writing teachers are here!"

Don spent a part of his visit in my room, with Bert and the other kids in section 8C. No one in 8C moved off into one of the conference corners that day — a first. Instead, they sat at their desks, writing away in absolute and eerie silence. Every now and then one writer or another chanced a glance to locate Don as he moved among them conferring, all of them dying for Don to drop by and whisper the magic entrée, "Tell me about your piece." Bert's anticipation was rewarded. Don knelt by his desk for a long chat about Bert's passion for sci fi and Frank Frazetta.

It was a good day. Taking themselves seriously as writers, our kids expected that Mary Ellen and Don would take them seriously, too. At the end of the day Don came and stood in my doorway with his coat on, smiling. "What are you smiling about?" I asked.

"I'm smiling at you," he said. "You know what makes you such a good writing teacher?"

Oh God, I thought. Here it comes: validation, from one of the world's greatest writing teachers. In a split second I flipped through the best possibilities. Was he going to remark on my intelligence? My commitment? My sensitivity?

"What?" I asked.

And he answered, "You're so damned organized."

Then Don stopped smiling, probably in response to the way my face must have crumpled. "Look," he explained seriously. "You can't teach writing this way if you're not organized. This isn't an open classroom approach, and you know it. It's people like you and Mary Ellen who make the best writing teachers. You two always ran a tight ship and you still do, but it's a different kind of ship."

A writing workshop *is* a very different kind of ship. From the beginning of writing workshop, I've organized and reorganized my room and my teaching to support writing and learning. And as Don suggested, I've had to define organization in a new way. I don't mean neatness — a good thing, too, because meticulousness will never feature among my virtues. By organization I mean discovering what writers need, and providing plenty of it. I was more than assuaged by Don's explanation because it included me in the same category as Mary Ellen, and no one knows better than she how to provide in school what writers need.

Mary Ellen Giacobbe's classroom was the primary site for the N.I.E. study Graves, Calkins, and Sowers conducted at Atkinson Academy. Currently a doctoral fellow at Harvard, Mary Ellen is a great teacher, of children and adults, and that's no accident of birth. She works hard at teaching well, continually reflecting on and revising her teaching so it provides a closer and closer approximation of what learners need. In organizing to teach writing, Mary Ellen provides three big basics.

Before any student comes anywhere near my classroom at the beginning of September, I want to be ready for our writing workshop. That means knowing what I expect will happen, knowing how, where, and when I expect it will take place, and knowing who's expected to do it. Murray says, ". . . it is our job as teachers of writing to create a context that is as appropriate for writing as the gym is for basketball" (1983, p. 228). I organize this environment beforehand, establishing my classroom as best I can as a place that invites and supports writing process so when my students arrive they'll find what they need to become writers. Writers need Giacobbe's three basics of time, ownership, and response.

Time

I pulled my chair up next to Amanda's and she read me her lead. This was a new piece, about attending Neil Diamond's concert in Portland the previous Friday night with her parents and sister. It began:

> "Okay, you're here. Do you want Mrs. Cook's binoculars? If you do, there are three caps you can't lose. Be careful not to let anything happen to them because they're not ours. If you have to go to the bathroom go now, not during the intermission, so you won't get lost and it won't be so crowded. At the end, meet us by the place where the hockey players go in. Okay?"

I recognized Amanda's father's voice. When she finished reading his instructions I asked her to go on. She'd already filled two pages with close descriptions of the events of Friday evening and verbatim dialogue — her family's as well as the chatter of the people in the seats around them. I laughed and shook my head. "Amanda, however did you remember all this in such detail?"

"Oh, I didn't," she answered. She pulled out a spiral-bound notebook and flipped through its pages. "I knew before we went that I'd want to write about it, so I brought this along and took notes all night on what was going on."

Amanda writes every school day, Monday through Friday. She thinks about her writing when she's not writing. She is a habitual writer.

Robbie and Karalee write every school day, Monday through Friday. Robbie was at home watching television one night, and school was about the farthest thing from his mind. Out of nowhere he came up with the perfect conclusion to his "Bert and I" story. He grabbed the only paper he could find in his house and scribbled away. The next day he came to class armed with a brown paper supermarket bag bearing the perfect ending.

Karalee came to class the same week with the lead of a new narrative, scrawled on little pieces of telephone message paper. She explained, "The other night, when I was spending the night at Susan's, I thought up the whole beginning of my new story in my head. Luckily I remembered it until I got to paper." She reshuffled her tiny manuscript pages, frowned, squinted, and stared off into space. I recognized I'd been dismissed and moved on so she could pick up the threads of her story.

Robbie and Karalee think about their writing when they're not writing; they, too, are habitual writers. Writers need time — regular, frequent chunks of time that they can count on, anticipate, and plan for. When we make time for writing in school, designating it a high priority activity of the English program, our students will develop the habits of writers — and the compulsions. Janet came into class one day and wailed, "Ms. A., my head is CONSTANTLY writing."

Graves recommends allotting at least three hours or class periods a week in order for this habit of mind to take hold, for students to begin to rehearse their writing offstage and come up with their own topics with some degree of success (1983, p. 223). When David said, "I can best think of things to write about just before I go to sleep — ideas seem to float into my head like hot air balloons," he was describing a ritual that could never evolve if he were a one-day-a-week writer.

Regular, frequent time for writing also allows students to write well. When they have sufficient time to consider and reconsider what they've written, they're more likely to achieve the clarity, logic, voice, and grace of good writing. Sandy commented, "If a teacher says, 'Do a full draft by the end of class,' I answer not, 'Yes, I can,' but 'I guess I have no choice.' Having to rush my writing cuts down on thinking time, and then on quality." Her friend Jennifer agreed. "When I get stuck, I take a little walk. Then I come back and try it again. I quit and come back and quit and come back because I know I won't write as well unless I give myself time to think."

I know exactly what they mean. I'm not a great first draft writer. I might not pass a course where writing was consistently assigned to be completed in a single class period; even if the requirement were a piece a week, I might never compose anything I liked or cared about. But allow me time to think, rethink, seek others' responses, and revise, and the chances are I can produce something readable.

Sandy and Jenn and I aren't alone. Hemingway revised the conclusion to *A Farewell to Arms* thirty-nine times. He had and took the time he needed to go back and solve any writer's greatest problem: "Getting the words right" (Plimpton; 1965, p. 222). Kurt Vonnegut wrote about time as the great leveler: anyone willing to put in the plodding hours can make a go of it as a writer.

> . . . novelists . . . have, on the average, about the same IQs as the cosmetic consultants at Bloomingdale's department store. Our power is patience. We have discovered that writing allows even a stupid person to seem halfway intelligent, if only that person will write the same thought over and over again, improving it just a little bit each time. It is a lot like inflating a blimp with a bicycle pump. Anybody can do it. All it takes is time (1981, p. 128).

Katherine Paterson, author of the Newbery Award winning classic *A Bridge to Terabithia*, talked about the way a regular writer's plodding days create the setting for her "good days":

> Those are the days you love. The days when somebody has to wake you up and tell you where you are. But there are a lot of days when you're just slogging along. And you're very conscious of your stuff and the typewriter is a machine and the paper is blank. You've got to be willing to put in those days in order to get the days when it's flowing like magic (1981).

We need to acknowledge in our teaching the realities of writing. A crucial reality is that good writers and writing don't take less time; they take more. Too many accounts of professional writers' practices have been published — *Writers at Work* is probably the best known series — for us to continue to cling to school myths of polished, first-time final drafts or weekly assignments. We need to acknowledge, once and for all, that "there is no instant writing — not even in America" (Simmons, 1982, p. 61).

Regular, frequent time also helps writers grow. Even when students write every day, growth in writing is slow and seldom follows a linear movement, each piece representing an improvement over the last. But regular, frequent time for writing also means regular, frequent occasions for teaching and learning more about writing. In context, over a whole year, I teach one new skill or issue at a time; in context, over a whole year, my kids try out new styles, subjects, rules, modes, forms, devices, techniques, and strategies. With adequate time to take risks and reflect, writers begin to be able to consider what's working and what needs more work, to apply new knowledge, and to take control.

I continue to learn this lesson. After a summer of teaching teachers, advising them from my pedestal to be patient with their students because growth in writing takes time, I suffered a rude shock when I went back to my classroom. My classes were filled with the worst eighth grade writers who ever breathed air. I wrote one seriously depressed letter after another to Mary Ellen that September, complaining about my new kids. My head was still too filled with images of last year's students — writers who had grown a whole year by the time they left me in June — for me to recollect and consider the good advice I'd lavished all summer long. By November I was sending Mary Ellen ecstatic letters filled with anecdotes and writing samples; I didn't remember my own advice until I saw my kids begin to prove it, gradually experimenting, applying, and growing.

B.J. was one of my eighth graders that September. In May he fished out his writing folder from seventh grade and brought it to school to show me. He was beside himself: "Listen to this one. Can you believe I wrote this and thought it was finished? Or how about this one — five paragraphs to say nothing, and then it just stops in mid-air. And then there's — hey, this would make a great story." A year after he thought he had finished "Hospital Time," B.J. went back and redrafted, bringing to his new version of the story the expertise he'd acquired over another year of writing workshop. It was growth neither of us had been fully aware of until we put the two pieces side by side.

6/5/83

Hospital Time

When I used to live on Peaks Island I had to have tubes put in my ears. I got to the hospital in the morning at 7:30 A.M. so that they would be sure that I would be fine for the operation. Well, after I had been in my bed for about an hour I got quite bored of watching cartoons.

All of a sudden I heard someone crying and coming towards my room. Suddenly my best friend Torr came in with a nurse holding his right arm. He was crying so hard he couldn't tell me what happened. Finally I got hauled into the operation room.

I finally got out of my sleeping with my mother at my side. I asked her what happened to Torr. She said, "He got hit by a bus". And then I went back to sleep.

The End

In 1984, a completely different writer is at work: new voice, new style, new perspective, new sense of story. B.J.'s lead alone is twice the length of his earlier version.

6/6/84

Hospital Time

"C'mon, B.J., get in the car!"

"Huh? What?"

"Get in the car!"

"Oh," I replied sleepily. "Let me get this straight. You think I can go far? I don't get it!"

My mom grabbed my arm, opened the door, and yelled in my ear: "Get in the car!"

"Oh, ok. Boy, just because I can't hear," I replied irritably.

My mom jumped in the car after me. I couldn't understand where we could be going at six o'clock in the morning. Man, I didn't like it.

"Uh, mom, uh, where could we be going in the wee hours of the morning?"

"Urr, urr, rumble, rumble."

That was all I could stand. First she starts yelling at me like a crazed maniac at six o'clock in the morning to get up. And now she won't even tell me what's up or, for that matter, what's goin' down.

"Where are we going?" I asked again.

"The hospital," she replied.

"Oh, uh, are you, uh, feeling o.k.?" I asked quizically.

"No, but ..."

Oh, no! God, no! Whenever she says "no but" and then trails off, something is up and it's not me.

"What's wrong, mom? Please tell me! Am I dying? Oh, please, tell me, please?"

"Oh, stop your belly-whoppin'. You're just having tubes put in your ears to make you hear better."

"I knew it! I knew I had /ukĕm... huh? I'm just having tubes put in? Yay! Yay! Uh, mom? Uh...what are tubes?"

And the rest of the latest "Hospital Time" unwinds in five more pages of self-aware overreaction. B.J. isn't just growing as a writer. He's growing up too.

When students have regular, frequent time set aside to write, writing can play a crucial role in helping them grow up, making it possible for them to capture who they are and then come back and measure themselves against that earlier self. Regular time for writing also allows students some control over this distance between their pasts and presents. When they can count on time always being there, they learn how to use it — when to confront, and when to wait.

Jennipher waited. Jenn's father died when she was in seventh grade and in early December of her eighth grade year she began to write about him. She covered page after page of yellow newsprint.

> 12/2
> 1st
>
> I was thirteen when my father died of cancer. I was almost a year ago and now when I see or hear that word feel a sinking feeling in my heart.
> Oh God I can't do this i think I'm going to die or freak out or something. But I guess not 'cause it wouldn't do anybody any good, including me.
> Oh, well I guess I'll live I'll just put it behind me and that will be the end of it forever, But maybe I can't do that. I'm scared.
> Oh God I think I'm going to die again, Oops! I guess not.
> I going to go eat a ton of lots chocolate get fat, hyper, and ~~this~~ of zits all at the same time

> Then I'll starve myself until
> I'm skinny again.
>   I'm still scared. I get these
> feelings that I have to hug
> somebody. So I hug my teddy bear and
> everything's all right.
>   But It really isn't cause nothing
> is ever all right And never will

Without reading or sharing what she'd written, Jenn tucked the yellow sheets away in the back of her writing folder. "It's too soon," she said. "I'm not ready." She went on to other topics. Twice again, in January and then in February, she retrieved the yellow sheets, added more, then folded them up and slipped them back into her folder. In March, Jennipher said, "I think I'd like to write a formal piece about my dad, but not tell it first person. That's too close and too hard." So her formal piece told the story of a girl a lot like Jennipher, with a dad a lot like David Jones.

Why?

"You're too old to cry," she thought as she forced back the tears and tried hard to listen to what the minister was saying.

"But I'm only thirteen," her thoughts interrupted. "This can't be happening to me." Some strong force was building up inside her now, and she wanted to scream. "I can't cry; I can't cry," she thought, holding tightly to her mother's hand. Her mother and brother were both crying.

When the ceremony was finally over, she was the last one to walk down the aisle and out of the church. Her cousin stood by the door. She burst into tears as she hugged her tightly. She was shaking as her cousin helped her down the steps where crowds of people were standing, talking. They were mostly her friends and family. She was hugged by an aunt and started to cry again. "Pull yourself together," she commanded herself, straightening up, wiping the tears from her face.

"It's funny all the time I've had to think in the last couple of days," she wondered, "even with all these people around." But she had thought. She'd thought about all the good times with her dad, about the stories her dad had told her.

He'd died of cancer three days earlier. When her aunt had told her she had cried and kept crying. "But now," she thought, "I can't cry again."

Then she was back at the house after the funeral, fighting through the crowds of *his* friends and family: that was who they really were.

She had the chance to see a lot of people, and talk about him and them, and herself.

She remembered again the stories he'd told. She loved the tale about the time he'd gone to Texas for treatment; had sat down on the curb waiting for his brother, who was checking the time of his appointment. A kid had come up to him to bum money for bus fare. Her father had asked him where he was from, and the boy replied, "Vermont." Her dad had teasingly responded, "I beat you; I'm from Maine." The boy had said something about his mother coming from a small town in Maine. And it happened that the boy's mother and her dad had grown up in the same town and had dated each other in high school.

Her dad was like that: he could make the whole world seem smaller and happier.

Now, the flowers around the house reminded her of the plants and flowers that had bloomed and blossomed under his green thumb. She snapped out of her reverie to realize someone was talking to her.

"He really was the greatest," the voice was saying.

She nodded, dazed, wanting to dwell on thoughts of all the good things about her father.

"Why him?" she asked herself. "It's not fair!" The voices were screaming inside her now. It was pure fear.

She pushed the thoughts away and walked upstairs, where most of the kids were hanging out. She smiled and said "Hi" to everyone. And as they talked she forgot all her troubles. But later, when she went downstairs again, she heard someone say, "She has her father's looks, doesn't she?" and someone else replied, "Oh, yes."

"No!" she thought. But it wasn't true. She had his eyes, his complexion, his hair.

Later in the day she'd once again forgotten everything that was wrong. She was laughing and talking with the others, playing games and watching tv. But in a moment a word triggered all those thoughts of her father and they came crashing back down on her.

She was so scared — not like being-afraid-of-the-dark scared, but a really deep down, somebody's-dead scared. She knew she would live and keep on living. But she'd still be scared, and maybe she'd have to try hard not to cry sometimes. And maybe every time someone mentioned cancer, or she read the word in a book, there would be an empty space somewhere in her stomach. Maybe someday she'd forget, or maybe someday she wouldn't. But her heart held one, great hope: that when she grew up, she might be as good a person as her dad had been.

JENNIPHER JONES

Jennipher benefited academically and personally from the steady availability of time to write. She — and Amanda, Robbie, Karalee, Janet, David, Sandy, Jennifer, B.J., and all their eighth grade classmates — benefit as writers from a quirk of Maine public schools. One reason they're able to write for fifty minutes every day, Monday through Friday, is that they come to my classroom twice on each of those days, once for writing and once again for a fifty-minute reading workshop. Maine is one of the few states where reading is generally taught as a separate course from English language arts right up through eighth grade.

When I sit down with my planbook in August, I write "Writers' Workshop" every place on my schedule where it says "English." Writers' workshop isn't an add-on; it is the English course, where everything that can validly be described as English is taught as sensibly as it can be taught, in the context of whole pieces of my students' writing. The luxury of my atypical schedule ensures that my kids will easily have at least three hours a week for writing.

If my schedule were more typical — just one fifty-minute period each day for English, literature included — I'd continue to give over all my class time to writing and reading workshops. But I'd teach writing on three regular, consecutive days, providing my students with the sense of routine and continuity writers need so that every Sunday evening they would know, "Tomorrow is Monday. Tomorrow and Tuesday and Wednesday, we'll be working on our writing in class. What will I be working on?" And if I had five or six straight English classes each day, I'd regularly schedule half my writing workshops for Wednesday, Thursday, and Friday, because I think listening hard to writers and writing for six periods straight three days running would be an exhausting proposition; on Wednesday, the overlap day, I'd make sure Toby took me out to dinner. The other two days of each school week I'd devote to literature, to reading workshop, nudging students to take home over the weekend those books they'd read in class.

Time for independent writing — and reading — isn't the icing on the cake, the reward we proffer senior honors students who've survived the curriculum. Writing and reading are the cake. When we make time, giving students one of a writer's basic necessities, we begin to make writers.

Ownership

Neat stacks of class sets of literature anthologies, interspersed with the plants I brought back to school every September, once marched across the countertop that runs the length of one wall of my classroom. Pretty displays I put up and took down depending on the unit I was covering that week covered the bulletin board that runs the width of the room. And twenty-seven student desks formed a perfect oval with one end ballasted by my big desk. It was a work of art, my work of art. Sometimes, leaving school, I'd pause with my hand on the light switch and admire my room before plunging it into darkness and heading for my other home, also interior-decorated by me for my convenience and pleasure.

Donald Graves compares a classroom organized as a writer's workshop to an artist's studio (1981). The artist sets up her studio so it has everything she needs arranged to suit her and her art. In the midst of the messy and unpredictable act of creating, the artist knows just where to find the desired palette knife or brush or tube of color. The studio exists for the convenience of the artist at work there, just as the writing classroom should exist for the convenience of young writers.

I think about the September I decided not to put up my Welcome Back bulletin board as another hallmark in my evolution. I left bare the whole back wall of cork and told my eighth grade classes, "This is your room. That's your bulletin board. Feel free to fill it up." And they did, with their drawings and private jokes, with lists of books they owned and were willing to loan, with riddles, poems, announcements, newspaper and magazine clippings, kindergarten class pictures — with kids' stuff. I went down to the boiler room, found a half dozen cardboard boxes, loaded them full, and took my teacher stuff home. Even my plants. Then I shelved the class sets of anthologies in cupboards and cleared the countertops for more kids' stuff, this time for the stuff of writers and readers.

Stacks of individual paperback titles, about a thousand all told, and plenty of bookmarks and sign-out sheets now form the eighth grade classroom library along half of the countertop space. Appendix G, a list of the two hundred titles eighth graders consistently give high ratings, suggests a baseline classroom library for junior high.

The other half of the countertop became a place for writers to choose their materials: as many different kinds of paper as I can budget or scare up; cans holding markers, calligraphy pens, pencils, ballpoints, and rulers; cups of clips, tacks, and staples; a stapler and staple remover; scissors and tape; a date stamp and pad; boxes of stationery and envelopes; plenty of white-out liquid; collections of writers' resources and references including dictionaries, spellers, usage handbooks, lettering stencils, bookbinding materials and address files; in short, everything a writer might possibly need, each item consigned to its own space. Appendix *A* is the consummate list of classroom materials for writing and publishing — a sort of Sears catalogue Wish Book for writing teachers.

The bare bones materials for writing workshop are writing utensils, paper, scissors and tape for cutting and pasting, stapler, paper clips, correction fluid for ease in perfecting final copies, and manila folders. Each writer needs two, one a daily folder for work in progress and another that stays on file in the classroom to store the whole collection of a student's finished pieces with all their accompanying drafts and notes, September until June. My annual budget request, featuring money for writing supplies and new paperbacks to rejuvenate the classroom library, runs a half to two-thirds the size of my old budgets; for what it would have cost to replace a single textbook I can buy a dozen bottles of white-out fluid. This is one argument to use on reluctant administrators: writing workshop is cheap.

Finally, my students and I arranged and rearranged the room, using classroom furniture to establish the work places they need as writers. Graves says the workshop "expects writing" (1983, p. 270); like the studio that expects art, it has its own rules, organization, and structure. The best arrangement we could create in the confines of a classroom consists of seven areas.

First there's the counter space that became the center for writing materials, where students go to get supplies and tools, check references, and so on. Next to this are three stack-trays, one for each class, labeled "Writing Ready To Be Edited"; here students place pieces they've self-edited and want me to blue-pencil in preparation for finished copy and publication. A fourth stack-tray collects "Writing To Be Photocopied," final copies of correspondence and other publications which I'll xerox after school and distribute in the next day's classes.

Beside these stands a file cabinet to which each class has access to one drawer. This is the repository for permanent writing folders, filed alphabetically, then numbered too, making it even easier to retrieve and replace them. We collect and file everything, and writers have access to their files, so they and I have a basis for observing growth and setting goals through the year.

In the front corner of the classroom, as far from the hurly-burly of the workshop as we could put it, stands the table kids call "No Man's Land." Writers work here, their backs to the room, when they want solitude and no interference; pulling up a chair at this table is a signal to friends and me that a writer doesn't want to confer.

In the center of the classroom are students' desks, grouped so I can walk around them to confer with individual writers. Writers do most of their writing here, and while a writer at work can be called upon by another student for response, their conference won't take place here.

Figuring out how to accommodate both writers' need for quiet and their need to talk about their writing presented our biggest headache in arranging the room as a workshop. At first students wrote and conferred at their groups of desks. At least five times each period I'd stand up wherever I was in the room and announce, "It's too noisy in here." The volume level would lower for about five minutes; then I'd have to stand up and make my announcement again, and again. The solution was obvious: writers needed a place to talk. Now, when two or more writers have arranged to confer with each other, they pick up their writing, leave the central writing area, and move to one of four "Conference Corners," labeled areas formed by the lockers and coat racks that run along one wall. That there are just four places — areas I pass continually as I circulate around the room — keeps another check on the noise level of the workshop.

The seventh place is a carpeted area at the front of the classroom, the location of our daily group share meetings. We push back desks to make enough room for the whole class to sit on the floor; in a circle, we hear from and help one or two writers near the close of each workshop.

This predictable environment, with each area and its uses clearly established, sets the stage for students' experimentation, decision-making, and independence. Writers in a workshop can exert ownership because they're not waiting for the teacher's motivational pre-writing activity or directions for "fixing" a piece of writing; instead, they're using the tools and procedures at their disposal to motivate and improve their own writing. Their writing belongs to them and they are responsible for it. As Don McQuade remarked, "The good writing teacher isn't responsible *for* his students' writing. He is responsible *to* his students" (1984).

My students constantly remind me of my responsibilities to them. Brendan, who moved to Boothbay Harbor over the summer, drafted a piece about the best friend he left behind in Maryland. His writing touched on a couple of different memories at a time when I was nudging eighth graders to narrow the focus of their narratives to single incidents described in close detail. In our conferences I nudged Brendan hard: "You have memories of all these adventures, all these things you did together. Which is the one you'd like to tell really well?" Brendan dug in his heels. He liked his piece the way it was; his friend would understand. I came back with more nudges, he stood his ground, and I gave up, respecting his ownership and knowing I could nudge next time around, with his next narrative. As far as Brendan was concerned, "Memories" was a finished piece. He and I edited it, then he wrote a final which I photocopied for him to send to his friend.

Memories

Saying good-bye to your first and best friend has got to be one of the hardest things to do after all the times you've had together . . . like when you're five and you're out playing in the mud next to your house in the big field and you lose one of your shoes in the waist-deep mud. And you have mud on yourself everywhere it's possible to have mud, and it starts to rain. So you start to leave (as if the rain could hurt) and you each decide to go home with the other to stop your moms from killing you.

That, to me, used to be friendship, but now it's a memory. And the odds that I'll ever do anything like this again seem astronomical. And at any time at all, a memory will burst into my mind, some good, some bad. But I love every one, because I did every one with my best friend.

I'll never have another friend like him. Even the fights we had don't seem to scratch the record we have of being two great friends.

Then the thing I dreaded the most came to be: I moved! It was odd the way we never said good-bye; the way we just casually waved as he climbed into his sister's car. We'd thought we would see each other the next day to say good-bye, but we didn't.

Those are all just memories now, eight hundred miles apart in two different minds. I know I'll never forget these memories, or him.

BRENDAN KANE

I'd been so intent on my agenda for Brendan's piece I hadn't listened to him. Brendan wrote "Memories" as a gift; it took the place of the letter he couldn't write because he was too embarrassed to directly broach his feelings. This safer format matched his purpose. None of this dawned on me until his mother wrote me a note at Christmas and mentioned in passing that "Memories" was the first thing Brendan had written that meant anything to him. It was so important to him that she'd had a copy framed for his bedroom wall as a special Christmas present. If I'd insisted on revision and taken ownership of his piece, the chances are pretty good that I'd have robbed Brendan of his accomplishment and "Memories" of its meaning.

When we sit quietly, wait, and listen, our students will tell us what they're trying to do as writers. Our job is to give time and ownership, and then help them know what it is they want to use time to do. We help in the writing conference, the "workmanlike conversation about writing in progress" (Sowers, 1982, p. 76).

Response

At age thirty-seven Carolyn Chute just published her first novel, the best-seller *The Beans of Egypt, Maine.* A high school drop-out, Chute has been writing since she was eight years old but never wrote in school and never took any of her writing to school to show her teachers. She explains:

> My stories were so precious to me; I didn't want my teachers to touch them, because everything I ever did in school was attacked by them. I even had a nightmare when I was an adult that my home economics teacher was ripping all my stories up and throwing them around. I think it's because she threatened my dignity while I was in school. (1985, pp. 8–9)

Writers are vulnerable. That's the writer there on the page, his or her essential self laid bare for the world to see. A writer wants response that is courteous and gentle, that gives help without threatening the writer's dignity. Every adult remembers at least one real experience writing in school comparable to Chute's nightmare, when an English teacher's response took the form of an attack: red ink bled all over a piece of writing that represented the writer's level best.

At the same time writers are inquisitive. They want to discover how they can improve the essential selves they present to the world. A writer wants response that takes the writer seriously and moves him or her forward, again, response that gives help without threatening the writer's dignity. All of us also remember a time when something we did elicited a compliment that felt contrived; it didn't help because our own standards told us we could have done better.

In *Children's Minds,* Margaret Donaldson defines the conflict between disciplined, rule-centered, "formal" education on the one hand, and child-centered, "progressive" education on the other, and concludes: "I can only see one way out of this dilemma: it is to exercise such control as is needful with a light touch and never to relish the need" (1978, p. 126). Murray, writing about writing conferences, concurs: "I teach the student not the paper but this doesn't mean I'm a 'like wow' teacher. I am critical and I certainly can be directive but I listen before I speak" (1982, p. 159).

Writers need to be listened to. They need honest, human reactions. They need teachers who help them discover the meaning they don't yet know by helping writers discover and build on what they *do* know. Writers need response while the words are churning out, in the midst of the messy, tentative act of drafting meaning. And they need to be able to anticipate and predict the teacher's approach. As Graves says, "Writing is such an unpredictable, up-and-down affair, that the help structure should be highly predictable. The more unsettled the writer, the more he needs to find the teacher's approach predictable" (1983, p. 273).

At the end of September Sabrina started a new piece called "The Dream of the Dead." Sabrina's mother is Vietnamese and she tells Sabrina and her brother, Mark, stories about her growing up in Vietnam. One night she told them the story of a childhood dream, and Sabrina decided to write it. She began her first draft the next day in school, but stopped after only a paragraph.

The Dream of the Dead   ① 9/22/83

We're sitting quietly on Mark's bed, listening to the pattering of the rain. Mom starts with the funeral of her grandfather in her dream. She and her relatives went to a small house. She relizes it's her grandparents. To her surprize when she went in, she saw her grand father!

The next day Sabrina started again, taking a slightly different tack this time, directly quoting her mother's words. Again, she got only a little way into the piece before she bogged down.

The Dream of the Dead   ② 9/23/83

We're sitting quietly on Mark's bed, waiting for my mother to start. She begins "We're going to my grandfather's funeral," said Mom "In Vietnam, we wear black to ward off evil spirits and in America, to show your mourning." "I stayed with my grandmother all night, so she wouldn't be lonely."

Sabrina was busy making faces at her paper when I came along and parked my little conference chair next to her desk. "How's it going?" I asked, leaning on her desktop and meeting her eyes.

"Not good," she answered.

"Tell me about it." I propped my chin on my folded arms and waited.

"Well, I'm trying to write about this dream of my mom's that she told me and Mark about, but I can't get it to come out right. This is my second try and it's just not working."

"What's the problem?"

She bit her lip and looked from her second draft to her first. "I don't know all the little details and stuff," she decided. "I can't remember all that she told us."

I paraphrased what I'd heard Sabrina saying. "You're having a hard time telling your mother's story. She knows the details that you don't." Sabrina nodded. "That is a problem. What could you do about it?" And I waited again, to hear Sabrina's options for solving the problem of this piece.

"Well . . ." she hesitated. "I could go home tonight and interview my mom about the details and write down what she says."

"That's an option," I agreed. And, because I write and confer a lot with other writers, I know another option; I throw it into the pot for Sabrina's consideration. "Here's another. Sometimes, when I have just a glimpse of a situation rather than the whole big panorama with all its details, I'll try it as a poem, where what I want is a kind of shorthand version. That's something else to consider." Then I stood, picked up my conference chair, and moved off to confer with another writer in another corner of my room.

Sabrina hadn't written poetry before. She went to the materials center, got more paper, and started draft three of "Dream of the Dead," this time as a poem.

Draft three did what Sabrina wanted. When the content was exactly as she wanted it she edited; she published her final copy in the October issue of the school literary paper, *The BRES Reporter.* In November, during our first quarterly evaluation conference, Sabrina said "Dream of the Dead" was the best of her five pieces of first quarter writing. "It's good because it's so mysterious, and because it's a poem," she said.

The Dream of the Dead

We're sitting quietly on Mark's bed,
listening to the patter of the rain.
Mom begins to talk.
She begins with the story
of her grandfather's funeral in Vietnam.
(This is before she tells us of her dream.)
They pass before his body and
give the new widow gifts.
Mom does not look at him.
All are dressed in black
to ward off evil spirits.
When she goes home
to her own bed,
she dreams of a party
at her grandparents' house.
Her grandfather is there,
pale in color, strange looking.
Mom helps him cook a chicken.
It's crispy and brown on the outside.
When cut,
the inside is bloody and raw.
No one notices
except my mother.
Everything is quiet —
then everyone is gone!
Suddenly her grandfather becomes
a bat.

He starts to chase her.
She runs
and hurdles over a stool
into a void of darkness.
The void of darkness
turns into the soft bed of her parents.
And we — Mark, my mother and I —
are suddenly back on Mark's bed
in America.

SABRINA LEWIS

The before, during, and after of my conference with Sabrina is typical; its elements are repeated day in and day out in writing workshop conferences right from the first day of school. The before, during, and after of the conference quickly become a predictable pattern, one writers can anticipate as well as repeat in their conferences with each other.

One constant is immediacy of response. Students know I'll respond in person during the writing rather than in written comments at the end. The purpose of writing workshop is to help kids develop their abilities as writers, not to assign sink-or-swim tests of writing ability, denying help along the way. After-the-fact response comes too late to do a writer much good; it assumes that students will not only hold the teacher's advice in their heads until the next piece and transfer it to an entirely new situation, but also that they actually read teachers' written comments. All of us who've ever spent entire, dreaded Sundays commenting on class sets of compositions have suspected on occasion that we're shouting down a hole. Don Murray's suspicions were so strong he conducted a small experiment one Sunday afternoon, writing purposely bad advice all over his students' papers: "do this backward," "add adjectives and adverbs," "be general and abstract." When Murray passed back the papers not one of his students questioned his comments (1982, p. 158).

I never write comments on students' writing. My marks are limited to straight editing of final drafts — either correcting or indicating the errors students missed when self-editing. I never have dreadful Sundays. Because writers are working and finishing pieces at their own paces, usually no more than five or six papers are submitted for my editing each day from each class: a half hour's routine each afternoon after school. Writing workshop provides time in school for students to work on their writing; it provides time in school for me, too, to work *with* students on their writing.

Another conference constant is *where* I work with students. I go to them, to their desks. I move because I'm trying to keep conferences brief and see many students each day. I started out with a special conference table at the front of the room where I sat for the duration of the workshop, meeting with writers one or two at a time. There were problems. I couldn't get rid of students once they'd joined me at the table: they had Ms. Atwell at their disposal until they decided to return to their seats, and they had me taking too much responsibility for listening to whole pieces of writing, identifying problems, and coming up with solutions. I saw just six or seven writers each period and I was constantly distracted by what the kids on line for the conference table seats were up to, not to mention the behavior in the far corners of the classroom.

When I move I can better control the length of the conference, see almost every writer every day, and monitor classroom behavior in general. At Lucy Calkins' suggestion, I move in a zig-zag fashion around the room so my kids always know I could be anywhere in the room in a second.

I move carrying my mandatory piece of writing conference equipment, the plastic, primary student's chair I liberated from the kindergarten storage area. For the first two years of writing workshop I knelt alongside students' desks. By the end of the second year my knees had given out — I could still get down but getting up again was another story. Now I carry my tiny chair, park it for each conference, and look up into my kids' faces.

I need to look at writers' faces because I'm an inveterate English teacher. If I look at a draft-in-progress, it's all over. While writers are drafting, their primary and overriding concern is with meaning, and when a writer reads or talks to me about a piece, I can focus on his or her meaning. When I read a draft, my eyes are drawn inexorably to errors. I'll want to focus on errors eventually, but only after the meanings are worked out and the student has submitted to me to edit. So as I move I avoid looking at the writing and, early on, if a student hands me a piece-in-progress and says, "Read this and tell me what you think," I hand it right back saying, "I don't read drafts. I need to listen. Why don't you tell me what *you* think?" When I accept the piece to read, I've accepted responsibility for it; worse, I've established a pattern, and kids will expect me to read their pieces and take responsibility again and again.

As much as possible, responsibility for the conference transaction rests with the writer. My students know I'm going to ask them to describe or assess their writing, that I'll open every conference with one of the two open-ended questions that are a writing teacher's stock in trade: "Tell me about your piece," and "How's it coming?" (Calkins; 1983, p. 132). By November I often don't have to say a word. When I pull up my chair the writer starts right in telling me how it's going or reading the part that needs more work or the section that's working well. And the conference proceeds in an equally predictable fashion: I wait, listen hard, tell what I heard, ask questions about things I don't understand or would like to know more about, ask what the writer might do next, and offer any options I might know of.

The purpose of our talks isn't to get the writer to revise. I confer with them about their content to help writers consider what's working, what needs more work, and what — if anything — they might do next. One aspect of content at a time and, later on, one skill at a time, we build together on what the writer knows. My goal is what Vygotsky termed "mediated" learning: "What the child can do in cooperation today he can do alone tomorrow" (1962, p. 104). Tomorrow, Sabrina can choose poetry as her mode on her own.

Learning to wait and listen have been the hardest parts of conferring for me. Mary Budd Rowe's work with teachers has shown we generally wait less than a full second before responding to what a student has said (1974). Dead air in the classroom made me so nervous I'd blunder in with my judgments and advice, answering my own questions if the writer weren't fast enough and listening to what they had to say mostly so I'd know when it was my turn to talk again — a less than thoughtful response.

I've learned to relax, to use the predictable pattern of the writing conference to make room for deliberation and reflection. When I listen hard I don't have to worry about what I'm going to say next; the writer and what the writer is telling me or reading to me become my focus. If I get sidetracked, and I often did when I first began listening to writing, I ask the writer to tell me or read to me again.

I listen hard so I can tell back what I've heard, so I may reflect for the writer. Susan Sowers says, "When a teacher reflects on a child's writing, she mirrors the text. She may summarize, paraphrase, or restate" (1982, p. 77). If my summary, paraphrase, or restatement doesn't match the student's vision of the text, there's a problem. The image in the mirror is distorted and now it's the writer's turn to reflect on his or her text. I help here with general questions I have as a curious human being — "I don't understand this" or "Please tell me more about that" — questions that invite the writer to talk, to elaborate and clarify.

Finally, I give the writer a chance to talk about and try out his or her options. The first year of writing workshop I was struck by the answers my kids gave when I asked, "What could you do next?" Often the solutions they developed on their own were the same as those on the tip of my tongue; just as often they came up with solutions that had never occurred to me. The longer I write and confer with writers, the more I know about writers' real strategies and the greater the pool of resources I have from which to draw my options, offering them in the form of nudges in our writing conferences. I nudge and share what I know because this is another of my responsibilities to my students. Murray writes:

> Teachers should not withhold information that will help the student solve a writing problem. The most effective teacher, however, will try by questioning to get the student to solve the problem alone. If that fails, the teacher may offer three or more alternative solutions, and remind the student to ignore any of them if a solution of the writer's own comes to mind (1983, p. 233).

I'm working toward the day my knowledge and experience are such that I have three or more alternatives to offer. In the meantime I can offer my one or two options, then walk away. It's up to Sabrina to decide what she'll do next. I have other writers to see. Tomorrow when I circulate I'll see Sabrina again and ask her again, "How's it going?" In these short, daily conferences I'm not asking to hear every word every writer writes, not attempting to take responsibility for their writing. I'm making myself available to work with many writers, one issue at a time. When it comes time to deal with editorial issues, I'll focus in much the same way, conferring with individuals one skill at a time.

One day at a time I build a predictable pattern of response to my students' writing — always beginning with the writer's meaning, with ideas and information, then reflecting, concentrating on one or two concerns, nudging, waiting, coming back. They can count on me — and they keep coming back.

While I was in the middle of writing this section, illustrating with Sabrina's "Dream of the Dead," two letters arrived from Sabrina. In March of their freshman year, she, Kellie, and Julie were trying to find time after school and their homework to get together and write a short novel and Sabrina needed response:

> ...Jules, Kel & I are starting to write a story about three kids who go into a cave/tunnel and find themselves in an another world. The main characters are Kirk, Craig, + their sister Erin, and their dog Hershey. We're each starting the begining by ourselves. Mine starts like this:
>
> The darkness of the night surrounded the three Phillips children as they quickened their footsteps to the safety of a nearby cave. The cave sheltered Kirk 16, Craig 14, Erin 5, and their dog Hershey from the steady pounding of the drenching rain. Erin, the youngest of the three, huddled with Hershey their _____ dog in the corner of their damp musty shelter.
>
> Does that sound alright? Do you know of any kind of dog that's small but not a poodle, chehuahua, or beagle? Can you have a damp & musty place at the same time? Help!...

Sabrina knows how to approach me about her writing. She begins with content. She confers while the piece is in progress. She asks a writer's questions about information. And she knows how I'll approach her, reflecting her content, questioning, exploring options, and answering her writer's questions.

Sabrina's second letter came in this week's mail. In the midst of all the latest news she wrote, "We've sort of put a halt on our story because we just don't have any time to get together to work on it." Her life is full — of high school's extracurricular and social activities, baby-sitting jobs, friends, lots of homework. Sabrina is in earnest. She wants to write and in fact she has no time. Her English teacher seldom sponsors in-class writing. If Sabrina is going to continue to grow as a writer, her school is going to have to make time for her to write.

Getting Ready

At the end of every August I spend a week or two at school getting organized for writers' workshop. The time I spend in preparation saves me and my students incalculable time once school begins for the business of teaching and learning writing. I set up the different work sites — putting out supplies and references where writers will choose materials (and identifying these as mine with the loudest, fluorescent-colored labels I can find); taping signs up over the areas I've designated as conference corners and affixing a pocket holding paper for note-jotting to the wall by each area; labeling the trays or tubs where writers will put pieces ready for me to edit and photocopy; readying the writing folders. The permanent writing folders are easy: just label with writers' names and stack them alphabetically in the file drawer or box where they'll remain until June. The daily writing folders require more preparation. In addition to storing works-in-progress, they'll serve as a writer's organizational and record-keeping system. I run off and staple inside each daily folder three forms which become the writer's responsibility to maintain. (Graves, 1983, p. 287; Giacobbe, 1984).

On the inside right I attach two lined sheets, one headed "Titles and Dates of Finished Pieces" and on top of that, "My Ideas for Writing." Writers will keep track through the year of what they have written and what they might write. Chapter 6 gives examples of and information about the uses and usefulness of topic and idea lists.

On the inside left I staple another lined sheet titled "Things_____ Can Do as a Writer." This will become the writer's individual editing and proofreading list as I teach skills in individual editing conferences and these new skills become the writer's responsibility (Giacobbe, 1984). Chapter 5 gives examples of and information about editing conferences and skills instruction — as well as status-of-the-class conferences and general conference record-keeping. The last two are my responsibility, and in August I prepare the simple forms where I'll keep these records.

The status-of-the-class chart is a grid listing the names of all the students in a class down the left-hand margin, with a box for each day of the week next to each name. I run off forty copies, one for every week of the school year. This chart will be my daily lesson plan where I'll record writers' plans and activities at the beginning of every class.

My other record-keeping device is a conference journal, one for every eighth grade section. In these notebooks I allocate six to eight pages for each writer, in alphabetical order. Here, through the year, I'll record the skills I teach in individual editing conferences — information particularly interesting to parents — as well as other, anecdotal information about what goes on in content conferences — information particularly interesting to me as a teacher-researcher.

And that's it for record-keeping. I have no need for my grade book since I'm no longer evaluating individual pieces of writing, and my lesson plan-book mostly serves me as a reminder: my schedule is different every day of the week so I can never remember which class comes in when for writing or reading. It's the one disconcerting element in the workshop's otherwise comfortable routine.

The day after Labor Day, the routine begins. My students start out with what writers need, the interdependent triad of time, ownership, and response. All three have to be there in full measure — regular, sustained time, writers' own decisions about their processes and products, and opportunities to confer about works in progress — if eighth graders are to become writers.

At the end of the Atkinson study Graves wrote:

> . . . when all the data were in and the information brewed down to the most important finding, we recorded that:
>
> WRITING IS A HIGHLY IDIOSYNCRATIC PROCESS THAT VARIES FROM DAY TO DAY.
>
> Variance is the norm, not the exception.
>
> Good teaching enhances even greater variation. The more risks a writer takes, and the more tools at the writer's disposal to carry out an audacious intention, the more the writing will vary in quality (1983, p. 270).

Writing can vary — and writers can grow — when the environment is unvaryingly reliable. The predictable schedule, physical arrangement of my classroom, and patterns of my response combine with the predictable structure of each day's class — the subject of the next chapter — so that writers' minds can range. The workshop is constant, but it's rarely monotonous.

Last year near the end of the school year Brian said, "You know what I like best about this class? Anything can happen in here." He explained, "I never know what Danny or Eric or Mike have come up with when they ask me for a conference. What's even better is, I never know what I'll come up with." I get ready in August so Brian can surprise himself all year long.

A group share meeting

CHAPTER 4

Getting Started

"Who says kids can't write the first week of school?"
Mary Ellen Giacobbe

I took a year's leave of absence from my classroom to write this book, and during that year spent a lot of time in other teachers' classrooms, demonstrating writing workshop approaches. Altogether I probably orchestrated thirty first days, kicking off a year of writing workshop for thirty teachers and their students. In every classroom I visited, primary through high school in every kind of community, every student had an idea to write about that first day and every student wrote. And every time it happened I shed another layer of my old topic anxiety.

The annual prospect of getting my own students started writing annually sent me into a small panic. In spite of my belief in the centrality of writers' own topics and all my good experiences asking kids to come up with their own, I always feared I'd encounter the beast that lurked: The Class with No Ideas for Writing. It never happened. Like the students in the classrooms I visited during my leave, all my eighth graders wrote every first day.

Now, having taken the plunge with so many students in so many schools with such consistent results, I think I may have shed the final layer of first-day panic. I've come to thoroughly believe Don Murray's observation: "Our students *will* write — if we let them" (1982, p. 146). I've come to thoroughly trust Harold Rosen's maxim: "Everyone has a story to tell" (1983). And I've learned that getting students started writing is an easy thing to do.

Getting everyone started writing on a topic of his or her choosing is the main thing I hope to accomplish the first day of school. Sometimes other teachers suffering first-day nerves ask about starting kids off with assigned topics and gradually easing into self-selection. I advise not. Don Graves's metaphor holds true. When we assign topics we create a welfare system, putting our students on writers' welfare (1983, p. 98). The student who writes this week on a topic I provide is going to show up the next week and the next requiring more topic hand-outs. He's learned that I'll do his thinking for him. Although I know from experience that the cycle can be broken, I also know from experience that it can be a hard cycle to break. It just makes good sense to jump in, so that right from the first day of writing class, kids' own ideas lie at the heart of the course.

In addition to getting those first pieces of writing going, the first day's meeting serves to introduce three of the writing workshop's four routines: the mini-lesson, writing workshop proper, and the group share meeting that ends every class. The fourth component, the status-of-the-class conference, necessarily makes its entrance on Day Two. From that point on, writing class follows a predictable pattern of five-minute lesson, quick status-of-the-class check, at least half an hour for the workshop's main business of writing and conferring, and five or ten minutes for the concluding whole-class share session. The routines may require time to take on meaning, but the structure they provide is in place from the start.

This chapter describes a typical first day's writing workshop — what we do and why we do it. I've introduced in context the mechanics of mini-lessons, the workshop proper, and group share, all concepts which reappear throughout the rest of *In the Middle*. And, I hope, I've demonstrated why getting all this started is so easy. Given the chance, knowing he had all the time he needed to tell his story well, surrounded by other writers with stories to tell and trusting those others were interested in what he had to say, who wouldn't write?

The Mini-Lesson

Lucy Calkins (1986) came up with the idea of mini-lessons, a brief meeting that begins the workshop where the whole class addresses an issue that's arisen in previous workshops or in pieces of students' writing. It might be an editorial issue — how to punctuate dialogue or set up a business letter. I also use this time to talk about issues of process or technique — the difference between revising and recopying, or how to show rather than tell — and to introduce different modes and genres writers might want to try out for themselves, usually by reading short selections aloud. At the beginning of the school year, my mini-lessons deal with procedural issues — how to use the daily writing folder, what resources and materials are available to writers, how to self-edit and where to put writing ready to be teacher-edited, what to do in conference corners. In a mini-lesson on conferences I'll discuss helpful ways of responding, and role-play good and bad conferences with a couple of my kids. At first I lead the discussions, but as the year progresses students share their expertise, too. Mini-lessons generally last between five and ten minutes, just long enough to touch on some timely topic.

Mini-lessons are a relatively new element in my classroom. When I first made the shift from writing assignments to writing workshop, I stopped lecturing and abandoned whole-group instruction. I moved out of the driver's seat and observed as my students sat behind the wheel and took control. I had to stay out of their way for a while and learn from them, another necessary step in my evolution. But a time came when I felt confident of my new expertise and ready to move back up front, sharing control now with my kids. I learn from them and I share my knowledge when something I've learned will help them. One of the occasions when I share what I know is the conference; another is the mini-lesson.

And that's the point of the mini-lesson: sharing personal knowledge of writing. The problems my students come up against mirror problems I confront in my own writing; these are professional writers' problems, too. We all struggle with leads that will invite a reader's engagement, with dialogue that will express character, with the subtleties of transitions and the complexities of punctuation. In mini-lessons I share my own, professional writers', and students' real solutions to these real problems. When I see kids struggling to come up with satisfying titles for finished pieces, I'll show them on an overhead how I tried Donald Murray's technique of brainstorming many titles (1984, pp. 84–91), grounding my mini-lesson in practical experience. I offer the technique as an option they may wish to try. I don't require "mastery" of mini-lesson information; I don't expect every one of my students is going to take to heart every word of the mini-lesson and put it immediately into effect. Even in my old writing assignment days, when I taught pull-out-the-stops, forty-five-minute maxi-lessons, that never happened.

Instead, the mini-lesson creates a communal frame of reference. Shelley Harwayne compares the mini-lesson to the roll call officer's spiel that begins every episode of *Hill Street Blues* (1984). An announcement about an at-large felon might at first seem completely irrelevant to a particular cop on the beat, but a few weeks later, when the officer catches sight of a familiar face through the windshield of her cruiser, she'll probably make the connection. The mini-lesson exposes kids to sensible, relevant information in this same way, enabling me to say to a particular writer, "Remember a few weeks ago when we talked about Don Murray's method of brainstorming to find a title? Why not give it a shot?"

My first day's mini-lesson is a topic search activity, one Mary Ellen Giacobbe taught me to help writers' wheels start turning; Graves describes a similar activity (1983, p. 12). It's the longest mini-lesson of the whole school year, in part because I'm establishing a foundation of expectations for the whole year, in part because I want to give kids some time to do the thinking and talking that start wheels turning. This is a transcript of a typical first day's mini-lesson — what kids and I do that enables all of us to discover the stories we want to tell.

> You'll need some paper — it doesn't matter what kind — and something to write with. That's your choice, too. Everybody seems to have his or her own. I always write with a finepoint Flair, and I love white composition paper, you know, the kind with wide lines and no margins. Okay?
>
> This morning when I woke up I knew we'd be writing today. So right away I started rehearsing, thinking about the stories I could tell, turning over different ideas in my mind while I was getting ready for school.
>
> As usual my dog was sitting on my stomach when I woke up, so it naturally occurred to me I could write about her. I write about Books and Toby a lot. Toby is my husband, and Books is my dog. Now, Toby

spends a truly astonishing amount of his time teaching Books to do things dogs don't have any right knowing how to do. For example, this dog won't come when she's called but she can identify by their names and fetch thirty-seven different rubber toys Toby's bought for her. So when he tells her to get her Goosie . . . I take that back. He doesn't tell Books to fetch her toys. Books's toys call to her. Toby, the world's worst ventriloquist, screeches in this weird little voice, "Books! I'm a Goosie! Come eat me!" And she does.

Facial expressions are the latest addition to Books's repertoire. She pulls the corners of her mouth way back and bares her teeth when Toby tells her to smile. It's actually pretty grotesque. Of all the so-called tricks Toby has taught Books, the one story I'm thinking of telling is the first time I saw Books smile.

I'd been away for a week, and a week is enough time for Toby to teach Books something major, so I should have been prepared. I came in our kitchen loaded down with luggage and Toby greeted me.

"Get down on your knees! Get down on your knees and look at Books's mouth."

"Toby, can this wait?"

It couldn't wait. So there I was, crouched down on the floor on all fours, trying to get a good look at my dog's mouth. Books, in the meantime, is on all fours, too, and is very excited that I'm home. No way is she going to stop wiggling so I can see her face. And the whole time Toby is saying, "There, did you see that? Did you see it?"

So then . . . well, there's a lot more to tell. That's just the beginning of one story I'm thinking of writing.

While I was eating breakfast I was still thinking. I noticed the September calendar — some mountain somewhere — and I thought, that's it! I'll write a story about mountain climbing — about putting those things on my feet and pulling myself up the face of a mountain using ropes and things . . . But I can't tell that story. I've never been mountain climbing. I don't know anything about mountain climbing. Maybe some day, if I climb a mountain, I'll have a story to tell. I'm going to stick with things I know about — those are the stories I can tell really well.

Then, while I was rinsing out my coffee cup, I looked out the window over the sink and saw two neighbor kids go by on their bicycles on their way to the Southport school. They were really little kids — first or second graders — and suddenly I thought about the first time I rode a bike on my own.

It took me a long time to learn. The summer I was seven, my mother and I had a lesson almost every night after supper. When all the other mothers had finished the dinner dishes and were sitting on their porches drinking coffee, my mother walked me and my bicycle up and down and up and down the road in front of our house. I remember the smell of hot tar — the street had just been paved. I remember the light — that muted glow you see and feel on nice summer evenings, just before sunset. I remember my mother holding on to the saddle of my bike, walking beside and just behind me, talking about balancing this way and pedaling that way. And I remember the day we were going up and down and I turned to say something to her — and she wasn't there. That's another story I'm thinking of writing.

Now, would you sit quietly and think, as I thought this morning, about the stories you have to tell? Remember when you were a child. Remember laughing and crying. Remember frights and quarrels and loving people. Remember moments in your life you want to preserve.

Think silently for three minutes. It'll probably help you capture your stories if you jot down notes as you remember them.

*   *   *   *   *

Now, turn to a friend and take just two minutes to quickly tell your friend all the stories you're thinking of telling.

*   *   *   *   *

Time's up. Change roles and take another two minutes for your friend to tell you his or her stories.

*   *   *   *   *

Time's up again. Let's talk as a whole group for a few minutes. What are some of your stories?

S1: My dog.
 A: What will you say about your dog?
S1: About this time I came home from school. He was still kind of a puppy. He got in my room and pulled one of the drawers right out of my bureau, and he was eating my socks and stuff.
 A: Your dog broke in and made a meal of your socks? Now, that's a story. You're ready to write. Who else has a story?
S2: I'm gonna tell about Mt. Washington.
 A: What about Mt. Washington?
S2: Last summer we climbed it. Except when my father told me we're going to climb Mt. Washington, I thought he meant, you know, really climb it. But he meant drive the car to the top.
 A: When did you catch on to what he meant?
S2: Not until we were almost there. Then I was so embarrassed because my brother told everyone.
 A: So you were embarrassed for two reasons — because you misunderstood and your brother made it public?
S2: Yeah.
 A: It sounds to me as if you're ready to write. Who else has a story to tell?
S3: I'm going to write about this place I went to this summer up near Nova Scotia.
 A: What are you going to say about it?
S3: Well, how there were all kinds of things to do there. We took our camper, and you could go diving in the pool at this place we

stayed. And I met some kids from Quebec. One night we stayed up to watch the sun come up. And another night we had fireworks they got in Mexico.

A: So on this trip you swam and dived, and you met kids from Quebec, and you pulled an all-nighter, and you set off fireworks. It sounds like you did a lot.

S3: Yeah, I really did.

A: And you've got all these stories to tell. What's your favorite story, of all the things you did?

S3: I'm not sure . . . Maybe when we set off the fireworks.

A: So you could start there, with the story of the fireworks? Then, if you'd like, you could tell some of your other Nova Scotia stories in other pieces of writing?

S3: Yeah. I could do chapters about the whole trip.

A: Right. It sounds like you're ready to go. Who else is ready with a story?

S4: I am. I'm going to write about Head Start. I remember this time we were learning how to make hand prints out of dough for Mother's Day presents. Gail and I were in the same group and were supposed to wait for the teacher to come around and roll out the dough. And when she wasn't looking, Gail picked up this big piece of dough and put the whole thing in her mouth. So I saw her and I did it, too. Then the teacher comes along with the rolling pin and she starts asking us questions about the dough, but we can't answer her 'cause our mouths are stuffed so full. So Gail . . .

A: Whoa! I can tell you're ready to write. It seems to me this whole class is ready to go to it. Let's begin.

As I said, this first mini-lesson, an invitation to uncover and share topics, is a long one. It breaks into two parts, my topic modeling and their topic search.

I begin by modeling my own writing for the big, obvious reason — to start establishing myself as a writer who teaches writing and probably has some idea of what she's talking about. But I'm also hoping my kids will begin to see how writing is idiosyncratic. Every writer prefers certain materials, pursues certain subjects, accommodates certain habits of mind. I want to show kids the inside of my head, letting them see that above all writing is an act of thinking and considering. There's no great mystique about coming up with topics; ideas come because I anticipate I'll be writing and look for them.

I begin by modeling stories of personal experience because that's where I hope my kids will begin, by looking for the significances of the events of their own lives. I know this is where they can begin writing confidently and well. Eventually, as the year unfolds, eighth graders will write everything under the sun. But in the beginning I nudge toward what they know best and care about most — all the rich goings-on in their lives that Lucy Calkins aptly terms "the underground curriculum."

For this same reason I always model a story I can't write. Right from the first day I'm trying to head off what Graves calls the "garbage in-garbage out" syndrome of nonsensical, TV-plot-inspired-prose — some of which, I'm convinced, owes a debt to equally nonsensical "creative writing" assignments, a term often used, as Graves points out, "when children write about subjects they know nothing about" (1984, p. 79). I'm hoping my students will come to consider conviction, involvement, and voice as part of their criteria as writers, so that as they begin to write fiction, for example, it will resemble genuine fiction. They're aware by then, via mini-lessons, that most published first novels are semi-autobiographical, that fiction writers, too, begin with what they know best, and that qualities of good writing — conviction, involvement, voice — cut right across the modes.

The stories I choose to model concern pretty mundane topics — in this instance, my dog and learning to ride my bike. That's on purpose. I hope students will begin to engage in the important business of making sense of their ordinary, everyday worlds. I'm also hoping to dissuade them from a belief widely held among eighth graders that good writers are people who have had great experiences. All of us have heard students say, "I don't know nothing. I've never done nothing." If I model as a topic my first view of the Acropolis by moonlight, I'm not going to inspire kids' confidence in the significance of their experiences. I do, in fact, write a lot about my dog and my childhood, subjects that have more to do with who I am and how I live than my week's tour of Athens. These are common experiences that to one degree or another are shared by all my kids, and I want the stories I model to help students find their own. In each class about a third of the pieces started that first day will be direct spin-offs of the topics I modeled, and I'm happy to see it. Students have begun a kind of borrowing I'll encourage all year, attending to and adapting other writers' ways of doing things.

Finally, I model a humorous story — I try, anyway — because for some eighth graders the realization that they can amuse their friends is the single greatest spur to their involvement as writers. In our quarterly evaluation conferences, students regularly tell me their best piece is their best "because it's funny."

The second part of the first day's mini-lesson, the topic search, gives students a chance to think about, write down, and talk about ideas of their own. I've modeled my rehearsal; now I'm asking kids to rehearse and helping by giving them a way to begin. It's a tightly-timed, focused sequence so attention won't wander, writers will think hard, and each can begin to write that first day, when it's crucial that everyone become a participant in the workshop.

I make time for talk during the topic search because talking is something writers do. Right from the inception of the workshop I'm acknowledging the role conferences with other writers will play all year long — in trying out ideas, sharing pieces in progress, and listening and responding to others' writing. And when I talk with those four or five volunteers who share their topics, I've set into motion patterns of response students can anticipate from me all year long and eventually adopt as ways of responding to each other. I paraphrase what I hear ("So you were embarrassed for two reasons . . ."). I ask about what I want to know more about ("When did you catch on . . . ?"). I try to help writers narrow the focus of their writing ("You've got all these stories to tell. What's your favorite . . . ?''). And I try to channel their story-telling from an oral medium to a written one ("Whoa! I can tell you're really ready to write").

How much of all this modeling do my students pick up on? A very few kids will make use of much of what I demonstrate that first day. The rest will begin to make sense in a general way of their options and my expectations. Again, the point of the mini-lesson is to expose students to ideas and information that I'll reinforce in individual conferences through the rest of the school year.

I conduct this particular mini-lesson *just this once*. The first day of the school year is the last day that all my kids will be at the same point in their writing, everyone starting a new piece. From this day on, if writing workshop is working as it should, students' writing will begin to represent a whole range of stages and phases — continuing a first draft, starting a second draft, abandoning a piece entirely, planning for a new piece, playing with leads, reconsidering a conclusion, adding information, re-sequencing by cutting and pasting, editing, proofreading, and so on. The mini-lessons students need now will reflect this broadening range of writers' activities.

Writers' Workshop

Writers' workshop is the heart of the writing class. The mini-lesson, status-of-the-class check, and share meeting exist to support what happens here. Of a typical fifty-minute class period, writers' workshop consumes about two-thirds; during this chunk of time, within the structure of the workshop environment, writers are on their own, calling their own shots.

On the first day I lay the foundation of this structure. At the mini-lesson's conclusion I quickly introduce the workshop procedures we'll follow all year, again understanding that I'll need to review and reinforce these procedures over the next days and weeks. I owe my basic workshop guidelines, too, to Mary Ellen Giacobbe and Lucy Calkins.

Let's begin. This year, we're going to have a writers' workshop every day. Every day all of you will be working in some way on your writing. And in this writers' workshop, we're going to have certain rules.

First, there's no erasing. Save that record of your thinking and how it's changed. I'm interested in how writers think and change their minds; when you change your mind, simply draw a line through.

Next, write on one side of the paper only. Writers often cut and paste — cut their writing apart and reorganize the pieces. That's hard to do when there's writing on the other side of the page.

The next rule is, save everything. You're creating a history of yourself as a writer this year, and what you decide against is as much a part of your writing as what you decide to keep. So hold on to all those false starts and ideas that don't work out and notes and doodles and preliminary drafts.

You should also date and label everything. By label I mean mark it DRAFT #1, DRAFT #2, and so on. Or NOTES, which is how I'd label the ideas for stories you just jotted down.

The next rule is, speak in quiet voices only. Beyond all else, writing is thinking. It's hard to think as a writer thinks when your thoughts are interrupted. During writing time I'll always speak softly and expect you to do the same. If you'd like to read your writing to a friend, there are places to go to quietly confer. All your writing conferences with each other will take place in the four conference corners.

And the final rule of writing workshop is, *work really hard.*

Then I sit down at an empty student desk — so kids can clearly see what I'm doing — with my favorite white paper and my favorite Flair pen. I label my manuscript DRAFT #1, put my head down, and start writing one of the stories I'd considered in the mini-lesson. I don't look up. I'm not watching to see who's writing and who isn't. I'm busy, I mean business, and my posture demonstrates that I'm expecting everyone else will become a writer and join me.

And they do. After ten minutes or so, when I finally look up from my own writing, everyone is writing. Always. That's when I begin to establish another of my workshop rules. I put my own writing aside and begin to move among my students, quietly conferring. If ever a student were still not writing by then, I'd move there first and conduct a brief topic interview.

I wish I had long enough class periods that I could write with my students every day. I can't, especially at the beginning of the school year when they need me most and our writer-to-writer dialogues are just getting off the ground. As the year progresses I'll find pockets of time when no one needs me and when I trust that they don't. Then I can sit at an empty desk, pull the latest draft of a story or poem or article from my bookbag, and write among the writers. More often I'll bring to the workshop for student response something I've written the night before — possibly an even more effective demonstration of my seriousness as a writer since it involves homework. Always, though, my primary responsibility in writing workshop is conferring — from day one I'm circulating quietly, listening hard, telling back, waiting, moving on.

The first day I won't get to every student. That day's mini-lesson and my own writing have consumed a lot of my time. But after tomorrow's briefer mini-lesson, I'll begin conferring by circulating among the students I haven't yet seen. It doesn't hurt to circulate with a clipboard in hand, noting this kind of information; keeping track of conferences is another way the status-of-the-class form comes in handy.

Group Share

The first day hasn't ended yet. Seven or eight minutes before the bell I ask my students to finish the sentence or conference in progress and assemble with their writing at the front of the classroom. There, we push desks back to make a clearing on the carpet — the spot where our group share meeting will daily unfold — and sit in a circle on the floor. During this first group meeting my students will also take possession of their daily writing folders.

I pass a folder to each writer, explaining:

> This is your daily or working folder. I said writers save everything, and this is where you'll save it — all the drafts and notes for the piece you're currently working on. Bring this folder to class with you every day, starting tomorrow. Inside, I've stapled three forms for your records: a sheet for you to list the pieces you've written this year, another to list all the skills you learn this year, and a third headed "My Ideas for Writing," your official place to keep track of topics for future pieces. We'll be talking more about how to use each sheet. In the meantime, the most important thing for you to know is that your writing folder is your text for this course. Take good care of this folder and *do not lose it.*

Then it's on to the main business of group share. Group share is another means for helping writers improve their writing — and more. Calkins calls share meetings "a vehicle for helping children become good writing teachers" (1983, p. 126). Here, I model for the whole group ways of listening and responding to writers; here we confer together about conferring, about responses that help and do not help writers.

Writers use group share for many reasons, most of which evolve as the year progresses — auditioning something new for the group's ears, sharing a technique that worked, trying out on an audience alternative ways of approaching a problem, hearing a range of perspectives on a piece in progress, following up on information introduced in mini-lessons. On most days a couple of students share their writing. Sometimes writers request group share. Sometimes I invite writers to bring something to the meeting — another kind of nudge, when I think they need to hear reactions other than the teacher's — and they agree. I've learned to make these arrangements beforehand, while I'm circulating during the workshop. Otherwise I risk an embarrassed, deadly silent circle of eighth graders, and group share becomes a pointless game where I coax and they resist. In fact, some students will never arrange to share, and that's all right. Except for the first day, when my motives are a little different, whole-class participation isn't the point; the goal is selective sharing for specific reasons with a group of peers.

Two important general purposes of group share are served right from day one: to bring closure to the workshop, and to find out what other writers in the workshop are up to. And right from day one I work especially hard to make the group share meeting a safe place. Eighth grade writers — all writers — need to know when they read aloud that their ideas will be heard and that nothing bad will happen. So the very first group share has a different format from those that will follow. I make this meeting an occasion for a fast airing of all the ideas the day brought us, saying to the circle, "Take half a minute to look at your draft and decide where the beginning ends. That's called a lead. Find the point where your lead ends — the point where a reader has a pretty good idea of what this piece will be about — and put a dot." That's a sufficient first explanation of a term we'll clarify for the rest of the school year. Then I tell the kids about behavior during group share, rules based on sensible guidelines Lucy Calkins and a group of Atkinson students modeled during a demonstration lesson (1981), and invite a low-risk initiation into sharing with the group:

> Group share is how our writing workshop will always end. We'll all meet every day to listen and respond to each others' writing. The rules will always be the same: make a circle, sit with your bottoms on the floor, put your paper face down if you're not reading, look at and listen to the writer who's sharing. Usually one or two writers take advantage of the special help available in group share. Starting tomorrow, that will be our format.
>
> Today I thought we'd take a few minutes to whip around the circle and hear what everyone came up with — what stories you decided to tell. We'll read our leads one right after another, right around the circle. Stop when you hit your dot. We won't stop between writers, or make any comments. Instead, watch the face of each writer as we go around the circle, and listen to what he or she tells.

It takes no more than three minutes for all of us, including me, to read around the circle. Then I quickly sum up, telling what I heard:

> The writers in this workshop definitely have stories to tell. You know about little sisters, learning how to drive a jeep, babysitting, playing the trumpet, bad dogs, chasing cows, blacksmithing, motorcycle crashes, Monhegan Island, the Windsor Fair, what it's like to be a big eighth grader . . . you know a lot. I'm looking forward to learning from you. Tuck those drafts inside your folders, and I'll see you and your folders tomorrow.

In this one class period we established a rhythm for a year's worth of writing workshops. Each day we'll begin together, meeting for the mini-lesson; each day writers will have a sustained chunk of time to go their own ways, writing and conferring; each day we'll come back together again at the workshop's end. Each day we begin as writers, proceed as writers, and conclude as writers. In subsequent workshops writers' wheels can start turning, gaining momentum over the year.

"Can" is a crucial modifier. Although my kids and I share the front seat, I own the vehicle; keeping it running is my responsibility. Writing workshop can break down. Everything depends on how I solve — and ask my kids to help solve — problems that inevitably arise.

When I think about all of this year's first days of writing workshop, I feel more than a little guilt — and a lot of envy. At the end of each of those thirty days I departed, and a teacher was left to confront the abyss of Day Two. Day One may be the scariest to contemplate, but in practice Day One is a cinch. Day Two and Day Three and Day 179 present the real challenge. They also admit the enviable possibility of a community of writers growing and learning together.

Nancie Atwell and writers in conference

CHAPTER 5

Responding to Writers and Writing

"A good teacher has been defined as one who makes himself progressively unnecessary."
Thomas J. Carruthers

"Let's face it," the workshop leader announced. "The point of a writing conference is to get the kids to revise." I stopped taking notes and looked up from my seat in the audience. She continued. "What you want to do is ask questions in such a way that students won't have any choice but to go back and make changes in their writing." I closed my notebook and capped my pen.

The point of a writing conference isn't to get kids to revise. In fact, there isn't any *one* point to be made by a writing conference. A whole range of different kinds of talk, suiting different purposes, goes on in a writing workshop. The nature of talk in my writing workshop depends on what a writer needs or what I need as a teacher of writers.

Students, for example, need to try out the content of their writing on others and on themselves as readers, hearing what they've said and considering what they might say next. They need to find new topics, to know what it is they know. They need to learn relevant editing and proofreading skills in the context of pieces of their writing. As their teacher I need to know what each of my students is doing each day. I also need to evaluate their growth and establish quarterly grades and goals for each writer.

Most often conferring happens one-to-one, a dialogue between me and a writer or between two students. Exceptions are the status-of-the-class conference, where the whole class reports its plan for the day, group share, and writers' responses to their own writing. Most often the responder's role in a conference is to listen, tell back, and ask questions. The exception here is the editing conference, where I talk more because I'm teaching new skills.

Although the point of each of these conferences differs, the goal is the same. Whether it is discovering meaning, mapping a plan for the day, learning new skills, or examining and evaluating growth, the goal is helping kids grow to independence. Independent writers can decide for themselves what's working and what needs more work. They aren't dependent on the teacher to do their thinking for them. Good writing teachers use the conference as a springboard for student initiative.

In this chapter I'll describe and give examples of each of the different kinds of conferences, each with its own structure, each designed to make writers' autonomy a daily possibility. Throughout, I've drawn on Donald Murray, Donald Graves, and Mary Ellen Giacobbe, my three best teachers when it comes to talking about writing.

The Status-of-the-Class Conference

When I abandoned my writing assignments and whole-class deadlines, I confronted an unnerving situation: period after period of twenty-five students working at their own paces, each on a different project, each at a different stage. How in the world was I going to map all that in one of the little boxes in my lesson-plan book? And how could I ever hope to keep records up to date as kids' plans progressed or changed or bogged down? One of my new roles as a teacher in a writing workshop is to know each student's status. The status-of-the-class conference, adapted from Don Graves (1983, p. 302), is my new lesson plan, a way to quickly and comprehensively map where each writer stands each day.

I begin recording the class's status on the second day of writing workshop. I come prepared with a chart, attached to a clipboard. Down the left-hand side I've written my kids' names. Next to each is a box for each day of the week. I run off forty of these status-of-the-class grids, one for every week of the school year, so that week by week I can see what students are doing and have done. My mini-lesson on the second day of school is explaining how the status-of-the-class conference works:

> Each day, before you go your separate ways, I'll ask each of you to tell me very quickly what you're working on and where you are in your piece. This is called a status-of-the-class conference. It's my way of keeping track of who's doing what and how I can best help you do what you're trying to do.
>
> Today, what will you be doing? You might be continuing draft one, the piece you started yesterday. Maybe you're starting draft two, a new version of this piece. Perhaps you're revising, considering what you wrote yesterday and making changes right on your first draft. You might be having a conference with a friend or me, getting response to what you've done so far. Or you may have come up with a topic you like better and wish to abandon yesterday's piece and start a new first draft. Please take thirty seconds to look at what you wrote yesterday and decide what you'll be doing today . . . .
>
> Now, when I call your name would you tell me your topic — what your piece is about — and what you intend to do in today's writing workshop? Please don't talk while others are reporting their plans, so I can hear them and so you can hear, too, what others are doing.

Writers need a little bit of training as to what their options are before they can be expected to formulate and articulate their plans. I use a writer's jargon right from the start because this is the vocabulary they'll need to accurately describe their activities in the workshop, words such as *draft, revise, topic, conference, response,* and *abandon.* That last is an important concept to introduce on the second day of writing workshop since kids who've had little experience selecting their own subjects often make poor choices at the start, settling for risk-free topics they don't genuinely care about or topics so broad they could never do them justice. Teachers have been criticized for years for assigning kids to write "What I Did on My Summer Vacation." It's amazing how many students choose this dinosaur on their own, biting off much more topic-wise than they could ever hope to chew in one piece of writing.

Another reason I introduce writers' options and terminology is to speed up the conference. By giving kids words, I'm cutting back on responses that go on and on in an attempt to explain a writer's intentions. The main purpose of the status-of-the-class conference is to quickly check in with each writer. If the whole-group conference takes longer than a maximum of three minutes I've defeated my purpose and I'm wasting writers' time. The period has only forty-five minutes. If a student hesitates or isn't sure, I leave a blank and come back to him or her once the others have started writing.

I think the status-of-the-class conference is worth three minutes of the whole class's time. I can't begin to know all the ways my students find ideas for writing, but I do know that eavesdropping is right up there. When they make their plans publicly, writers naturally teach others about new options for topic and genre. When Kevin told me he was working on a first draft of a parody of a vacation brochure, parodies of vacation brochures, advice columns, and pop songs, including Mike's version of Bryan Adams's song "Heaven" called "Kevin," cropped up during the next days' workshops.

Figure 1 shows a reproduction of a typical week's status-of-the-class chart. At the bottom is a key that explains my code for jotting down what students tell me. It serves as another way to speed up the conference. There are a couple of other noteworthy aspects of this particular chart. Jamie is the first.

On his worst days Jamie was the kind of student who would make any teacher think twice about converting the classroom into a workshop. He rarely did homework, accomplished little in class, and needed lots of prodding. He could easily have slipped through my fingers. But because I'm recording writers' plans and saving the charts from week to week, I could see at a glance that Jamie hadn't turned in a piece to me to edit — the final step in the process – in almost two weeks. Furthermore, from our content conferences it was clear that he wasn't anywhere near completing anything. His daily folder was filled with half-hearted beginnings. So on Monday Jamie and I set a deadline, for him alone. In the status-of-the-class conference I asked him, "When can you have a piece ready for me to edit?" and he answered, "Friday," which was agreeable to me. Across from his name, under FRIDAY, I wrote "Due to me to edit."

You can follow Jamie's progress through the week. On Monday he began an essay, thinking he'd try his hand at an essay contest I'd announced in the morning's mini-lesson. On Tuesday he came to class with the first draft of a

Status of the Class

8C

	MONDAY 4/2	TUESDAY	WEDNESDAY	THURSDAY	FRIDAY
Rachel	a.b.	D.1 - "Superman"	S.E. poems D.1 "Superman"	ED CON REWRITE(S)	D.1 "Superman"
Luanne	Yearbook poetry D.1 of essay	Fin. poetry	D.1 - Essay	Essay (S)	Revise D.1 of essay
Michelle	D.1 - new topic	D.1 - Short story / Res.	Conf. self Response	Revise D.1	a.b.
Carol	D.1 - "Aerosmith"	D.1 - "Yrbook Story"	D.1 - Yrbook	D.1 - Yrbook Response	D.2 - Yearbook
Scott	D.3 - poem	S.E. poem	ED CON REWRITE	a.b.	D.1 - new poem
Ernie	Fin. D.2 - "Damariscove"	Response D.3? (S)	S.E.	ED CON REWRITE	D.1 - parody
Tony	Revise "Today" parody	S.E.	Finish S.E.	ED CON REWRITE	Start D.1 - new topic
Jane	Poetry poster	D.1 - new topic	Cont. D.1 - "Tracy's Party"	Response Revise?	Revise SE.?
Jon	S.E. "Sugarloaf"	Fin. S.E. D.1 - new top.	ED CON REWRITE	Revise poem- format	S.E. / D.1
Jennipher	D.1 - "Art Club"	Revise "AC"	Conclusion - "AC" (S)	Cut & paste S.E.	ED CON REWRITE
Jamie	D.1 - Essay Contest	D.2 - poem	D.2 - poem	Revise poem	DUE TO ME TO EDIT / S.E. AFTER SCHOOL
Arelitsa	D.1 - "Greek Church" (S)	Cont. D.1 - "G.C."	Revise Booth- bay Project	D.1 - "Greek Church"	Revise D.2?
Steve	Revise parody	D.1 - s. story	D.1 - s. story	Cont. D.1	Response Cont. D.1
Bean	Fin. petition	S.E.	ED CON REWRITE	D.1 - Computer piece	Cont. D.1
Suzy	ED CON REWRITE	D.1 - new poem (S)	Poem	Poem - D.2	S.E.
Tracy	D.1 - play	Cont. D.1 - play	a.b.	a.b.	Cont. D.1 - play (S)
Shane	a.b.	D.2. of letter	S.E. letter	ED CON REWRITE	Add. envelope, mail, D.1
Dede	D.1 - poem or story?	Cont. D.1 - s. story	Conf. self Revise?	D.1 - part 2 (S)	Fin. D.1
Mike	Suspended	D.1 - "Next Day"	Cont. D.1	Cont. D.1	Response
Hilary	Revise S.S. Response	Revise S.S.	Conf. self D.2?	a.b.	a.b.
Leslie	ED CON REWRITE	D.1 - new poem	Cont. D.1	Conclusion of poem	S.E. poem
John	Finish final	D.1 - book review	Cont. D.1	Revise D.1 So far	Cont. D.1
Darren	Fin. D.1 - "Who Did It?"	Response Revise?	S.E. D.1 - Résumé	EDCON REWRITE D.1 - Résumé	Fin. rewrite
Patrice	—	—	D.1 - s. story	Cont. D.1	D.1 Response

KEY TO ABBREVIATIONS

Figure 1

D.1 : FIRST DRAFT
D.2 : SECOND DRAFT, ETC.
ED CON : EDITING CONFERENCE WITH THE TEACHER,
REWRITE: THEN WRITING FINAL COPY OF THE PIECE
RESPONSE: CONTENT CONFERENCE
(S : SCHEDULED FOR GROUP SHARE
SELF-CONF: CONFERRING WITH SELF
S.E.: SELF-EDITING

poem and said he intended to work on draft two. For three days he claimed to be re-drafting and revising a six-line poem. On Friday, when Jamie hadn't completed his poem (self-editing in preparation for submitting it to me for final editing), I assigned him to come in after school and make up his work, just as he'd have an after-school if he didn't complete his math or social studies homework.

Patrice is another student worth noting. She moved to Boothbay Harbor during this particular week, joining 8C on Wednesday morning. I added her name to the bottom of the chart, then proceeded to take the status of the class. Patrice listened hard. When I got to her name and called, "Patrice?" she called back, "First draft, short story."

At the end of the status-of-the-class conference, each student and I have a verbal contract. The student has said, "This is what I'll do today," and I've noted that plan. The structure no longer looks like those I'd created in the little boxes of my plan book; if anything, it's tighter and more comprehensive, about as far as it could be from the chaos I'd envisioned. Most importantly, it didn't emanate from the teacher's big desk. Deciding and acting on decisions quickly become the writer's domain, and my plan book mostly serves now to remind me of the predictable nature of writing workshop. Each day I fill the boxes in my book the same way:

WRITING WORKSHOP

1. Mini-lesson: _____
2. Status-of-the-Class Conference (See chart on clipboard)
3. Write/Confer (I circulate)
4. Group Share (5–7 minutes before the bell)

Conferring About Content

Arelitsa was tackling a new subject — God — and she was stuck. I carried my conference chair to her corner of the classroom, settled beside her desk, and waited.

"Hi," she said. "I think I need some response. I'm pretty confused with this piece."

"Okay. What's up?"

She waved her first draft at me. "You know how when you're little you have these funny ideas of how things work? Well, the other night I had a flashback. I remembered what I used to think about God. I used to have this picture of Him in my mind, like the Jolly Green Giant or something. And now I don't have a picture. He's just sort of everywhere."

I told back. "So you're trying to write about two things: how you used to see God, your image of Him when you were a little kid, and how you perceive Him now that you've grown up. There's no specific image, but He's all around you now."

"Yeah," she agreed. "It's really two parts. Like S. E. Hinton, that was then and this is now."

"So what will you do next?"

"Umm . . ." she hesitated. "Probably second draft, with two parts."

Arelitsa's first and final drafts of her poem appear in figure 2. Except for my checking in to ask how it was going and her confirming she was on the right track, we didn't confer at length again. Our talk had served its purpose, helping her get unstuck so she could proceed on her own.

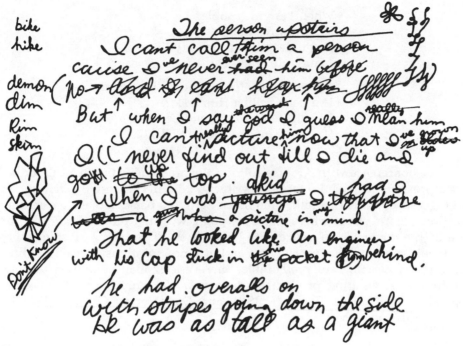

Figure 2

The Guy Upstairs

When I was a kid,
I didn't have much of a brain:
I thought He was an engineer
(the kind that runs a train).

He wore overalls
with stripes down the sides.
He was as tall as a giant,
and Heaven is where He'd hide.

He was easy to make friends with,
although He'd never talk back.
Some people got responses
(I guessed they had the knack).

But now that I've grown older
He's harder to define.
I can't really explain Him —
He's just there, in my mind.

"Please no embarrassments!"
"Please don't let it hurt!"
I close my eyes and beg Him;
I stammer and I blurt.

When I am in trouble
He is always there.
He guides me through my life —
I guess He really cares.

(Have you noticed through this poem
I've been calling Him a He?
For all I know He could be an It.
Hey — or maybe even a She!)

ARELITSA KAZAKOS

The conference with Arelitsa follows the predictable pattern I described in the previous chapter. I invite the writer to talk, in this case by waiting and making a space for her to talk, then listen hard, tell back, and ask a clarifying question — here, about where Arelee is going with the piece. Again the purpose of the content conference is to help writers discover the meanings they don't yet know, to name problems and attempt solutions. Because conferences about meaning are predictable, there are explicit guidelines teachers can follow in ensuring productive dialogues. I'm grateful to Mary Ellen Giacobbe (1983), Don Graves (1983), and Don Murray (1982, 1985) for much of this good advice.

Content Conference Guidelines for Teachers

1. Keep conferences short, just a quick minute or two. At first, as you get the hang of conferring, they may run longer. It's important to remember that you're not asking to hear every word every student writes; if you do, you're taking control and making each of those pieces of writing your responsibility. Instead, ask kids to tell you about the piece. Ask them to read or talk to you about the lead or conclusion, a part that's working well, or a part where they need help. If you begin with long conferences, listening to and trouble-shooting whole pieces at a time, writers will quickly come to count on this kind of response, they won't learn how to find and solve their own problems, and you'll see only a few kids each day.
2. See as many writers as possible. If you can't get to everyone on a given day, make a note on the status-of-the-class chart of who you didn't get a chance to check in with and see them first in the next workshop.
3. Go to your students, so you can control the length of the conference and see many writers. Circulate among them in a zig-zag pattern, from one area of the room to another. It's like a commando raid: they never know where you'll be next.
4. Make eye contact with the writer. This means kneeling or sitting alongside their desks as you talk and listen. Because the student and the

student's reaction are the focus of the conference, don't look at or read the paper or allow the writer to give it to you.

5. Don't tell writers what should be in their writing or, worse, write on their pieces. Remember the centrality of ownership in students' growth as writers. The piece of writing belongs to the writer.

6. Build on what writers know and have done, rather than bemoaning what's not on the page or what's wrong with what is there. Remember that in general students do the best they can. As you help them move forward, their best will get better.

7. Resist making judgments about the writing. If you tell a writer her first draft is good, why should she bother doing anything more with the piece? And how can she be expected to develop her own criteria for good writing if she's dependent on her teacher's judgments to tell her what's good? Avoid generalized or contrived praise, too. It's a way many of us were trained to talk as teachers — congratulating kids on their opinions, stroking verbally as a reward for desired behavior, deeming everything our kids do "Good!" or even "Very good!" — and it's not a way human beings talk to each other. Instead, praise by becoming involved in the writing, by paying and calling attention to what students know. And praise by describing the effects specific techniques have on you as reader/listener: "Your lead brought me right into the piece," or "When you read the part about the discovery of the raccoon nest, I could see it happening."

8. In questioning students, ask about something you're curious about as an inquisitive human being. Forget you're an English teacher and focus on the meaning. What would you like to know more about? What didn't you understand? Then focus on just these one or two issues, taking care not to overwhelm the writer, asking open-ended questions that will allow the writer to talk. For example, a string of questions along the line of "When did you go? With whom? Did you have fun? Did you have anything to eat? What?" elicits a string of one- and two-word answers. A global question such as "Tell me more about X" or "I don't understand Y" gets a writer thinking and talking about her piece.

Specific writing situations call for more specific questions. These relate to typical kinds of problems that emerge in pieces of eighth graders' writing. In the chart below I've identified typical situations and given examples of questions that have helped my kids tackle each problem.

Questions That Can Help

Situation	Conference Approaches
The piece is unfocused: it covers several or many different days, events, ideas, etc.	• Do you have more than one story here? • What's the most important thing you're trying to say? • What's your favorite part? How can you build on it?

Situation	*Conference Approaches*
There isn't enough information in the piece.	• I don't understand. • Please tell me more about it. • What else do you know about your topic? • How could you find out more about your topic?
There's too much information in the piece.	• Is all this information important to your reader? What parts don't you need?
The piece is a list of events and includes little of the writer's reflections.	• How did you feel when this happened? • What do you think about this? • Why is this significant to you?
The lead holds the reader at arm's length, going on about contextual details rather than introducing the writer's thesis.	• Does this lead bring your reader right into the piece? • Where does your piece really begin? Can you delete other information and begin there instead?
The conclusion is either too sudden or drags on and on.	• What do you want your reader to know or feel at the end of your piece? Does this conclusion do it? • Where does your piece really end?
There are no or few direct quotes in a piece in which people talk.	• What can you do to show how these people spoke, so your reader can hear their voices?
You want to bring closure to the conference and understand what the student is taking away from the conference situation.	• What do you think you'll do next?

Group Share Sessions

The group share meeting that ends each writing workshop features all the elements of individual conferences, with one difference. Here many listeners respond to a writer's work. Group share exists for those occasions when a writer needs to hear a range of perspectives or speak to a wider audience. For writers who need this kind of help, a group meeting can be a godsend.

It's important for both teachers and kids to remember that group share isn't a show-and-tell session, that it's a purposeful dialogue. Teachers shouldn't believe every writer must eventually share a piece; the point is making a place for kids who require a wider response on a given day. Nor should kids believe group share is an occasion to perform. Again, they have to have a reason for coming before the group.

I mentioned some of the reasons eighth graders seek group response in the previous chapter: to get many perspectives on a problem simultaneously, to try out something new on a group, to share a successful new technique, to run a couple of alternative solutions past a wide readership, to celebrate a finished piece. Phil arranged with me to read in a group share meeting one afternoon because he wanted to know if the class could find any flaws in a plan he'd hatched.

In a mini-lesson that week I'd conducted a quick topic search, asking kids to consider a question I'd borrowed from Don Murray (1980): "What problems need solving? Who might have solutions?" My aim was to introduce another genre, helping kids begin to understand the possibilities inherent in persuasive writing for changing their worlds. Phil decided to pursue one of the topics he'd brainstormed: the problem of no mini-bikes or motorcycles allowed on school grounds. Six or seven minutes before the bell I called, "Time for group share," and we pushed desks back and assembled in a circle on the floor. Following group share procedures that I'd reviewed and re-reviewed until students caught on, Phil kicked off by telling what he'd written, where he was in the piece, and what he wanted from the group.

"Okay. This is a letter to the school committee about asking them to let kids ride mini-bikes to school. It's my first draft. What I want to know is do you think this would convince them?" He read:

> To the Members of the Something Something School Committee:
> I am writing to ask why motorcycles are not allowed to be ridden to school. They are no different than bicycles. If the problem is bikes getting hurt or stolen by other students, we should be able to take that chance. I think you ought to have a rule that you can ride to school as long as you have a note from your parents with their permission.
> If you will not let us ride our motocycles to school you should at least choose one day we can like field day or the last day of school.
> Motorcycles are a lot of fun, and we riders would like to include them during a long and boring day of school.
> A BRES Student, Phil Webster.

When Phil finished reading, three hands shot up. Phil called on Willie, who began by telling back. "You think the school committee should let kids ride motorcycles to school if their parents write a note saying it's okay, or on a special day like field day. And the reason you think they should let us is because school is so boring."

"Right," Phil agreed. He called on Jenny next. She asked, "So how do you think the school committee is going to feel when you tell them the reason you want this is because their school is so boring?" Treb chimed in. "Yeah, I don't imagine they're gonna be too thrilled." Phil laughed and I asked him what he was going to do next with his letter.

"I think I've got to do something with that last paragraph. Be more convincing somehow," he answered.

I asked him, "Have you ever heard the cliché, 'You can catch more flies with honey than with vinegar'? Think about how sweetness might be more convincing."

The bell rang, and the class dispersed. In the following day's group share meeting Cathy read a draft of a petition to the principal requesting a spectator bus for away basketball games, then Phil read his new conclusion to the group. He'd deleted the paragraph about school's long and boring days and substituted some honey:

> I wish you would give consideration to my ideas and try to work something out. Please write back.
> Thank you.

Topic Conferences

In a small, revealing piece of research I asked my three classes of eighth grade writers to name their best pieces of writing and tell how they came up with the topic. I was interested in knowing where good ideas for writing come from when students are allowed to write on subjects of their own choosing. Kids' answers described a writers' environment — all of the circumstances, arrangements, and provisions that enable writers to find and explore their own ideas. The list below summarizes that research, showing what we did in general, day in and week out, to enrich the classroom environment and keep good topics coming.

Establishing a Writer's Environment

- Schedule daily whole-group sharing times and encourage peer conferences so students discover the topics, modes, and audiences other writers, including the teacher, have chosen.
- Publish their writing, so students discover the topics and modes other writers have chosen. *Publication is crucial*: writers most often write to be read. Appendix *B* is a list of ways Boothbay students have gone public with their writing.
- Ask that students maintain and have handy running lists of potential topics, jotting down ideas as they come on a special sheet stapled inside their daily writing folders.
- For future reference, ask that students keep lists of the topics on which they have written, again on a sheet stapled inside the daily folder.
- Talk with students about how they come up with their ideas for writing. In conferences, ask them how and why they chose a particular topic, helping them to become more conscious of their sources of ideas.
- Talk with students about how professional authors come up with their topics for writing, drawing on published accounts of professional authors' processes and, when possible, inviting professional authors to come into the school to talk with student writers.
- Keep informed of and share with students calls for manuscripts from student authors — all those magazines and books that publish children's

writing, as well as student writing contests. Appendix C describes a range of places junior high teachers can submit students' writing.

- Read to students, provide frequent time for independent reading, and make available in the classroom a large assortment of books encompassing a variety of modes and subjects.
- Introduce new modes and techniques in mini-lessons.
- Conduct occasional whole-group topic searches in mini-lessons, asking kids to record the ideas they generate for future reference.
- Encourage students to view and use interests relating to other areas of the curriculum as sources for topics: to write about subjects traditionally associated with science and social studies, for example, in the writing workshop.
- Provide a variety of writing materials. Different kinds of utensils and papers will suggest different kinds of formats and genres.
- Allow students to abandon pieces and move on to other subjects.
- Provide regular, frequent blocks of time for students to think, plan, become ready, and write.
- Acknowledge that every student has something to say. Let kids know you care about and are interested in their ideas, experiences, and areas of expertise.
- Expect that every student will have ideas for writing.

Given the richness of this environment, students still get stuck. When an individual is having trouble with topic selection I offer some options for getting unstuck. I might suggest that the writer read through the permanent writing folder or look at the list of topics on which he or she has previously written. Sometimes an old piece suggests new ideas. I might show the writer how to brainstorm, how to write down as quickly as possible as many ideas as possible, piggy-backing one idea on another and not censoring anything. I might give the writer my clipboard and ask him or her to spend ten minutes circulating among other writers, surveying them about their topics. Or I might ask the writer, "Who could you talk to for a few minutes who might best help you think of something?" or interview the student myself. This special interview is a topic conference.

In a topic conference the interviewer asks a few open-ended questions about a writer's experiences, observations, and areas of interest and expertise and briefly notes the interviewee's responses. I printed a sheet of such questions and stuck copies in the scrap paper pockets in the four conference corners. When a student asks me or another student for a topic conference these sheets are a ready reference, if we need them. The interviewer chooses and asks several of the questions on the list and follows up with related questions, trying to get the writer thinking and talking in a focused way.

Questions for a Topic Conference

- Tell me about your: weekend
  family
  friends
  pets

- Tell me about your: neighborhood
                        likes and dislikes
                        earliest memories
                        hobbies
                        skills
                        jobs and responsibilities
                        fears
                        birthdays
                        Christmases
                        favorite books
                        favorite movies
                        favorite poems
                        favorite sports
                        favorite subjects.
- What kinds of writing would you like to try?
- What's a story you tell again and again?
- What can you remember doing for the first time?
- What can you remember doing for the last time?
- What are you good at?
- What have you read/heard/seen/felt that you can't forget?*
- What would you like to know?
- What problems need solving? Who might have solutions to those problems?

Lance asked me for a topic interview near the end of class one day in March. He'd spent the period brainstorming and hadn't hit on an idea he was interested in. He and I went off and sat together in one of the conference corners.

LANCE: I think I've got . . . what do you call it? Writer's blues, or something like that?

ATWELL: Writer's blues sounds pretty good to me. Or you could call it writer's block. What's happening?

L: Well, I've been trying to think of a good topic. Something different from what I usually write, you know, like "The Day I Blah, Blah, Blah."

A: Yeah, I think I see. You want to try for something bigger, something more important.

L: Yeah.

A: You know, you could write about your own life without it being "blah, blah, blah." One thing writers do is discover what's important, what's really significant, in everyday life. Like, what have you done lately, apart from school?

L: The usual nothing. Hang out.

A: Um-hmm.

L: Work.

---

*The last three questions are courtesy of Donald Murray's "Questions to Produce Writing Topics" (1980).

A: At home?

L: Yeah, vacuuming and dishes and stuff, but selling flowers too. Usually every Saturday.

A: Do your parents have a shop, or what?

L: Yeah, but I work with Todd. We park the car on the strip between Cook's Corner and Brunswick and wait for people to come by.

A: Is that you guys? A big, white Cadillac?

L: Yeah. Todd and me.

A: I've wondered about that car. What's it like doing that?

L: It's a drag. You sit there all day with nothing to do. The worst was Valentine's Day. We had to take off school and go down there for the whole day.

A: It was bad?

L: Yeah, really stupid. We didn't have any choice. We practically froze. And it was even more boring than usual. Todd read basketball stats at me all day. I had this Valentine's present for Amanda, a necklace, that I couldn't give her. My big thrill was when Todd gave me a Valentine by writing "Happy Valentine's" with ketchup on the table at McDonald's. And there was this guy who thought Todd and me were Moonies 'cause we were selling flowers. Really weird.

A: Well, think about that one. This could be more than "blah, blah, blah" — the contrast between how you could've spent Valentine's, here at school with Amanda and the other kids, and what you did instead because of that job, hour after hour after hour in that car with Todd. And you've got some specific details that could show the contrast — Todd reeling off stats, the ketchup Valentine, the necklace you couldn't give her, the Moonies guy . . . .

L: They could be, like, symbols that show how I was feeling.

A: Right. So, what do you think you'll do now?

L: I'm going to try this as a piece. I'm going to try to figure out what it all means.

A topic conference gets a writer talking by following the general principles of content conferences: a few open-ended questions, follow-up questions, waiting, and telling back. In this conference with Lance my job isn't to tell him what he should write but to help him find out what he knows, show him I'm interested in what he knows, and then give it back to him from my perspective. In the piece that grew from our topic conference, Lance did something new for him as a writer. Rather than just reporting events he tried to discover significances and write layers of meaning.

Happy Valentine's Day

I turned to look out the window as I sat there on the cold car seat. Why was it always Todd and I who had to work on the holidays? I thought about it for a while, just staring out the window at the snow-covered ground. To tell the truth I thought about a lot of things then, like why we had to sell flowers on Valentine's Day especially. I mean, we sold them on Christmas Day too, but at least school wasn't in session then.

I thought about school and what everyone might be doing at that point. Probably passing Valentines around. And then I turned to look out the other window, thinking about Amanda. She was the main reason I wanted to go back to school. I had to give her the necklace I'd bought her for a Valentine's present. Of all the days, I *had* to miss school on this day! I missed school; I missed Amanda.

My thoughts were interrupted by Todd giving me basketball stats from the magazine he was reading. "And Dr. J scored 37 points . . ." he continued. I like to hear about sports and stuff, but at that point I didn't really care. I knew it was going to be one of those days in the big cold Cadillac.

The flowers outside on the hood of the car started to freeze up a little, but I didn't pay much attention. I picked up a book and began reading it for the sixth time. Todd turned on the engine to try to get some heat circulating. The exhaust filled the car fast, so fast that three or four times I started to doze off and almost fell asleep. I remembered how car exhaust could kill, sat up, and opened the window for fresh air.

It was only 12:00. We had five more hours to slave through until we could leave. "Lance," Todd suddenly said. "Moses did a 360 dunk last night; I snuck down and watched the game after mom and dad went to bed." There was no sense telling him to shut up because once he got started, he wouldn't stop. So I put him out of my head and turned away.

Just then a car pulled up and I jumped out. The customer, a man, bought some flowers. As he was leaving he paused and said, "Hey, kid. Come back here." I didn't know what to think so I went back over. "Ummmmm. I'd like to talk with you for a moment," the guy said, acting a bit strange.

"Go for it," I said, trying to sound like a professional flower salesman. He pulled out a camera, a taperecorder, and a microphone and then questioned:

"Are you from the Moonies?"

"Wha?" I didn't know what he was talking about.

"Are you, kid? You know, you could get in trouble for this!" he continued and looked me directly in the eye. It seemed almost as if he were trying to hypnotize me.

"No, I guess not," I replied. I was still curious as to what he was talking about.

He grabbed my arm and said, "What do you mean, you 'guess not'? Just give it to me straight. This is important!" I pulled away from him and hurried back toward the car. "I'll get you for this!" he shouted after me.

Another crazy customer. They were mostly like that. I locked the doors and picked up my book.

The day dragged on and on. Finally it was five o'clock and Todd and I, without hesitation, put the unsold flowers in the back of the car and took off. I started laughing to myself as I realized where we were heading. We were going to McDonald's to celebrate Valentine's Day with a meal of McDonald's special thirty-cent hamburgers.

I followed Todd into the restaurant and took a seat after we'd ordered. I thought about the both of us. I wasn't thinking about school much then, since it was long over. What I thought about was how responsible I felt with Todd. It was the first time we had been in Brunswick together, without our parents having driven us in for the day.

Just then Todd started laughing and said, "Look, Lance, look!" I couldn't figure out what he was talking about at first, until I looked down on the table.

I started laughing, too: in squiggled letters he'd written "Happy Valentine's Day" on the table with ketchup.

When we walked out of McDonald's to head back home, in my right hand I held a take-out supper for Brant, my little brother. In my left, I carried the box with Amanda's necklace in it.

LANCE DADALEARES

Conferring with Oneself

One day I watched as Jake wrote furiously for half an hour, put down his pen, picked up his paper, jumped up from his desk, and approached a friend for a writing conference. Watching more closely, I observed this same sequence time and again with other students. I was worried.

Writers were bypassing their most important readers — themselves — and depending on others to identify and solve problems in their writing. Paul Eschholz of the Vermont Writing Project compares this "I'm done; give me response" syndrome to the case of a patient who instructs his physician, "Fix me, Doc," without ever describing where he hurts.

"Having a Writing Conference with Yourself" is a guide I wrote for my students with their help. It's based on questions we ask each other in writing conferences, questions posed by Graves, Giacobbe, and Murray, and questions I ask myself about my own prose writing. The focus is on content. As always, mechanical issues come later, once the writing says what the writer wants it to.

Each student keeps a copy in his or her writing folder, and I encourage its use in addition to conferences with their peers and me. I introduce each of the categories of questions in a separate mini-lesson so kids can get a handle on one issue at a time; just giving them the list one day and requiring they ask themselves all of these questions of each piece they write would overwhelm and would defeat my purpose, which is to develop discriminating writers whose own careful readings of their pieces will aid them in requesting specific help in conferences with others — authors who have some ideas about "where they hurt."

HAVING A WRITING CONFERENCE WITH YOURSELF

Read your piece to yourself, at least once but probably several times. The best writers spend a lot of time reading over and thinking about what they've written.

Your next job is to make some decisions about what's down there on that paper: the weaknesses of the piece — the parts that need more work — and its strengths — those parts that work so well you want to do more with them. In other words, your next job is to have a writing conference with yourself.

A writer's biggest question is always, "What is it I'm trying to say here?" The questions below may help you find and shape what you're trying to say.

Questions About Information

Do I have enough information?

What's the strongest or most exciting part of the piece and how can I build
    on it?
Have I shown (not told) by using examples?
Have I told my thoughts and feelings at the points where my readers will
    wonder?
Have I told where, when, and with whom this is happening?
Have I described the scene and people with enough detail that a reader can
    see it happening?
Is there any part that might confuse a reader? Have I explained each part
    well enough that a reader will know what I mean?
Does this piece need conversation? Did people talk? Have I directly quoted
    the words they said?

Do I have too much information?

What parts aren't needed — don't add to my point or story? Can I delete
    them?
What is this piece really about? Are there parts that are about something
    else? Can I cut them?
Do I have more than one story here? Which is the one story I really want to
    tell?
Is this a "bed-to-bed" piece, going through every event of the day? Can I
    focus on just the important part of the day and delete the rest?
Is there too much conversation? Too many fussy little details? Have I ex-
    plained too much?

Questions About Leads

Does my lead bring my reader right into my piece, into the main ideas or
    action?
Where does the piece really begin? Can I cut the first paragraph? The first
    two? The first page?

Questions About Conclusions

Does my conclusion drop off and leave my reader wondering?
Does my conclusion go on and on?
How do I want my reader to feel at the end of the piece? Does this conclusion do it?
What do I want my reader to know at the end of the piece? Does this conclusion do it?

Questions About Titles

Does my title fit what the piece is about?
Is my title a "grabber"? Would it make a reader want to read my piece?

Questions About Style

Have I cluttered my piece with unnecessary adjectives and adverbs?
Have I said something more than once?
Have I used any word(s) too often?
Are any sentences too long and tangled? Too brief and choppy?
Have I paragraphed often enough to give my reader's eyes some breaks?
Have I broken the flow of my piece by paragraphing too often?
Is my information in order? Is this the sequence in which things happened?
Have I grouped together ideas related to each other?
Does the voice stay the same — first person participant (I did it) *or* third person observer (he or she did it)?
Does the verb tense stay the same — present (it's happening now) *or* past (it happened before)?

Editing Conferences

Charles Cooper recently wrote, "It's easier to persist with commas if you know you're engaged in some fundamentally important human activity that has very great consequences for your full development as a human being" (1984). It is my favorite quote about editorial issues, funny and absolutely the truth.

When students understand the importance of what they're trying to say as writers, they also care about how their words go down on the page. They know that in the end what they've said and how it looks each contribute to a reader's appreciation of text. I think we do our kids a disservice to contend that a reader's appreciation is an either/or proposition; that readers either respond to content (in school we usually call it "creativity") or to format (in school, called "basic skills"). Readers respond to both. If we teach simplistic formulas for good writing we leave students wide open to readers' disdain or, worse, their disinterest. Who, other than a teacher, will read an illegible or unpunctuated text? What reader will read, very far anyway, a mechanically perfect text that says nothing?

While writing is personal and expressive, it is also social and transactional (Britton, *et al*, 1975). We use writing to discover what we know, think, and believe. We also use writing as a social discourse, to conduct transactions with the rest of the world, sharing what we know, think, and believe. When we emphasize either "creative writing" or "fundamentals" we bypass real writers' highly sophisticated reasons for composing texts and real readers' equally sophisticated responses to texts. We need to help our students learn the importance of both content issues and editorial issues, but each in their own time and place.

Editorial issues should be addressed after the content of a piece of writing is set. When the writer is satisfied with what he or she has said, whether it has taken one draft or twelve, then the writer attends formally and finally to the conventions of written American English. Asking students to edit before the content is set reflects a misunderstanding of what writers do. Teachers and students who focus on editorial issues in early drafts are deemphasizing information and disallowing the real possibility that revision will allow for changes of such magnitude that the final draft will be significantly different. As Donald Murray remarks:

> The greatest compliment I can give a student is to mark up a paper. But I can only mark up the best drafts. You can't go to work on a piece of writing until it is near the end of the process, until the author has found something important to say and a way to say it (1982, p. 161).

Once the content is set, the writer edits first. Early in the school year I use a mini-lesson to explain that writers edit because they want the writing to invite reading and to mean to others what they intend. They also want to prevent the errors or awkwardness that will distract readers and interfere with meaning; they've learned that readers come to the page with certain expectations.

Students in the writers' workshop edit in a pen or pencil different in color from the text, showing what they know on their own, before submitting their writing to the teacher for final editing. When I edit I correct or indicate any errors that the writer missed, then choose one or two high-priority concerns to address in an individual editing conference in the following day's class. During the status-of-the-class conference I tell those writers their plan for the day, which I've recorded on my grid the night before: editing conference with me, then a rewrite. After the status-of-the-class conference I start circulating by going first, their pieces in hand, to the students who gave me writing to edit the day before. In conference I explain these new skills as to their function in the particular piece. The writer adds the new skills to the list stapled inside his or her daily folder, assuming responsibility for editing in these areas on subsequent pieces of writing (Graves, 1983, p. 298; Giacobbe, 1984), then writes or types a perfect final copy from the corrected text. Editing pens, individual skills lists, and white-out fluid are students' essential tools when taking on the roles of editor and proofreader.

Although I correct or indicate in a third color ink every error on pieces submitted for editing, I address just one or two concerns at a time during our editing conferences because I've learned that my kids can learn this many new skills at a time. If there are ten kinds of errors in a piece and I teach all of them in one conference, the chances are pretty slim that the student will comprehend or apply any of them. When I teach a couple of conventions at at time, the student slowly builds a list of new skills he or she has a pretty good chance of understanding and putting to use in future writing.

My editing is *editing* in the strictest sense of the word. As Murray says, I mark up the paper. I don't write comments about content. I've made my responses orally, during content conferences. I give the student exactly what the student has asked for: my expertise as an editor, so he or she may get the piece ready for a real reader's eyes and expectations. And because I'm marking up a paper the writer has already edited and submitted to me to be marked up, there are none of the heartaches associated with teachers' corrections. An editor's blue pencil serves a very different function from a teacher's red pen. As editor, I'm one of the last stops on a writer's way to an audience he or she cares about and wants to affect.

When I finish editing a piece of writing, I make two kinds of notes in my editing conference journal in preparation for the editing conference. I note the skills the writer has used correctly — what this writer knows and can do — and the new skills I'll teach in the next day's class during our conference. This record is crucial. I've learned that public relations-wise, it's not enough to announce to parents at conference time, "I teach skills in context." Parents deserve specifics. They want to know that their children are learning what students in an English class are supposed to be learning, and in my editing conference journal I can show exactly what their children are learning in the context of pieces of writing over the days and weeks of the writing workshop.

Figure 3 shows one page from one of my editing journals, a loose-leaf notebook containing four or five pages for each student. The format is one Susan Sowers shared with Boothbay teachers when she visited our school. In the first column I record the title of the piece, the date, the mode, and any observations of interest to me. This last is strictly for my purposes as a teacher-researcher: the journal gives me a place to capture interesting goings-on in the behavior of individual writers. The second column is a record of skills I see the student is using correctly. This column forces me to focus on, and then celebrate, what my kids can do, rather than falling back into my old deficit-model perspective. An arrow in the "Skills Used Correctly" column shows me the writer is applying a skill I taught in a previous conference. In the third column I jot down the areas I plan to address with that student the next day in our editing conference. A circled number in the "Skills Taught" column signals that this is a skill I'm having to re-teach.

The editorial issues I teach in individual conferences run the gamut, from syntax to usage to spelling, punctuation, format, and stylistic concerns. There is no one set of editorial concerns, no grade eight skills scope and sequence. There are individual writers with varying degrees of editorial expertise. By teaching in context, one-to-one, I can go right to the heart of what an individual writer needs. My job as a teacher of skills is to focus on the writing, on the individual piece, and make a judgment about where this writer has come from and where he or she needs to go next. It's surprisingly

Figure 3

TEACHER'S CONFERENCE RECORD FOR __Kelli__

TITLE OF PIECE & DATE (COMMENTS)	SKILLS USED CORRECTLY	SKILLS TAUGHT (NO MORE THAN 2)
9/12 "My Mind" (poem) (K. published the final as a poster for the bulletin bd.)	Lines Rhyming words at ends of lines it©s Spelling fair Name, date, draft #	Edit in pen or pencil different in color Capitals on first, last, and important words in a title; no quotes
9/13 "Listening to Mr. Burgess" (poem) ↑ (Wrote both poems last night at home, so excited about reactions to "My Mind" poster.) ↓	Quotes around words said aloud; dialogue correctly punctuated → Edited in a different color pen → Caps on title, correctly Acrostic format	② No quotes around the title Lie: people lie down Lay: people lay things down
9/13 "Sometimes in the Dark" (poem)	Lines and rhyming words at ends Stanzas	
9/22 "My Friend, My Victim" (p.e.n.) (Four kids in 8A described this same incident – four dif. pts. of view. Published together.) Kel asked me about this – about what it did – in her novel in reading last week.	→ Caps on title, no quotes Edited for spelling, circling words not sure of Quoting & #ing dialogue ! * * * to show shifts in time and place #ing Used # symbol when editing Apostrophes on possessives	Semi-colon between two sentences where she wants to show a relationship (comma splices)
9/30 "Day After Day" (Poem – parody of Cyndi Lauper song. Kel drafted this poem as a #. My hunch: attempting a line-by-line parody of Lauper presented more than she cd. handle at one time.)	Spelling → End-stop (NO comma splices) → ; No quotes on title Dash to show abrupt change	Remind her: On a rhymed poem, no indents; rhyming words at ends of lines; stanzas

easy to make such judgments. As a reader first, I have expectations too, and the ways a writer eases my way, or disconcerts me, fairly jump off the page. Figure 4 shows a student's editing list. I've listed below that a sampling of the kinds of skills I've taught my students, skills they've recorded on their individual editing lists at the end of each of our conferences.

Figure 4

SKILLS LIST

THINGS THAT ___Steve___ CAN DO AS A WRITER

1. Put quotation marks around words people say out loud.
   (ex. "Wow!" he exclaimed. "This liver is delicious.")

2. When the "he said" phrase comes first, it's always followed by a comma.
   (Ex. He said, "This school is driving me crazy!")

3. ¶ = new paragraph

4. Draft in paragraphs.

5. Use ' to show possession. (Jim's go-cart)

6. Use ' to show a missing letter (it's fun)

7. all right   a lot

8. Colon before an explanation. (ex. I saw a dim light up ahead: home.)

9. Three-line heading on any letter:
   • Country Club Road
   • Boothbay, Maine 04537
   • Date

10. Watch for over-use of !

11. Write numbers of one and two words as words. (Ex. ten, twenty-five, 206.)

12. New ¶ whenever someone different speaks.

13. Don't indent the greeting of a letter.

14. There a place (Let's go there.)
    Their belongs to them (That's their dog.)
    They're they are (They're going to the movies.)

15. On a business letter, put a colon after the greeting, print my name under my signature.

16.

17.

18.

SAMPLE SKILLS TAUGHT IN EDITING CONFERENCES
(from Students' Skills Lists)

- Edit in a pen or pencil that's a different color from my piece.
- Put the date and draft number on every piece.
- Write on one side of the paper only so I can cut and paste.
- Two left-hand margins on my prose pieces, one for regular lines and one for indents.
- Use ⁋ when editing to indicate new paragraphs.
- Watch for too-short, choppy paragraphs. Combine these.
- Watch for paragraphs that are too long. Give my readers more breaks.
- Draft in paragraphs.
- Use really short (1–2 sentence) paragraphs to stress a point or idea.
- Circle any words I'm not sure of and then go back and look up their spellings.
- Write numbers of fewer than three words as words.
- After a *C*, it's *EI*, not *IE*.
- All right = two words. A lot = two words.
- Put capital letters on the first, last, and important words in a title.
- When I need parentheses within parentheses, ([   ]).
- When splitting words between lines, split them between syllables. See a dictionary to find out how a word splits.
- Don't split a one-syllable word.
- Keep the voice of my stories consistent: either he/she *or* I.
- Keep my pronouns clear so readers can tell who "he" or "she" refers to.
- Keep my verb tense consistent: either past (it happened before) *or* present (it's happening now).
- ____, ____, and *I* as a sentence subject (not *me*).
- Read my pieces softly to myself and put periods where I hear my voice drop and stop.
- Proofread softly to myself, listening for missing words and missing sounds at the ends of words.
- Use a semi-colon between two sentences where I want to show a relationship.
- Watch for comma splices because a comma isn't strong enough to hold two sentences together. Use a period or semi-colon.
- Use apostrophe *s* to show something belongs to someone.
- Use an apostrophe to show a letter is missing.
- Use ellipses to indicate a long, dramatic pause.
- Use a colon to show a list is coming.
- Separate interjections from the rest of the sentence with a comma.
- You're = you are. Your = belongs to you.
- It's = it is. Its = belongs to an it.
- On a rhymed poem, one left-hand margin. No indents, except for left-overs that won't fit on the line where I want them.
- On a rhymed poem, rhyming words go at the ends of lines.
- Put a comma after the closing of a letter.
- Don't indent the greeting of a letter.

- On every letter I write, the same heading: my address
  - my town, state and zip
  - today's date
- On a business letter, put a colon after the greeting and print my name under my signature.
- Put a capital on only the first word of a letter's closing.
- Put quotation marks around the words people say out loud.
- Between a quote and its "he said" phrase, put a comma, exclamation point or question mark, never a period.
- When the "he said" phrase comes first, it's followed by a comma.
- A quote and its "he said" phrase usually belong in the same paragraph.
- Start a new paragraph every time the speaker changes.
- Use single quotes when quoting inside a quote.
- When I proofread, listen for too many "ands."
- Proofread for clutter: too many adjectives and adverbs.
- Watch for saying the same thing more than once.

Since I started explicitly teaching skills in the context of pieces of kids' writing, not only are students more skilled at mechanics, but I'm more knowledgeable about how mechanics work. Because I have to explain conventions as to their function, I have to understand inside and out how mechanics function. For example, rather than parroting *Warriner's* rules about punctuation, I show kids why punctuation was invented — essentially to show readers what to do with their voices — and how the different marks work to that effect. Rather than reciting *Warriner's* seven models of paragraph formation (models seldom found, by the way, in the real world of published prose) I tell how paragraphs were developed to give readers breaks. I show how the paragraph symbol was inserted in early illuminated texts, before indentation became a convention, to make breaks for readers and signal new themes or information, and I ask writers of unparagraphed drafts to decide where to divide their prose so it's easier for a reader to take in. The following transcripts of editing conferences illustrate ways of approaching some typical editorial issues — run-on sentences, illegibility, and rules for paragraphing dialogue — from the perspective of function.

ATWELL: Sandi, there was one big problem I noticed last night when I edited this piece, and it had to do with periods and other end-stops. Can you tell me what a period does?
SANDI: It comes at the end of a complete sentence.
 A: How can you tell a complete sentence?
 S: If you have a complete subject and a complete predicate.
 A: Right. So . . . what does that mean?
 S (long pause): I'm not sure. It's a rule we learned in sixth grade.
 A: Well, let's take a look at "Body in Gull Lake" and see if you can learn a rule you can apply. Punctuation, like periods and commas and exclamation points, shows people how to read a piece of writing — what to

do with their voices. A period usually shows a reader where to drop and stop her voice. Do me a favor. Read this paragraph softly aloud and listen: Where does your voice drop and stop?

(Sandi reads.)

A: Could you hear the periods?

S: Yeah. I see what you mean.

A: Without periods, what you've got here is called "run-on sentences." Your reader's voice just runs on and on. Periods are probably the single most important punctuation mark because they signal the stops. Would you add this skill to your list, that from now on you'll proofread softly to yourself and make sure you've put periods where your voice drops and stops?

S: Sure.

*   *   *

ATWELL: I had major difficulty editing this for you, Bri. Your handwriting really had me stumped. It took me about three times as long to edit as the other pieces I read last night because I just couldn't make out the words.

BRIAN: Everybody else can read my writing.

A: So I'm the first reader who's complained?

B: Yeah.

A: Let me tell you exactly what happened when I read this. The letters are very small, so I had to squint and strain my eyes to see them. The *m*'s and *n*'s are written just alike so I couldn't tell which is which, and the letters with closed circles, like *o*, *a*, *d* and *b*, weren't closed so I couldn't figure out which letter you meant a lot of the time. All in all, I almost missed a great story because your cursive got in my way. Do you have any idea what you could do about this, so other, future readers won't be turned off and just pass by what you have to say?

B: I could write neater.

A: Um-hmm.

B: Take my time.

A: You could. Can I suggest another alternative?

B: What?

A: Well, rather than re-learning cursive, which would take a tremendous amount of practice and would take time away from *writing* writing, why don't you print? How's your printing?

B: I think it's pretty good. But we're not supposed to print in school.

A: That's not a rule in my class. Let's face it. After all the time you spent on cursive in third grade and fourth and fifth, by the time you get to high school and college your teachers won't care whether you print or use cursive, just as long as they can read what you've written. Probably the only thing you need cursive for is your signature. Would you be willing to print final drafts and see how that goes?

B: I guess so.

A: How are you going to put that on your skills list?

B: I'll say something like, "Print my finals so other people can read what I've written."

A: Sounds good.

*   *   *

ATWELL: I noticed you did a pretty effective job here of using quotation marks around the words people say aloud. Every time someone speaks you've indicated it's a direct quote with marks where they begin and marks where they stop.

TIMMY: I finally got the hang of that.

A: Let me show you something else about writing dialogue. In this part, who's talking here, in this sentence?

T: Um . . . I am.

A: And who's talking here, in this next sentence?

T: David.

A: Do you know the way writers usually show readers that one person has stopped talking and another has started, besides starting a new set of quotation marks?

T: Uh-uh.

A: Writers start new paragraphs whenever the speaker changes, so readers will have an easier time following the conversation. It's a way of signaling readers that one person has stopped talking and now another will start. You go down to the next line and indent each time there's a change.

T: And you just leave all this space blank?

A: Right.

T: Doesn't that waste a lot of paper?

A: Well, I don't think it's a waste if it helps a reader. What book are you reading these days?

T: *Where the Red Fern Grows.*

A: May I see it? . . . Look, Rawls does just what I was talking about. See? The boy and his grandfather are talking here, and as they converse back and forth each gets his own paragraph.

T: I never noticed that before.

A: It's probably one of those conventions that you never took particular notice of. It's always been there, helping you follow the story. So, could you add "new paragraphs when the speaker changes" as a skill on your list?

T: Okay.

Evaluating Writing in Conference

In evaluating writing, I know my grading system has to take into account all the abilities that come into play when a writer writes. Writing isn't one ability but a combination of many — experimenting, planning, choosing, questioning, anticipating, organizing, reading, listening, reviewing, editing, and on and on. I also know that one piece of writing can't provide an accurate picture of a student's abilities but represents one step in a writer's slow growth.

Reliability — fairness to my students and my understandings of writing — is one of my concerns as an evaluator. Validity is another. My grading system has to reflect the expectations I communicate to kids in each day's writing class. If evaluation is to be valid I can't turn around at the end of nine weeks and impose "objective" standards for "good" writing on the pieces in their folders, grading accordingly. When Melissa tries her hand at a letter to the editor, attempting to persuade readers of the local paper to vote to close Maine Yankee, our nuclear power plant, it's the attempt I value first. The writer is trying a new mode, persuasion, and risking a wide, critical audience. I'll help her track down and order her information. I'll ask her to consider the attitudes and needs of her readers. But when Melissa's letter isn't particularly well argued, I won't punish the attempt in my grade book or view it as a failure. My students' and my own writing have taught me that writing growth is seldom a linear progress, each piece representing an improvement over the last. I know it's hard to write well when trying new genres and chancing complex topics.

If I'm to do justice to writing and writers, I can't grade individual pieces of writing. So, wanting my students to risk and experiment, I abandoned my rank book. In six years no eighth grader has asked me to rate a piece of writing. A student writing about the death of his coonhound, expertise as a lobsterman, anger over the principal's decision banning junior high dances, or love for his grandfather isn't writing for a grade.

However, four times a year I am required to put grades on report cards. These grades reflect as closely as I can what their writing program asks students to do. Their program asks writers to demonstrate growth in many areas — topic selection, level of involvement, clarity and grace of language, degree of effort and initiative, completeness of content, consistency in editing and proofreading. To look for growth we collect all of each student's writing and file it chronologically in the permanent folders. Kids number their drafts and clip these to the finished pieces. Eighth graders typically accumulate between four and seven finished pieces in their folders each quarter, so by the end of each nine weeks we have a mass of each writer's writing to consider. I know nine weeks isn't a very long time, even when students write every day, for judging growth. But given the constraints of a traditional reporting system, these collections of writing are the most reliable basis I have for individual evaluation.

During the last week of each grading period I conduct each morning's status-of-the-class conference, then put all my other writing teacher roles on hold. I ask students to rely on each other for response to pieces-in-progress and spend five days of class time conferring with individual writers on their work of the past nine weeks. I hold evaluation conferences because I need to talk with individuals about their specific accomplishments and goals, and because they need a time to sit back and give some serious thought to what they have done and want to do next in pieces of their writing. The conferences are for both of us.

The quarterly evaluation conference begins as an interview. About a week before grades close I decide on the four or five questions I'll pose this time around. I view the interview part of the conference as a research task. Kids will be generating data from which I'll discover patterns in their writing or just learn more about their learning. Three of my questions remain the same, every quarter of the school year, because when kids' answers to these questions change it shows me something about my teaching and their learning.

Each quarter I ask every student, "What does one have to do in order to be a good writer?" I want to know how eighth graders will perceive and articulate an effective writer's processes over the forty weeks of writers' workshop. I also ask, "Which is your best piece of writing from this past quarter? What makes it best?" because I'm interested in knowing students' changing criteria for good writing. Finally, I always ask, "What are your goals for the next quarter? What do you want to try to do as a writer?" Their responses to this question, essentially a self-evaluation, become one of the bases for the second part of the evaluation conference, where we set goals for the next nine weeks.

The other question or two that I ask in the interview depend on what I'm particularly interested in looking into or following up on from a teacher-researcher's perspective during this quarter. For example, one winter I was particularly interested in kids' topic sources. I wanted to know how and where they came by their ideas. So I asked each writer during January's evaluation, "Where do your ideas for writing come from?" And they couldn't tell me, except in vague and general terms. The problem was my vague and general question. At the end of the next nine weeks I got more specific, and so did they. I asked, "Which is your best piece of writing of this quarter? What makes it best? How did you come up with the idea for this piece?" Now they could tell me. Their responses became the basis for an article in *English Journal* (Atwell, 1985) describing the resources on which adolescents draw in discovering writing ideas. Data generated in response to questions about connections kids found between what they were reading and their writing became the heart of Chapter 11 of this book.

Just recently I asked each eighth grader, "What's the most important or useful thing you learned as a writer during this first quarter of writing workshop?" What I thought they would give back to me is what I thought I had given them. I thought I'd stressed leads and conclusions, self-editing, and a writer's need to be her own first critic — things I thought the whole class needed to know. Instead, in one class students named over thirty different areas of growth, from specific skills ("ellipses to show a long pause," "circling words I'm not sure of and looking up their spellings," "the colon rules," "probably the thing about not connecting sentences with a comma," "how to set up a business letter") to specific writing techniques ("trying new things like flashbacks and embedding context," "metaphors: they're hard and it makes you think how to write it," "different kinds of leads — action, reaction, dialogue," "conversation — I used to just write what happened") to general writing concerns ("looking at my writing from a reader's point of view; I didn't do that before," "taking as much time as I need," "working on individual pieces more, rather than writing a lot of pieces"). I learned a lot about individual variance among the writers in any one group, about how it's not possible to teach something a whole class needs to know. And, once again, I learned how a standard sequential curriculum, no matter what the sequence, puts limits on kids' learning by mandating that everyone learn the same one thing at a time.

The week before evaluation conferences I tack the list of interview questions to the bulletin board and conduct a mini-lesson explaining what I mean by each question and what data I'm trying to get at this time around. I tell kids, "You're responsible between now and your conference with me to think about these questions and decide how you'll answer them." When I began evaluating in conference I purposely surprised my writers with these questions. I'm not convinced the surprise element added anything to the interviews except long, long pauses as kids groped for answers. Now, because of the thoughtfulness and seriousness of their responses, I'm convinced it's crucial that students rehearse and are made responsible for coming prepared to talk.

In this first half of the evaluation conference I ask my four or five questions, working from a pre-printed form, and write down students' answers. I've reproduced one of these forms in figure 5. I know, again after trial and error, that I want to take dictation during the conference rather than tape record and transcribe later. First, by writing as kids speak I slow down the conference, giving the writer a chance to continue thinking and talking while I'm writing and giving me a chance to continue thinking too. In general, my follow-up questions come to me in those seconds when I'm jotting. Second, the one time I taped conferences and then took everything home I discovered it takes me at least ten hours to transcribe one hour of tape. I'd much rather conduct my research in school as the data unfolds than do my imitation of an unskilled secretary night after night at my kitchen table.

When the interview is finished we go on to set goals for the next nine weeks. Prior to the conference I've noted one or two specific things a writer needs to work on next, goals based on what I've observed in the student's writing and behavior of that quarter. I limit myself to one or two high-priority goals because at least one more goal will be set by the student in response to the final interview question and, again, because I know kids can only work on so much at one time. If they're overwhelmed by objectives they won't be able to attend to and accomplish any of them. I come to each conference with a half sheet of paper headed "_____ Quarter Writing Goals for _____" on which I've written down those one or two areas of concern. I also bring another of these slips, left blank, so that at the end of the conference the writer can make a copy for his or her records and return the original to me. Often kids staple their copies to the covers of their daily writing folders so they'll have a prominent reminder of just what it is they're supposed to be concentrating on during the next nine weeks. Goals run the gamut — from mechanics and format to technique, process issues, procedures, new modes and topics, and so on. Following figure 5 is a list of specific writing objectives I've set for eighth graders or they've set for themselves.

Figure 5

<u>EVALUATION CONFERENCE NOTES.</u>

NAME *Mike* _____   QUARTER *2*___

DATE *20 January*_____   GRADE *B*___

- WHAT DOES SOMEONE HAVE TO DO IN ORDER TO BE A GOOD WRITER?

  Grab the reader's attention right off with an interesting lead. Then keep the pc. going w̄ important or surprising facts. Good description. Know how to use the language — about punctuation, using a dictionary, that stuff. Have a good ending — something surprising that leaves the reader writing in his head.

- WHAT'S YOUR BEST PIECE OF WRITING OF THIS QUARTER?   *"Computer Camp"*

- WHAT MAKES IT BEST?

  It's different from my other personal experience narratives because it doesn't tell about the camp. It's about what was going on inside me — all my negativeness and worries and stereotyping the other campers. Plus I think I handled the dialogue pretty good.

- I NOTICE YOU MADE <u>THIS</u> CHANGE IN CONTENT (*deleted refs. to "rip off co."*) IN THIS PIECE OF YOUR WRITING OF THE PAST QUARTER (*letter to baseball env. co.*). WOULD YOU BE WILLING TO CHANGE IT BACK TO THE WAY YOU FIRST WROTE IT?   *No*

- WHY OR WHY NOT?

  Because the first way I wrote it was rude. I was being smart and letting off steam. They wouldn't take me seriously or give me my money back if I really wrote that.

  I didn't want to sound like an 8th grader.

- WHAT ARE YOUR GOALS FOR THE NEXT QUARTER? (WHAT DO YOU WANT TO TRY TO DO AS A WRITER?)

  Last year I was going to try it and this year I think I really could do it : a fantasy - adventure pc. like David Eddings.'

SAMPLE WRITING GOALS

- Work on sticking to one topic, narrowing the focus of your pieces.
- Tell more in your writing. Give more specific information so readers can see, hear, and feel your stories — more conversation and descriptions of actions, thoughts, and feelings.
- Experiment with alternatives: several different leads (or conclusions or titles) and then choose and work with your best.

- Try some new kinds of writing, beyond personal experience narratives: research, essays, letters, editorials, poetry, plays, parodies, etc. Check out the list of "Kinds of Writing That Have Emerged in BRES Writing Classrooms." (Appendix *D*)
- Brainstorm topics. Write down as many ideas as you can, as fast as you can. Then choose the best.
- When you read, start noting how professional authors begin and conclude their novels and short stories.
- Try a sustained piece of fiction: characters who change, logical plot, theme, the works.
- Try some more poetry, both rhymed and free verse.
- Try some idea writing; investigate one of your special areas of knowledge.
- Continue to work on context, embedding the who-what-where-when-and-why amidst the dialogue and action.
- Tell more about your thoughts and feelings, about why these events or ideas are significant to you. Give your readers a way into your pieces.
- Confer with yourself more, trying to be more independent in deciding what works and what needs more work in pieces of your writing.
- Get some group response to drafts-in-progress — or at least response beyond one friend.
- Spend less time conferring. Limit yourself to one conference each class period.
- Spend more time at home on your writing: at least _____ evenings each week.
- Work on finishing more pieces of writing. Try not to abandon quite so soon.
- Start keeping and maintain a list of potential topics. Jot down ideas as they come.
- Ask a serious writer/friend to interview you when you're stuck for a topic.
- Work at organizing yourself. Take time at the end of each day's class to straighten your folder and file your papers. Make a special place in your locker to store your folder.
- Record your new skills on your skills list immediately after each editing conference.
- Take more time and care with final copies, and proofread when you're finished with a pen in your hand.
- Proofread in particular for missing words and missing word endings (*s* and *ed*).
- Work on legibility, closing, *o*'s, *a*'s, *d*'s, etc. and extending the tails of *t*'s, *f*'s, *p*'s, etc.
- Make more use of direct quotes, bringing speakers to life rather than paraphrasing their words.
- Draft in paragraphs.
- Watch for too many paragraphs.
- Watch for comma splices. Start a new sentence or, when appropriate, use a semi-colon.
- Self-edit for spelling by circling and then looking up any word you're not absolutely sure of.

- Put punctuation — *!* or *?* or *,* — between a quote and its "he said" phrase.
- Apostrophes on contractions to show missing letters: I'm, I'll, let's that's, etc.

At the end of the next quarter I base a writer's grade on progress made toward the individual goals established in the evaluation conference. Prior to each evaluation conference I review the goals the writer and I set last time around, then assign a letter grade reflecting what I've observed in the student's work of the intervening nine weeks. If a student has completely accomplished his or her goals, the grade is an A; if there's been good or more than adequate progress, a B. Adequate or fair work receives a C, and so on. At the end of each evaluation conference I tell students their grades and explain how I arrived at the grade in terms of progress made toward goals. The conclusion of my conference with Mike, the boy interviewed in the evaluation notes of figure 5, illustrates:

ATWELL: Okay, Mike, your goals for this past quarter were to try some new kinds of writing, going beyond personal experience narrative, and to work on proofreading finals so you didn't end up making a lot of new mistakes on the published copy.

MIKE: I really spent a lot of time on that.

A: Believe me, I noticed. I appreciate it. When I read your stuff — at the very end, when I could read it as a reader, not an editor — I didn't find myself distracted the way I did last quarter. The mistakes didn't get in my way.

M: Yeah, my mother noticed that too.

A: So, that's a goal you've conquered. That's something you can do. What about the other goal, trying something new?

M: I really didn't do too much on that. Except for my letters, my pieces are still mostly stories about me. But I am going to try fiction this quarter.

A: Your David Eddings-type piece?

M: Yeah. And I also think I'm going to write two more letters. One to that guy who invented Logo . . . .

A: Seymour Papert?

M: Yeah. And one to the company where I got this last program. They totally screwed up on Logo.

A: Sounds good. So, looking back again for a minute, I'd call this good progress. It's B work. You completely accomplished one goal and did some work toward the other, with your letters to the baseball company. Let's see what you can do this coming quarter toward your new goals and toward an A for next time.

M: Okay.

Mike established as one of his goals for the next nine weeks a very specific task, writing a fantasy-adventure short story. One week into the new quarter he read a magazine article about Halley's Comet that moved him to abandon his short story to conduct and report on his own research into the comet's history and trajectory. I can't penalize a writer for taking this kind of initiative. In a quick conference we changed that evaluation goal to reflect Mike's new project. The goals aren't carved in stone, and if something happens that they require alteration the writer and I alter them.

At the end of the very first quarter, grades cannot be based on goals because there's been no time or occasion to set goals. In this set of conferences I look for growth over time in the basic activities in which writers engage, activities defined by Donald Murray and Donald Graves in an unpublished manuscript from a few years ago:

- finding a subject
- collecting specific information on that subject
- ordering that information
- presenting that information with clarity and grace
- following the customs of spelling, mechanics, and usage.

To these I add three criteria of my own:

- amount of time and effort spent on writing
- degree of risk-taking and initiative
- preparedness.

I copied these criteria onto an overhead transparency and during the first weeks of school present a mini-lesson on evaluation, explaining that students' progress during the first quarter will be measured in these general areas. Everyone starts the school year with the same basic goals.

Other methods exist for setting grades. At the suggestion of Mary Ellen Giacobbe some writing teachers develop point systems, giving various weights to the qualities they've stressed in a quarter's writing workshop, then review all of each student's work of the quarter, assign points accordingly, and confer with individual writers on the results. For example, a teacher might weigh the work of a quarter by dividing 100 points into categories appropriate to her particular kids and teaching focus:

20 pts.	CONTENT	Supplies appropriate and significant information
20 pts.	CLARITY	Organizes and presents content to meet a reader's needs
20 pts	MECHANICS	Spelling, punctuation, margins, paragraphing, legibility
15 pts.	FOCUS	Narrows topics
15 pts.	COMMITMENT	Uses time productively; confers with self and proofreads
10 pts.	RISK-TAKING	Willing to try new modes, topics, forms, techniques, etc.

Another alternative, suggested by Hasse Halley (1982), is to begin with a base grade, a C for example, assigned to students who produce a satisfactory volume of writing. Writers then choose their best piece of the quarter from their writing folders, revise, and submit these to the teacher for evaluation at the end of the quarter. The base grade goes up if the final draft is better than a C. For example, a student who meets the basic requirements and submits a B paper earns a B. Halley's system rewards both effort and excellence and, as she notes, "The important issue is that I do not have to wonder about the grade. It comes naturally as part of the process and is usually no surprise to the student" (p. 150).

Evaluating writing using any of these systems takes time. I think the time is worth it. When we give over our English courses to writing, and when our writing programs are based on what writers do and need, we're giving our students clear signals about the importance of hands-on experience and sustained practice in a writer's development. Making evaluation an occasion for students and teacher to analyze the writing together provides a chance to extend writers' involvement and development. Just as important, the evaluation conference, as with any of the dialogues between writer and teacher, is another opportunity for us to learn more about students and their writing.

Heather conducts the day's mini-lesson.

CHAPTER 6

Writing Mini-Lessons

"Don't say the old lady screamed. Bring her on and let her scream."
Mark Twain

The first time I taught a graduate course for teachers, one of my students was a male elementary school principal. Fred confirmed all my worst stereotypes of male elementary school principals. He lectured and tried to intimidate female members of the class, stood up in the middle of sessions to pontificate on whatever subject had just entered his head, and talked a lot in a way male elementary school principals can about *his* teachers, *his* kids, and *his* school. One morning he stood up in the middle of a presentation and announced, "When I get back to my school, I'm going to fire all my third grade teachers." I bit the insides of my cheeks and asked him why in the world he'd want to do that.

Fred answered, "Because my art teacher tells me that kids in kindergarten, first, and second grade produce wonderful artwork. It's free, really creative and imaginative. Then these kids hit third grade and they lose it. Suddenly they don't like what they draw. All that spontaneity and self-confidence go right out the window. They produce these crabbed little pictures squeezed into the corner of the page. They erase until the paper rips. Something's going on with those third grade teachers to undermine my kids, and I'm going to replace every one of them."

Fred is right. Something is going on at grade three. But it's going on with third graders, not their teachers. Having passed through the developmental stage Piaget labels egocentricity, students are on their way to adulthood and sociocentricity. They're growing up, and their maturity is reflected in their approaches to artwork — and to writing.

Young children, usually younger than grade three, are egocentric in their orientation to the world. A sense of playfulness dominates their creative endeavors. There's little planning ahead or looking back. They draw and write mostly to please themselves, and they usually like whatever they do. When I visit first grade writing workshops at Boothbay Elementary and ask writers, "What do you think of your story?" the standard response is "Good," and they mean it.

When I visit third grade writing workshops at our school, I'm more likely to be asked by writers, "What do you think of my story? Is it good?" These students want to be accepted and want reassurance that what they do is acceptable. They've become aware of audience — of others' opinions — and realize others will look at and judge what they've done. They care about these judgments. In addition, they have standards of their own or at least become aware that standards exist. Donna Maxim, third grade teacher at Boothbay, calls this "the year of metamorphosis — when the safe cocoon of childhood begins to crumble" (1986).

In a situation like the art class at the school Fred administers, third graders suddenly realize their stick figures don't look like real people. They see that their landscapes look flat and primitive. They understand that it's possible to draw accurately and realistically, and few have the natural talent to pull it off. Translated into a writing situation, this is the onset of writer's block, a phenomenon rarely encountered in the primary grades.

Older writers — those of us in grades three through eighty-eight — need help breaking through this paralyzing self-consciousness to take advantage of the new powers and levels of awareness that maturity brings. Teachers can provide that help by responding sensibly and sensitively to students' writing, by modeling ways students can respond to each other, by helping kids make choices, by giving enough class time to writing that writers can work through and solve their problems. To complete Donna Maxim's cocoon metaphor, "At third grade, kids' wings emerge and begin to unfurl. The unfurling happens if the classroom is a safe enough place to take that risk, to reveal these gorgeous, delicate wings." Teachers can also help by teaching, by showing students techniques they can use to better achieve their new standards. This is how and where mini-lessons come in.

By way of response to Fred's complaint I said, "If I were you, Fred, I'd talk to the art teacher, not the third grade staff. And I'd suggest to her that these kids need some simple lessons: how to use one- and two-point perspective to create the effect of three dimensions, how to use light to shade objects so they look round, how to draw a face — how the human face is shaped like an up-ended egg with the eyes falling roughly in the middle of the egg and with just enough space for one eye between the two — and so on." With some practical techniques at their disposal, teachable techniques, kids can use new skills to recapture and depict the worlds of their imaginations. These are mini-lessons for an artists' workshop.

In writing workshop, mini-lessons serve similar ends. I use the five-minute presentations to introduce new concepts and techniques as I see writers need them. These brief occasions for teaching allow me to bring to light information that will aid struggling writers, helping kids understand that all of them are capable of producing writing that works both for themselves and for their readers. In the process, writers can rediscover their earlier playfulness as they learn ways to control and shape it.

The original source of mini-lesson information is Lucy Calkins' very useful book *The Art of Teaching Writing* (1986). In this chapter I'll explore ways I've used mini-lessons in eighth graders' writing workshop. In looking back over three years of writing lessons, I found three categories of presentations. Sometimes I present procedural information, talking about how the workshop works and how students function in a writers' workshop. Sometimes I discuss the craft of writing, showing techniques, style, and genre. And sometimes I teach skills, introducing conventions that will help writers communicate as they intend.

Procedures of Writing Workshop

I precede all discussion of anything about writing workshop procedures or expectations with a small piece of research. The very first morning I distribute a brief, open-ended survey designed to get at kids' opening sets as writers — their criteria, attitudes, and self-assessments. I've reproduced this survey as Appendix *E*. I administer the survey as soon as students are seated that first morning, because I want as clean a slate as I can get, my first picture of eighth graders' knowledge and experience. In May, before end-of-school craziness takes over, I readminister the survey, then return both versions to each student and ask writers to describe and explain any changes, as a piece of research of their own. Their statements provide a quick, rich evaluation of the overall writing program, of my teaching and their learning.

At the beginning of the school year, for at least the first several weeks, most of my mini-lessons will be procedural. Students need to learn how the workshop works — what I expect of them and what they can expect of me. As the year progresses, fewer and fewer fall into this category as kids get the hang of workshop routines. One of my first lessons is a straightforward explanation of expectations. I distribute and talk about two lists:

EXPECTATIONS FOR GRADE 8 WRITING

Part I: Your Role

1. To come to class each and every day with your daily writing folder, in which you'll keep all drafts of your pieces-in-progress.
2. To take care of your folder: it's your text for this course.
3. To write every day and to finish pieces of writing.
4. To make a daily plan for your writing and to work at it during class and at home.
5. To find topics you care about.
6. To take risks as a writer, trying new techniques, topics, skills, and kinds of writing.
7. To draft your prose writing in paragraphs.
8. To number and date your drafts of each piece.
9. To work hard at self-editing your final drafts and to self-edit in a pen or pencil different in color from the print of your text.
10. To maintain your skills list and to use it as a guide in self-editing and proofreading.
11. To make final copies legible and correct with decent margins.
12. To take care with the writing materials and resources I've provided you.

13. To make decisions about what's working and what needs more work in pieces of your writing; to listen to and question other writers' pieces, giving thoughtful, helpful response.
14. To not do anything to disturb or distract me or other writers.
15. To discover what writing can do for you.

Part II: My Role

1. To keep track of what you're writing, where you are in your writing, and what you need as a writer.
2. To grade your writing four times this year, based on your growth and effort as a writer.
3. To write every day and to finish pieces of writing.
4. To prepare and present mini-lessons based on what I see you need to know next.
5. To help you find topics you care about.
6. To provide a predictable class structure in which you'll feel free to take risks as a writer.
7. To organize the room so it meets your various needs as a writer.
8. To help you learn specific editing and proofreading skills.
9. To be your final editor.
10. To give you opportunities to publish your writing.
11. To photocopy finished pieces you want photocopied.
12. To provide you with the materials you need to write.
13. To listen to you and to respond to your writing by asking thoughtful, helpful questions; to help you listen and respond to other writers' pieces in thoughtful, helpful ways; to make a record of what happens in my conferences with you.
14. To make sure no one does anything to disturb or distract you when you're writing or conferring.
15. To help you discover what writing can do for you.

One thing I don't expect is that my kids will do everything listed under "Your Role" the first week or even month of school. This is a general statement, background on which they and I will build together. It's also a helpful summary for parents, one I distribute during Open House in September.

This framework of expectations suggests other procedural lessons. One has to do with writing process itself. I'm careful never to talk about *the* writing process because that article implies there's just one process through which every writer goes. I know I can talk only in general ways about what writers do, or in specific ways about what I or other writers do on specific occasions. But I also know I have to give my kids some guidelines for using writing as process if they've never been asked for anything other than a first-time-final draft. One of my early mini-lessons outlines writing as process. I make a large poster that tells what writers in my workshop generally do:

WHAT WRITERS DO

WRITERS:

- rehearse (find an idea)
  - draft one
    - confer
      - draft two/revise
        - confer . . .
          - decide the content is set
            - self-edit
              - teacher-edit
                - final copy/go public

I'll explain this poster in a first-week mini-lesson, telling kids it suggests a guideline for what they'll be doing. Then I take the poster down after two or three weeks. *This is crucial.* Once kids have a general idea of procedures, and some of the language of the workshop, I want them to make their own decisions about what to do next as writers by looking at and thinking about pieces of their writing. If they're still consulting the poster after a month of writer's workshop, they're not deciding.

Students' writing folders are another basis for a variety of quick presentations on procedural issues. On one day I explain the difference between the two folders — one a portfolio of finished pieces, filed chronologically, that we'll keep in the classroom all year so they and I may see their growth; the other a working folder that comes to class each day with a writer and holds all of the writer's current works-in-progress. On another day I'll describe how the topics list stapled inside the folder works, asking writers to list the titles or topics of their finished pieces so they can see at a glance what they've accomplished and so they have another resource in finding ideas for future pieces. And on other days I'll explain the skills list — each writer's growing list of editing and proofreading skills which shows the conventions writers have learned and for which they're to become responsible — and the "Ideas for Writing" list, a place I provide for writers to capture ideas that would otherwise be lost. I talk about these issues as they become issues — for example, introducing the skills list the day of my first editing conferences and addressing the topics list on the first day that several kids have finished pieces to record there.

Explaining what students do with finished pieces is another procedural mini-lesson, one of a whole range of presentations dealing with the classroom itself, with where things are and what they're for. These presentations include:

- where students put pieces ready for teacher editing (in the top shelf of their own class's stack tray);
- where students put pieces they'd like photocopied (in a box marked accordingly);
- where I put pieces I've edited or photocopied (in the bottom shelf of their class's stack tray);

- what students do when a piece is finished (in my classroom, publish it if it's going public, then staple all the drafts together, with the final or its photocopy on top, and place in a box on top of the file cabinet. On Fridays I clean out the box, note the date and genre of each finished piece in my grade book, then file in writers' permanent folders);
- where to find such references as dictionaries, usage handbooks, and Spellex spellers (kept together in a small blue bookcase);
- other references on file in the blue bookcase (a folder of writing contests and places to publish, a listing of pen pal agencies, zip codes for Maine communities, an atlas, lettering stencils, etc.);
- materials available to writers and their uses (a can of red and green pens for self-editing, a variety of stationery and envelopes for different kinds of correspondence, white-out liquid for errors on finals, scissors and tape for cutting and pasting drafts, a stapler and clips for keeping drafts together, a range of different kinds of lined and unlined paper for drafting, ditto masters, poster paper and magic markers for publishing, a date stamp and pad for dating drafts, an address file box to which students and I contribute addresses through the year, etc.);
- the classroom bulletin boards and their uses (students' own, to be filled by them with their announcements, cartoons, drawings, poems and poetry posters, photographs, jokes and riddles, grafitti, etc.); and
- the classroom's three work areas: the writing area, No Man's Land, and the conference corner.

In each mini-lesson I try not to violate my own mini-lesson dictums. That means keeping the presentation brief — five to seven minutes is typical — so I don't use too much of kids' valuable writing time. I do all or most of the talking, presenting the salient points of the issue I've raised, sharing my authority. But I give time at the end for students to ask questions or voice concerns. Finally, I have to remember that my lessons aren't meant to be definitive explanations. They serve as introductions, background information to which I can make reference later in individual conferences. Just because I've done a mini-lesson on the classroom's three work areas doesn't mean I've "covered" the topic. I know I'll be reminding kids about how to use the room all through the year. The transcript below of my presentation on the three work areas illustrates these mini-lesson principles:

> One thing I've learned as a writer is that writers engage in different kinds of activities. Writing isn't just sitting silently at a desk putting pen to paper — although sometimes quiet and solitude are exactly what you want. Writing also involves talking, as you try out ideas on other writers, and listening as they give their responses. And writing involves collecting the materials you need as you need them.
>
> This classroom is organized so you can do most of the things writers do. In addition to the materials center I've set up three areas. The first is your cluster of desks, where you're all sitting now. This is a place to write. It's a fairly quiet place. If you're working here and decide you need a conference, you won't have it here. You may approach others seated here, to see if they're willing to respond to your writing, and if

they say yes you'll both move to a conference area. These are the four places between the coatracks that I've labeled as conference corners. When you talk to other kids about your writing, this is where you'll talk. I've hung pockets of scrap paper in each corner so you can take notes if you need to while you're conferring. When you've finished responding and receiving response, return to your desks so the corner is freed for the next writer who needs it.

The final writing area is the table up front. This is No Man's Land. You'll work here when you're hot on a topic and don't want to be disturbed. If you park yourself here, you're signaling other writers that you don't want to be distracted in any way, asked for a response, and so on. No Man's Land is for days when the writing is intense.

So you have clusters of desks for writing, approaching, and being approached. You have four conference corners for talking about writing. And you have a table for days when you want to singlemindedly pursue your writing.

What are your questions?

Another set of procedural mini-lessons deals with what happens in the conference corners. I do a lot of talking at the beginning of the year about responses that help writers and responses that don't. I describe the principles of conferring — how the writer reads and how responders listen hard, tell back, and ask questions about things they don't understand. And, with kids' help, I role-play successful and not-so-successful conferences. Three or four times during the first month of school I'll ask a writer to join me at the front of the room and read a piece of writing aloud for my response. I'll model appropriate response first, looking at the writer's face, listening, paraphrasing, then asking just a couple of questions about something I'd like to know more about. When I'm finished I ask the rest of the class to describe what they saw me doing. The next day I'll model a truly awful response to the same piece of writing. This time, as the writer reads, I make all the mistakes I made as a novice responder and all the kinds of remarks kids make when they're not helping each other with their writing. I look at the piece of writing instead of the writer, or I look around the room. As soon as the writer finishes reading I jump in with a story about a similar experience of my own. I make judgments: "Well, that was boring," or "Great. Really great. Really, really great. Really." I tell what should be in the piece and what the writer should do next. At the end of the conference I ask my kids to describe and discuss what went wrong. If a teacher with whom I'm working comments that his or her students aren't adept conferrers, I suggest role-playing conference situations during the first weeks of school. Kids will need training, models, reminders, and time to get better at responding, just as we teachers do. Through the school year I keep coming back in mini-lessons to role-play, for better or worse, what I hear as I pass the conference corners.

Other procedural mini-lessons are announcements of interest to writers, which take place through the course of the entire school year. I'll take five minutes at the beginning of a period to read the rubric and rules for a magazine that publishes student writing or an announcement about a new writing contest I discovered on the teachers' room bulletin board. I'll introduce and show recent books and magazine and journal articles I think writers might want to know about. And I'll distribute and explain my own calls for manuscripts.

These calls are dittoed sheets outlining the requirements for themed magazines I'll be publishing. I explain the particular theme — kids' earliest memories, sports experiences, adventures with friends, ideas about the world around them — or genre. If it's a poetry or short story collection there's no single theme. I ask for legible, edited copy and I set a firm deadline. Everyone who submits a piece that meets these guidelines gets published; the point is publishing a class magazine, not canonizing the best writers. Depending on the theme, between ten and forty-five writers have contributed to various class magazines, with poetry anthologies consistently the most popular. I've had good luck persuading parent volunteers to type the final ditto masters. High school business and work-study students have also typed a lot of our magazine copy.

Five times a year I use procedural mini-lessons to discuss evaluation. The first time I share my general evaluation criteria, and the next four times I explain the questions I'll be asking during evaluation conferences at the end of weeks nine, eighteen, twenty-seven, and thirty-six. I put evaluation criteria and questions on overhead transparencies.

I put much of the material I cover in mini-lessons on overheads and make frequent use of an overhead projector. I taught for almost ten years before I ever used an overhead and I don't see now how I got along without one. I can show writing to a whole class when I use a transparency, pointing out exactly what I want everyone to see. It takes only seconds to make a transparency using the school photocopier. I have a well-earned reputation as a bungler when it comes to a-v equipment, but making and using overhead transparencies is easy even for me. I encourage writing teachers to prowl around media storage rooms and school basements, where all those overhead projectors schools bought back in the late fifties are gathering dust, and invest in a few bulbs and a box of transparencies. If the school copier doesn't make transparencies, it's time-consuming but simple to make your own by tracing over the piece of writing with a marking pen. There's no comparable method for demonstrating writing lessons, particularly issues of craft.

The Craft of Writing

I categorize as *craft* mini-lesson presentations that touch on matters of technique, style, and genre. These are my favorites — when I can share tricks of the trade with eighth graders. Some are my tricks, lessons I've learned through my own writing. Some are students' tricks which they or I share as mini-lessons, and some come from professional writers. Donald Murray's *Write to Learn* (1984) and William Zinsser's *On Writing Well* (1985) are my best professional sources for information and advice about the craft of writing.

Showing students writers' techniques has the same effects and benefits as demonstrating artists' methods in art class. Both help kids begin to develop a repertoire of their own strategies. Eventually, as students discover how and when to apply them, the strategies become second nature. Just as an experienced artist doesn't have to contemplate the principles of perspective each time she draws a vanishing point, the experienced writer can naturally turn to a writer's tricks, brainstorming titles or cutting and taping a draft. In mini-lessons I introduce information about techniques and style, and in conferences I help kids learn how to apply it to their pieces and intentions.

For example, I've learned from observing and questioning them that when students don't revise, sometimes it's because they don't know how. They don't have ways they can physically manipulate the page — to add information, delete it, or move it around. In mini-lessons I show techniques for revising, demonstrating with a piece of my writing or by composing on the blackboard or overhead. These are basic revision devices:

- Carets (^) are invaluable when inserting a new word, phrase, or line.
- Arrows allow writers to connect with the remaining empty spaces on the page: in the margins or on the back.
- Asterisks or other codes are good for inserting chunks, something bigger than a caret or arrow can accommodate. Often kids will develop a whole system of symbols or numbers, inserting these into the text where appropriate, then heading up sheets of paper with the corresponding symbols and writing the additional material there.
- Spider legs are another method for adding. Spider legs are strips of paper on which a writer writes new material; these are stapled to the draft at the appropriate points in the piece.
- Cut and tape allows writers both to insert new chunks of text and re-order sections of a text. It can also save a writer from having to recopy when moving on to a new draft. Workable sections from an early draft can be retrieved and reattached to subsequent drafts. (Of equal benefit is the implication that revising doesn't mean recopying.)
- Writers can also circle sections of text in different colored inks as a way to reorganize. Especially when writing about ideas, my kids' drafts jump from topic to topic and back again. When revising they use fine-point markers and circle in one color all references to one topic, circle in another color all references to another topic, and so on. On the next draft they can combine each of the sections marked with a particular color.
- Writers circle, too, to indicate what they'll keep of a given text. For beginning writers, deleting — crossing out — is much harder than adding. Once those words are finally down on the page they become golden. I encourage reluctant deleters to circle what they like and want to keep.

Crossing out is tough, but writers need to be tough-minded if they're to get better at writing. Sometimes crossing out is tough because it messes up the page. Students who have never seen a good, messed-up draft will naturally be reluctant to cross out, make inserts with carets and arrows, or cut and paste their manuscripts. Kids need visual proof that this is what writers do, and there is no better or more convincing model in a junior high writers' workshop than the teacher, this adult expert who knows that writing is thinking and messes up the page in an effort to unscramble her thoughts. I base a lot of my craft mini-lessons on my own manuscripts.

In showing kids Don Murray's techniques for brainstorming titles, (1984), I'll reproduce a piece of my writing on a transparency and ask kids to help me generate possible titles. I write down every title that's suggested, then choose the one that best fits the piece and that I think would most appeal to readers. Figure one is a draft of a poem I wrote for *The BRES Reporter* along with the list of titles one class and I came up with in a mini-lesson.

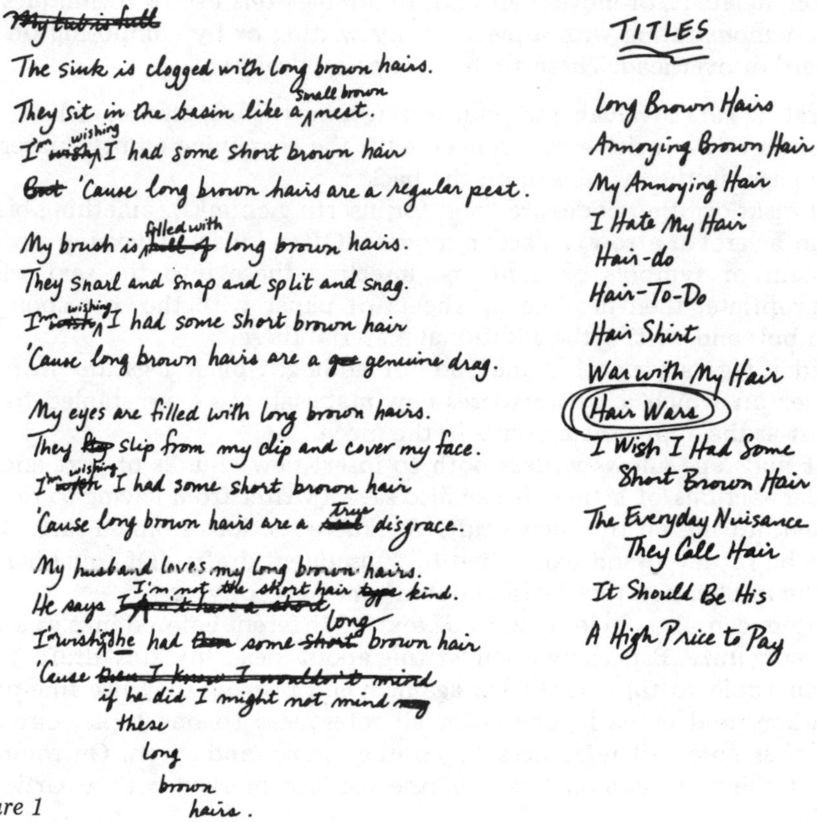

TITLES

My tub is full

The sink is clogged with long brown hairs.
They sit in the basin like a nest. *small brown*
I'm *wishing* I had some short brown hair
Cause long brown hairs are a regular pest.

My brush is *filled with* long brown hairs.
They snarl and snap and split and snag.
I'm *wishing* I had some short brown hair
'Cause long brown hairs are a genuine drag.

My eyes are filled with long brown hairs.
They slip from my clip and cover my face.
I'm *wishing* I had some short brown hair
'Cause long brown hairs are a *true* disgrace.

My husband loves my long brown hairs.
He says *I'm not the short hair type* kind.
I wish he had some *long* brown hair
'Cause if he did I might not mind
these
long
brown
hairs.

Long Brown Hairs
Annoying Brown Hair
My Annoying Hair
I Hate My Hair
Hair-do
Hair-To-Do
Hair Shirt
War with My Hair
(Hair Wars)
I Wish I Had Some
    Short Brown Hair
The Everyday Nuisance
    They Call Hair
It Should Be His
A High Price to Pay

Figure 1

I also use pieces of kids' writing in craft mini-lessons. When I see a student doing something of potential interest to the class, I'll ask permission to make a transparency of the piece for the next day's workshop. When Jennipher tried Murray's techniques (1982, p. 99) of drafting many alternative leads and working with the best, I showed my three writing classes this new variation on brainstorming using Jenn's drafts (figure two). Jenn became so frustrated with the lead that she finally *drew* what happened that day on the t-bar. (She eventually settled on her seventh beginning.) On another day, when she came up with a way to take and use notes in drafting a complicated narrative, Jenn made her own transparency and presented the mini-lesson herself.

Bert and Ernie on the T-Bar

① If sounds funny, doesn't it? My title I mean. I got the two characters from Sesame Street for the people in my story. But they
aren't the ones.

② Bert and Ernie got on the t-bar behind Andy and I. I looked
back at them just as Ernie fell off—10 feet after getting on.

③ As I got on the T-Bar for the first time I knew it was going to be
interesting. I did all right, I mean, I didn't do so bad. I was riding
with a friend of mine. More friends got on behind us.

④   Tale of the T-BAR
    "The T-bar is going to be interesting."
    Those were my thoughts as

⑤ I turned around to look at Ernie and Bert to see Ernie falling off
the T-bar. Andy told me to turn around before I fell off too. I
decided right then that I didn't like the T-bar.

⑦ "Look," said Andy, the guy I was riding the t-bar with for
the first time. "There's where Bert and I fell the last time."
I looked at the transition on the side and
laughed, thinking about when we'd climbed on. Bert and Ernie
had taken the lift behind ours, and Ernie had fallen off after
about five feet because of the difference in their sizes.
Lord, I thought. This thing could be dangerous."

Figure 2

Brainstorming and drafting alternative leads — and conclusions — are techniques for generating information. I also use mini-lessons to help kids generate topics, eliciting ideas that they can add to the lists in their folders and pick up on later if they'd like — a writer's version of money in the bank. I'll talk with kids about the legitimacy of returning to pieces of writing and topics from other years' writing workshops. Much of my own time as a writer is spent circling back through issues I've explored before and want to explore again from new perspectives. Or I'll throw out a question like "Who would you like to write a letter to some day?" and ask kids to talk to a friend and list ideas for five minutes. Or I'll read a piece like Julie Clifford's "I Never Had a Chance" and ask writers to discuss and brainstorm their own earliest memories of school, adding their recollections to their Ideas for Writing lists.

I Never Had a Chance

The big, yellow bus rolled up to our step,
And I was out the front door with a skip and a hop.

It was my first day of school; how fun it would be!
Well, at least that was what my mom had told me.

When I got on the bus, it seemed really neat,
As I looked to the back and saw seat after seat.

Some big kids started talking to my brother, Mike,
Asking him questions like, "Who's that little tyke?"

He said I was his sister, and it was my first day of school;
Mike made me feel really cool.

A big, white building soon came into sight.
My brother got up and said, "See you tonight!"

I didn't know whether to get off or stay on;
I wondered, should I go where my brother has gone?

Then the bus driver said, "Kindergarten, you stay here."
As the bus rolled on I choked back a tear;
In a moment the Boothbay Town Hall drew near.

I'd seen the Town Hall a million times for sure.
But this time it was different, not like ever before.

It was bigger and meaner and it made a bad face.
I thought to myself, why do I have to go to this place?

Then I thought of my mother and the lunch she had packed —
The fluffernutter sandwich and the cake for a snack.

I suddenly thought school might be o.k.,
So I picked up my lunchbox and started on my way.

I was in such a hurry to see this new place
That I missed the last step and fell flat on my face.

I got back on my feet and brushed off my dress;
Then I opened my lunchbox and, boy! What a mess!

I had a sandwich soaked with kool-aid, and a soggy piece of cake.
Glass rattled in my thermos, and *they* said it wouldn't break.

That was the beginning of my school career:
Riding a bus, eyes full of tears,
Looking at big kids and fearing their jeers,
Falling on my face in front of my peers,
And a growling in my stomach as lunch time drew near.

I never had a chance.

Some of my craft mini-lessons address questions of style. Most of the time I'm presenting solutions I found in my own writing, with the help of Murray and Zinsser. And much of the time these are lessons I learned by unlearning things I had been taught in school. Cutting clutter — showing rather than telling — is a good example of a style mini-lesson. One morning on the way to school I stopped at the grocery store and bought an apple to use as a prop in helping kids understand the difference between showing and telling. When I got to school I copied out a piece of advice from Mark Twain onto the blackboard: "Don't say the old lady screamed. Bring her on and let her scream." Then I began the mini-lesson:

I remember when I was in second grade, we had writing the last Friday of every month at the very end of the day. My teacher would bring in some kind of object or picture, and we'd get to write a paragraph describing it. But first we'd always have a lesson in adjectives and adverbs.

Mrs. Perkins would hold up, say, an apple like this one and tell the class, "Now, boys and girls, let's see how many words you can think of to describe this apple." Let's role-play. I'll be Mrs. Perkins and you be her class. What words can you boys and girls come up with? I'll write your suggestions here on the board.

Then Mrs. Perkins would say, "Very good. Now, I'd like each of you to write your very own sentence using just as many of these words as you can. These are called adjectives, and good writers use lots of them."

The problem is that good writers don't use lots of adjectives, or adverbs for that matter. Telling a lot, embedding describing words, is a teacher's idea of good writing, not a writer's. Good writers show, rather than tell. They let us see people and ideas in action rather than depending on this kind of description. They give us specifics, little stories we can see and hear. A good writer would take that sentence about the apple and get rid of those obvious adjectives — obvious because they don't really show readers anything. Of course, an apple is red, round, crisp, shiny, and juicy. This is called clutter, and a good writer would cut the clutter. And then the writer would create a showing sentence. For example, "When I sank my teeth into the apple its juice hit me square in the eye." Now we have strong verbs and nouns; now we know something about this apple. The quote from Mark Twain points up this lesson. You can tell us the old lady screamed, or you can bring her on so we can hear her scream: "Arrrgggghhh!" You could tell: "I was really hot." Or you can show: "Sweat dripped off my glasses." You could tell: "He turned pink." Or you can show: "He blushed" — now we can see him. Here's an example from a piece Heather wrote last week. In her first draft she told that "Daren's voice sounded funny." In her final draft she wrote, "Daren's voice echoed and boomed as if he were talking into a megaphone." Now we can hear him.

This is more a revising technique than a first draft strategy. At some point you may want to read through your draft and mark in the margin anywhere where you find yourself telling. Think about how you could show instead.

Other style mini-lessons I present as writers need them have dealt with voice; for example, the difference between first and third person and the need to keep a consistent voice. Young writers' first attempts at fiction often shift back and forth between first and third person narrators. I've conducted a similar lesson in verb tense and the need to keep a consistent tense, past or present. At the same time I'll discuss flashbacks and foreshadowing, because it's most often when they start to experiment with complicated sequences that kids temporarily lose control of verb tense.

I talk frequently in mini-lessons about ways writers involve readers in the writing. A common problem in eighth graders' writing is a lack of reflection. They will list facts or describe a string of events without helping readers understand the underlying significance of their knowledge or experiences. A stylistic technique that helps readers become involved is a writer's showing what the writer, or a main character, thinks and feels. I'll show an author doing this — for example, by reading a passage from *Where the Red Fern Grows* where Wilson Rawls takes us inside the boy's heart and mind. And I'll ask kids to mark points in their pieces where they think a reader might need to know what the writer is thinking and feeling.

Especially at the beginning of the school year I also talk about focus. When writers start choosing their own topics they invariably make choices that are too broad — a whole week at their family's camp rather than just one interesting experience, or everything there is to know about motorcycles rather than one aspect of motorcycling. The "bed-to-bed" narrative (Graves, 1983, p. 156) is another typical problem of beginning writers. The writer tells everything about one day, from getting up in the morning to going to bed at night. He buries in this list of events the special experience that drew him to the topic in the first place, and the reader can't tell why the writer cared about the topic — or why the reader should care. Beginning writers often sacrifice depth for "coverage," the result being sketchy information, a lack of specifics that make it hard for a reader to engage with the writing. Tiffany's first draft, below, is typical of a writer new to topic selection.

Maggy

I remember the day my mom got a dog. It was named Maggy. We got her in New Hampshire. She was a red Doberman. Then we moved back to East Boothbay and she was so hyper she went to the bathroom all over the house! I remember when I was on the lawn and there was a rope that was attached to two trees and Maggy's leash was on that. She would chase her own leash. Maggy was too hyper for us. We couldn't find a home for her and we were more patient with her then I think anybody else could have been. So we had to get her put to sleep a couple of days ago. I love her very much, and I miss her.

Although Tiffany sees just one topic, Maggy, in fact she has five: the day they got the dog, the dog messing in the house, playing together on the lawn, trying to find another home for Maggy, and having her put to sleep. I've copied this piece of writing on an overhead transparency. In a mini-lesson I point out the number of topics the writer is trying to describe, how she overwhelms us with little bits of information rather than selecting one experience that will really show her feelings about Maggy. Students need to know that writers select. An analogy to photography helps:

Like a landscape photographer, a writer is confronted with a huge chunk of scenery; like the photographer, the writer chooses where she will focus, which piece to narrow down to and depict with care and grace. Once that selection is made, the photographer begins to explore the details of the new scene he has framed and the writer begins to explore the specifics of the narrowed topic. The end result is a highly detailed view of one aspect of a landscape or, for the writer, one area of knowledge or one special experience. Tiffany's second draft of "Maggy" focused on the day she and her mother brought the dog home. The final draft was a three-page account of that one day, rich with specifics showing Tiffany's love for her new dog.

I'll conclude the focus mini-lesson by reassuring students that this is a revising technique, one they can use to find the topics within their own and others' pieces. I don't want to make first drafts so self-conscious that the flow of language stops. Year after year I've seen kids begin the year writing unfocused first drafts, then discover their true topics by reading over and considering what they've written. With mini-lessons about focus, and with follow-up references to focus in our content conferences, students gradually internalize this procedure. They no longer have to write first drafts to discover their topics, but can focus and delete in their heads.

Mini-lessons on leads and conclusions gradually help students internalize these stylistic concerns too. I read aloud good, varied beginnings and endings from novels in the classroom library, from essays on the "Op Ed" page of *The New York Times*, from articles in *The Nation*, from short stories by John Cheever and John Updike. I talk a lot about options, about how writers create and play with alternatives rather than settling for the first introduction or conclusion that comes to mind. On overheads I'll experiment with different ways into and out of a given piece of writing. For example, in a mini-lesson on narrative leads I tell students:

I think the lead is the crucial part of any piece of writing. The lead is the point where readers decide if they're going to keep on reading. It's also the point where you establish your topic, the direction you'll take, your voice in this piece — everything. You want your lead to bring your reader into your piece by creating a tension — some kind of problem that the reader solves by continuing to read the writing. Later on you can embed the context, filling in the who-what-where-when-why a reader will need as the piece progresses.

And then, over the next three days, I'll write on an overhead four alternatives for kicking off a piece of writing: a lackluster lead that puts all the who-what-where-when-why information up front, then three leads beginning with a character in action, reaction, or dialogue, so kids can see how the alternatives work in a given writing situation, as below:

LEADS

I. TYPICAL

It was a day at the end of June, 1984. My whole family, including my mom, dad, brother and me, were at our camp at Rangeley Lake. We arrived the night before at 10:00 so it was dark when we got there and unpacked. The next morning when I was eating breakfast my dad started yelling for me from down at the dock at the top of his lungs about a car in the lake.

II. ACTION: A CHARACTER DOING SOMETHING

I ran down to our dock as fast as my legs could carry me, my feet pounding away on the old wood, hurrying me toward the sound of my dad's panicked voice. "Scott!" he hollered again.

"Coming, dad!" I gasped, and picked up my speed.

III. DIALOGUE: A CHARACTER OR CHARACTERS SAYING SOMETHING

"Scott! Get down here on the double!" my father hollered.

"Dad?" I hollered back. "Where are you?" I was sitting at the kitchen table eating breakfast our first morning at our Rangeley Lake camp, and from someplace outside my dad was calling for me.

"Scott! MOVE IT. You're not going to believe this," dad's voice urged me. I gulped down my milk, pushed away from the table and bolted out the door, slamming the broken screen door behind me.

IV. REACTION: A CHARACTER THINKING ABOUT SOMETHING

I couldn't imagine what my father could be hollering about already at 7:00 in the morning. I thought hard and fast about what I might have done to get him so riled up. Had he found out about the cigarettes I'd hidden in my knapsack? Or the way I'd talked to my mother the night before, when we got to camp and she'd asked me to help unpack the car? Before I could consider a third possibility my dad's voice shattered my thoughts.

"Scott! Move it! You're not going to believe this!"

Other style mini-lessons are suggested by the individual questions in "Having a Writing Conference with Yourself," which appears in chapter five, Murray's *Write to Learn*, and by Zinsser's *On Writing Well*.

Finally, some craft mini-lessons explore genre. If I want students to move beyond personal experience narratives, one way I can help is by introducing other kinds of writing in mini-lessons. I give kids copies of the list of "Kinds of Writing That Have Emerged in Boothbay's Writing Workshops" (Appendix *D*) to tuck into their writing folders, and I talk about some of these different modes from time to time throughout the year.

When kids begin to try their hands at fiction, their first attempts are often flops. Beginning writers assume that fiction means anything goes. Logic, specifics, and character fly out the window. Giant Martian saucers land in a back yard in Hawaii, ghosts run after people for no reason, good robots battle bad robots. As soon as students start writing short stories or reach the point when I'd like to nudge them to experiment with fiction, I talk for a couple of days in mini-lessons about keys to writing good fiction:

1. Write what you know. These are the stories you can tell best and make most believable. Remember that most first published novels are semi-autobiographical.
2. Create and stay with one main character: a someone for your readers to be with, a someone inside whose head we go to see, hear, participate in, and react to the events of the story.
3. Describe your main character's thoughts and feelings.
4. Spin a believable plot. Even science fiction makes sense on its own terms. Create an internal logic, with reasons for things happening as they do.
5. Establish a narrative voice. Will it be first person (*I* did this or that) or third person (*He/She/They* did this or that)? Keep the narrative voice consistent.
6. Develop a theme. What will you show about life through what happens to your main character? How will your main character change?
7. Remember that all the elements of effective personal experience narratives apply to fiction, too: specific information, context (who-what-where-when-why), description, dialogue, action, motivation, graceful language, a "grabbing" lead, a satisfying conclusion.

I also save copies of pieces of student fiction that work because they follow these principles, especially the need to write what one knows, or through writing to discover more about what one knows. I have a story Lance wrote about two boys climbing a water tower, based partly on his own experiences climbing the tower in Boothbay Harbor. I have Justine's story about a daydreaming girl whose daydreams are much like Justine's. I have Daniel's story "Trapped," about two boys out cruising on their motorcycles who get caught in a blizzard; in it Daniel used his experiences as a motorcyclist and a knowledge of techniques for building fires and treating frostbite he gained as a Boy Scout. I'll read these short stories aloud on different days and explain a bit about how each writer used personal knowledge to create the fiction.

A wonderful advantage I had the second year of writing workshop was a wealth of student writing on which I could draw to illustrate mini-lessons. Whenever a student finishes a piece I think is interesting, I photocopy and file it. Kids can learn a lot from professionally published writers, but I'm convinced they learn best from local authors — from pieces of other students' writing or from the teacher's — because the situations are more relevant.

For example, my best aids in introducing resumé writing are job applications written by previous years' students. Every spring, when eighth graders begin to line up summer work, I present a couple of days of mini-lessons on resumés and cover letters, illustrating with photocopies from the year before. I explain:

> Resumés have two important functions: to obtain an interview, and to demonstrate to prospective employers how your experience and knowledge and achievements can satisfy their needs. A resumé isn't an autobiography or a complete listing of your social history. It's selected information, designed to get you a job interview. A resumé can go a long way in helping you get the job you want.

> Your letter of application is going to be your employer's first impression of you. Make sure it reflects your strongest assets. Tell the contribution you can make to the employer. Indicate the position you're applying for and the reasons you think you can do the job well. Use simple, direct language. Organize and present your information just as clearly as you can. Then make sure your final one makes a good impression — that it's neat and correctly spelled. If you can't type it or get someone else to type it, print it just as legibly as you can.

> There are two kinds of job application letters. First, there's an independent letter like Darren's. Darren decided not to use a resumé, but to tell his prospective employer about his skills and assets in a letter. He didn't feel as if he had enough experience to list it on a resumé.

Box 77, Route 27
Boothbay Harbor, ME 04538
April 26, 1984

Mr. George Werner
McKown Point
West Boothbay Harbor, Maine

Dear Mr. Werner:

I am a fourteen-year-old native of Boothbay, and I'm interested in doing all your yardwork at your summer home. Chris Paine told me about the job and told you about me. I am a very hard worker and responsible, too. Other jobs I have held include lawn mowing (for Lorraine Smally and my father) and snow shoveling for various local people.

I think that I could handle the responsibility of your big lawn. At the end of last summer, Chris showed me how your tractor and weed whacker work, and how to mow all sections of your lawn.

I am very interested in the job, and I am also interested in your reply. I can be reached to set up an interview at the address above or by calling 633-4602 after 3:00 p.m.

Thank you. I look forward to hearing from you.

Sincerely yours,
Darren Winslow

Notice how Darren gave Mr. Werner four important pieces of information. He explained that he could do the job, he told about his work habits and other job experience, he asked for an interview, and he let Mr. Werner know where, when, and how he could be reached.

Luanne decided to write a resumé — a formal series of statements about herself, her social history, and her job experience. She borrowed the format from a reference she found in the blue bookcase, a booklet titled *All About Letters* (NCTE, 1982). She puts her name, address, and phone number up top and provides a brief summary of her qualifications. Then she summarizes her education, experience, and assets, making a case for herself as someone who is responsible and cooperative.

Luanne Bradley

Eastern Avenue	207-633-1161	Boothbay Harbor, Maine

Offering to scoop and dish ice cream: a strong sense of responsibility; the willingness to learn any assigned task; energy; and a cheerful outlook. Seeking position of a waitress, etc.

EDUCATION — Will graduate in four years from Boothbay Region High School. Best grades and most enjoyed classes: reading, algebra. Honors and mostly A's throughout the year.

SUMMER AND PARTTIME EMPLOYMENT — Last summer helped with pogie fishing around Boothbay. The previous summer, a sternman, lobstering. All employers were complimentary about the quality of my work and my general helpfulness.

RELATED EXPERIENCE — The only experience I've had with serving food is at home when I sometimes make dinner. Once in a while I'll serve at bake sales.

OTHER ACCOMPLISHMENTS AND ASSETS — Since I was little, I have been in both Brownies and Girl Scouts where I have learned many responsibilities. Most enjoy myself when very busy . . . Teachers say I'm a fast learner . . . Have always made friends easily . . . Missed days of school only because of dentist appointments . . . In late November, appeared at the Rotary Club with a presentation of the Boothbay Writing Project . . . In January, participated in an assembly program honoring the B.R.E.S. Special Olympians.

PERSONAL DATA   Born 1969. Excellent health. Well-groomed. Enjoy reading, downhill skiing, basketball, tennis, softball, and music.

Finally, a job applicant sends a cover letter along with the resumé. It should be short and to the point, emphasizing the appropriate skills you mentioned in your resumé, introducing the employer to your resumé, and asking for an interview. You can see how Carol handled this in her cover letter.

Seaview Road
West Boothbay Harbor, Maine 04575
March 23, 1984

Mrs. Linda B. Kerns, Personnel Manager
Patterson's Wharf, Inc.
Southport, Maine 04576

Dear Mrs. Kerns:

I am writing to you in order to apply for a job at your restaurant as a parttime summer ice cream waitress. I am willing to do any job assigned to me, cheerfully and enthusiastically.

My updated resumé is enclosed with more information.

I would appreciate it if you would seriously consider me for this position. I am waiting for you to contact me concerning possible employment. I can be reached at 633–2404 weekends and after 4:00 p.m.

Thank you.

Sincerely,
Carol Creaser

Last year, after a few days of mini-lessons on job applications, four or five students in each of my classes decided to write their resumés. The others worked on whatever interested them. They had no need to write resumés at that moment. But they knew something about resumé writing and could find out how to go about writing their own when the time came. The information I present in mini-lessons is seldom immediately useful to more than a handful of kids because their agendas as writers vary so.

Other genre mini-lessons address different poetic forms — free verse and a range of rhyme and syllable schemes. I also introduce interviewing, from generating questions through synthesizing results. When it comes time for

Maine's annual assessment in writing, I really hit persuasive writing hard, preparing kids for the exam. In November this piece of writing appears on every eighth grader's agenda.

I have no qualms about prepping kids for the state test, spending a few days prior to the exam talking about strategies for taking exams. I don't think prepping has that significant an effect on kids' scores if the test calls for a writing sample. Kids can't learn how to write in preparation for a test, but they can learn how to better control the test situation. This is a writing task they'll encounter throughout their careers as students, one they'll need to control to some degree. But because it's not the most important writing task they'll encounter in school, we don't spend more than a couple of days of mini-lessons immediately before the test discussing procedures. For example, we've established that the best way to use the hour the state allows is to write one draft, skipping lines, and then to revise and edit this draft, recopying it in the test booklet as the final. Knowing that one of the rubrics will call for a piece of persuasive writing, I came up with a simple set of procedures for persuasion:

1. Brainstorm your arguments, quickly listing all the reasons you can think of to support your point of view. Try to be convincing by taking positive positions.
2. If it's a letter (and persuasive prompts usually are) use friendly letter format, with your three-line heading. If the prompt provides an address for the party to whom you're writing, use business letter format (your heading and then the inside address with a colon after the greeting).
3. Begin by providing context: a paragraph in which you tell why you're writing.
4. Organize your brainstormed list by numbering arguments in the order you want to present them, then present them, each to its own paragraph.
5. Use transitional words and phrases (e.g., in addition, also, etc.) to connect your paragraphs.
6. Close by telling them what you'd like them to do next, and thank them.

Finally, writing about ideas is brand-new territory for many junior high kids. Essays require a logical development very different from the chronology of narrative. I talk about essay writing in mini-lessons both when I announce a class magazine featuring idea writing and when I have news of an essay contest. One spring I shared news of five separate essay contests during mini-lessons, competitions sponsored by Rotary, a local conservation group, the Maine Press Association, the humane society, and the U.S. Olympic Committee. Then I read aloud good essays — editorials, letters to the editor, and columns from *The New York Times* and *Boston Globe* — and talked about what the essayists did, the specific strategies they employed.

In effective essays authors keep the issue in question at the front of their minds; they don't write everything about everything. They use many of the same elements as good narrative writers — a grabbing title and lead, a conclusion that satisfies readers but keeps them thinking, too. They develop examples that show what they mean, rather than telling. They develop their examples as paragraphs, separate chunks of ideas that readers can take in one at a time. And they connect their examples with transitional words and phrases, the cement that glues together the separate chunks.

Then we looked together at three pieces of idea writing on transparencies and found a good variety of ways writers helped readers make wholes out of parts — phrases like *in addition, I also believe, I further think, for example, it's clear that, in conclusion, at the same time, yet gradually, so, now, above all.* Kids don't naturally note these conventions. When I point them out in mini-lessons, eighth graders can begin to see them for themselves, understanding how a genre works and how they can use its conventions to better communicate with their readers.

Skills

Introducing conventions that will help writers communicate with readers is what skill mini-lessons are all about. Here, too, the point is for the teacher to see what students need and then teach quick lessons about those issues. Because of the Boothbay Writing Project, my eighth graders have some experience as writers — more with each passing year — when they come to me in September. With each passing year they're more adept at mechanics; a mini-lesson I presented two years ago on capitalizing titles isn't appropriate for the kids I'm teaching this year because by and large they know how to capitalize titles. My point is this: I think we teach too many skills and not at the right time. We succumb to the temptation to cover English "content" because the surface features of written language are so obvious, teachable, and testable. Instead of regarding the corpus of English textbook content as the basis for our skills instruction, we need to look at our students' writing and begin to analyze what is and isn't going on there. When I edit my eighth graders' writing and analyze what isn't going on, I find bases for four different kinds of skill mini-lessons: format, punctuation, usage, and spelling.

By format I mean what the page is supposed to look like. Paragraphing and proper prose margins are format mini-lessons. In presenting them I talk to kids about why readers need indentations in a text — how setting off chunks of it gives readers breaks and also helps them organize and make sense of what they're taking in. I don't present textbook models of paragraphs because invariably the models don't hold up when compared with prose in the real world. I do ask kids to try to draft in paragraphs by guessing where they think the breaks should appear. In editing conferences, we confer on their guesses.

Setting up poetry margins is another format mini-lesson. Kids' first poems, especially among students who haven't read much poetry, often look like paragraphs. Students don't yet have a sense of line or line tension. They haven't noticed stanzas and the spaces that divide them. Sometimes they aren't aware that rhyming words appear at the ends of lines. Just as soon as I see September's first poem-in-paragraph-form I help the writer, in an editing conference, find her lines. When she has finished a final version, the poet puts both drafts on overhead transparencies and shows them to the class, explaining in a mini-lesson what she did to create a poetic format. Figures 3 and 3A show Heather's two versions of "Autumn Breeze," the first poem she ever wrote and the basis for the first mini-lesson she ever presented. Her friend Sarah presented a mini-lesson on rhymed poetic format, showing how she put rhyming words at the ends of lines, brought down and indented "leftovers" that wouldn't fit the width of the page, and skipped lines on her paper to separate her groups of rhymed lines into stanzas. Mini-lessons in reading workshop also help students with poetic formats, especially if they read a variety of verse, from a sonnet by Shakespeare to Cummings' "Buffalo Bill's defunct."

I also address smaller, more technical format issues. Dividing words between syllables at line breaks is one. Students don't have much trouble understanding that words have to be split between syllables or that one-syllable words can't be split. They run into trouble when they can't tell where one syllable ends and another begins. In this mini-lesson I make a transparency of a page from a dictionary, point out how words are listed already divided into syllables, and show how five or six of the projected words would have to be split in a piece of writing. I end the mini-lesson

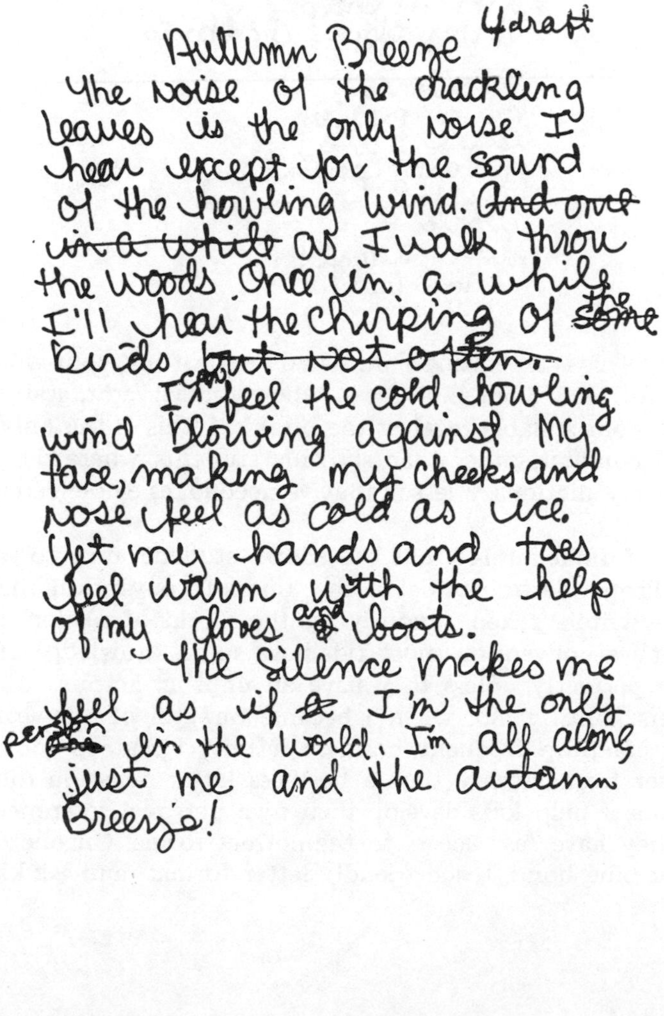

Figure 3

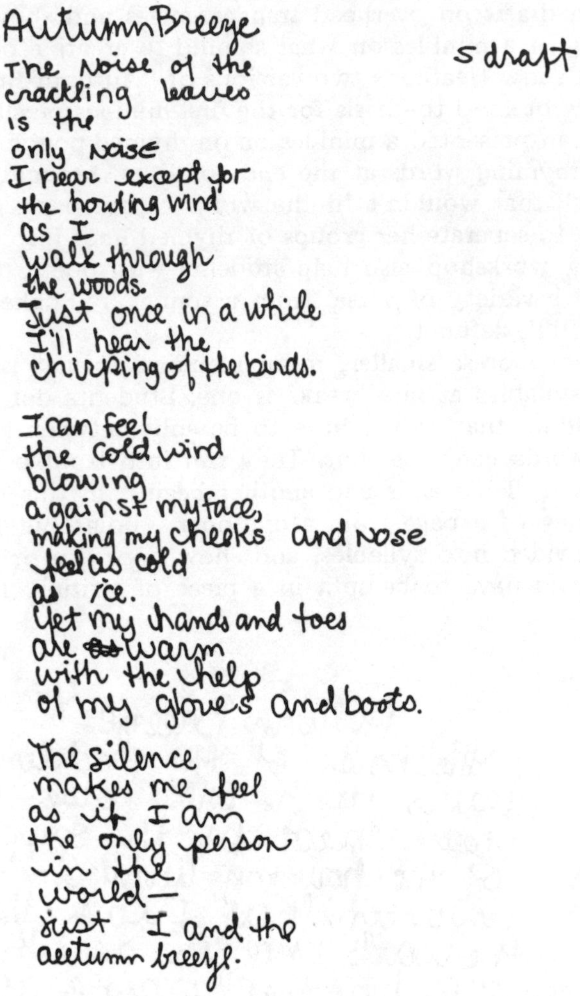

Autumn Breeze

5 draft

The noise of the
crackling leaves
is the
only noise
I hear except for
the howling wind
as I
walk through
the woods.
Just once in a while
I'll hear the
chirping of the birds.

I can feel
the cold wind
blowing
against my face,
making my cheeks and nose
feel as cold
as ice.
Yet my hands and toes
are so warm
with the help
of my gloves and boots.

The silence
makes me feel
as if I am
the only person
in the
world—
just I and the
autumn breeze.

Figure 3A

by observing, "This is an editing skill. As you're drafting, split words between syllables according to your best guess. When you self-edit, grab a dictionary and compare your syllables against the book's." This is the only dictionary mini-lesson I conduct, other than showing students where the dictionaries are. It's the only dictionary lesson they've needed, as evidenced by pieces of their writing.

In other format mini-lessons I've shown students how to set up correspondence. Proper letter format is the kind of convention that helps get eighth grade writers taken seriously by the world of readers beyond our classroom. It's a convention most kids have some knowledge of but which few produce perfectly unless they have an unusual amount of experience writing letters. Until 1980, when I became director of our writing project and had to compose frequent business letters, I had to look up proper business letter format every time a business letter occasion rolled around. In mini-lessons I help kids develop their own personal references for letter format so they have fast access to the correct forms. On one day I'll pass out pieces of blue bond, teach friendly letter format, and ask kids to set up a mock friendly letter on the blue paper, then file it in their daily folders for future reference. On another day I'll pass out yellow bond, teach business letter format, and ask kids to do a quick mock-up of a business letter, to be filed with the blue sheet. On a third day I'll give everyone an envelope and teach them how to address it. They clip the envelopes and the letter sheets together and put them in the backs of their folders, to use as and if they need them during the year.

My punctuation mini-lessons deal with two kinds of marks: those that kids could use if they were aware of them, and those that kids are aware of but don't use correctly. The first are pure pleasure to teach because they bring such voice to writing. Students aren't generally aware of the use of ellipsis marks to indicate a break in thought, or missing text. They're not aware of how dashes can signal an abrupt change, or emphasize or set off information. They don't know how colons can introduce explanations or lists. They haven't used parentheses to indicate asides, or encountered parentheses within parentheses. They haven't noticed how writers of narratives sometimes string a line of asterisks across the page to indicate a shift in time or place. And they've forgotten something they knew as first graders: how printing a word in caps or underlining it raises the volume. These are quick, helpful mini-lessons.

The punctuation marks my kids most often misuse or fail to use are periods, commas, quotation marks, and apostrophes. Some writers still aren't aware of what these marks do for readers, particularly the period and the comma. In a mini-lesson I'll try to show, in sentences written on a transparency, how a period indicates a full stop of one's voice, and a comma makes a pause. I'll also teach a semi-colon, the mark a writer uses when he knows he has two sentences but wants to show a relationship between them and so doesn't want a full stop. I'll bring up the dash and colon again, this time as ways writers attach sentence fragments to syntactically complete sentences. Then I'll follow up on mini-lessons in individual editing conferences with writers still having trouble with run-on sentences, comma splices, and fragments. This is a group of mini-lessons I'll abandon soon. Each year fewer and fewer of my students have problems with end-stop punctuation. They have a sense of sentences because they have so much experience writing.

Because the marks for conversation are so complicated, and because conversation is a major feature of eighth graders' narratives, rules for quoting dialogue consume a good bit of mini-lesson and editing conference time. On different days I've talked about the basic rule — that words said aloud take quotes — and introduced all the others: a comma after the explanatory phrase if it comes first; a comma, exclamation point, or question mark — never a period — between a quoted remark and its explanatory phrase; a capital letter at the beginning of a quoted remark; single quotes inside double quotes; how to paragraph speakers; how to punctuate a speech that goes on for more than one paragraph; etc. This isn't thrilling territory to cover but it is worthwhile. Knowledge of these rules allows writers to bring people's words to life on the page.

Usage mini-lessons include quick discussions of the differences between *lie* and *lay* and *sit* and *set*, distinctions that escape or confuse many young writers. Pronoun usage also comes up. Kids have trouble using the correct pronoun form when the subject of a sentence is compound (e.g., Danny and I, or Danny and me). I teach kids to test the pronoun by itself in the sentence, dropping the "_____ and" part of the phrase, to see which form is correct. Students can understand and use this procedure, a welcome alternative to spending months drilling lists of nominative and objective case pronouns at the end of which most students still won't understand how to apply it in their writing.

Finally, I talk about spelling in skill mini-lessons, since misspellings seem to throw off readers more than any other error. I teach kids how to self-edit for spelling:

> Read through your last draft with a pen in your hand and draw a circle around any word that doesn't look quite right or any words you're not absolutely sure of. Good spellers are people who have a pretty good sense of what words should — or shouldn't — look like. Then grab a dictionary or Spellex speller and look up each of your circled words. See how close you were, notice how the word is correctly spelled if you did misspell it, and write the correct spelling on your draft if you weren't correct. I know it's hard to think beyond today, this week, or even this year, but I won't be here as your final editor after June. You don't have to become a flawless speller by June — no one can spell every word correctly. But you should begin to develop a sense of American spelling, of the ways words should look. And you should know how you can compensate for the fact that no one can spell every word correctly. You compensate by doing your best at identifying words you're not certain of; then you look them up.

I pull spelling mini-lessons from specific, frequent errors I find when I edit students' writing. As with all the other kinds of mini-lessons, I want to be as relevant as possible to the whole group and what it needs. At the same time I understand that not everyone in the group will learn what I teach. In mini-lessons I give a fast, pointed shot of information, then hope for the best.

The poet X. J. Kennedy recently cautioned, "Good writing occurs because a writer passionately desires to say something . . . Students do not need more abstract advice about how to write. They need somehow to have their feelings kindled" (1984). I copied out Kennedy's warning and tacked it over my desk. I have to remember not to let my mini-lessons become occasions for preaching abstract formulas and rules. More than that, I have to remember that mini-lessons are not the most important occasions of the writing workshop. It's very tempting to view mini-lessons as the answer, the ultimate method. They're not. Writing mini-lessons are a welcome, worthwhile addition to my repertoire as a teacher, but no substitute for the personal response, the conversations in which kids begin to discover what they passionately desire to say.

SECTION III
Reading Workshop

Libby in reading workshop

CHAPTER 7

Building a Dining Room Table, Part I: Reading Workshop

"My education was the liberty I had to read indiscriminately and all the time, with my eyes hanging out."
Dylan Thomas

My sister called with the good news: their offer had been accepted. She, her husband, and my nephew Eric were about to move to a new house, with a big yard, shade trees — and an above-ground pool. "Please," she asked. "Whatever you do when you visit us, promise you won't let on to Eric that Atwells don't swim."

Bonnie wants us Atwells to pretend that learning to swim is a natural part of life. Specifically, she wants to introduce Eric to their pool without any of his adult relatives betraying our longstanding panic about deep water. Bonnie remembers the swimming lessons of our youth — how our parents conveyed their own unease in the water, how their eyes worried, and how we kids kept our feet firmly planted on the bottom and refused to put our faces in the water. We were no fools. We believed our parents when they showed us that learning to swim was going to be difficult and dangerous.

My sister knows that her little son, like all humans, learns at least as much from the implicit as the explicit. In defining conditions necessary for learning to take place, Frank Smith refers to incidents of teaching, implicit and explicit, as "demonstrations." We humans are surrounded by demonstrations; everything anyone does "demonstrates not only what can be done and how it can be done, but what the person doing it feels about the act" (1982, p. 171-2). We learn by engaging with particular demonstrations, as I learned more by engaging with my parents' inadvertent demonstrations concerning deep water than from all of their good, explicit advice about stroking, kicking, and breathing.

In our classrooms each day, we explicitly teach and students learn; this is a fact, Janet Emig writes, that "no one will deny. But," she continues, "to believe that children learn *because* teachers teach and only what teachers explicitly teach is to engage in magical thinking . . ." (1983, p. 135). It is magical thinking for me to believe I convey to the students in my classroom only good, explicit advice about writing and reading. The information that

151

comes out of my mouth when I talk is at least equaled by implicit data, so that every minute they can observe me I'm providing demonstrations with which eighth graders may or may not engage. I'll never be able to account for what each learns through the ways I teach.

As my parents' approaches to deep water taught me tacit lessons about swimming, so the ways we approach literature in the secondary English classroom convey inadvertent messages to our students about reading — about what, why, how, when, and for whom people read. And our approaches to literature tend to be fairly standard in secondary classrooms across the U.S.

We select and assign texts, generally one chapter or chunk at a time, to be read by the whole class as homework, then discussed or formally tested in the following day's session, at the end of which another piece of text is assigned. We prepare and present lectures on literary topics and require our students to memorize various bits of literary information — the Roman equivalents of the Greek deities, characteristics of the New Criticism, lists of Latin roots, definitions, George Eliot's real name — followed by exams where students report back what we said and assigned them to memorize. We talk a lot, much of it about the importance of literacy, of reading well and widely, of language as a prism for knowing ourselves and our world. But we seldom make class time for students to read or accommodate their choices or knowledge, and seldom do our students see their teachers reading, captivated by another's written words.

Our kids are learning from us. The question is, what exactly are they learning? What inadvertent messages do we transmit via the standard approach to literature? I've started to try to make explicit the tacit lessons I learned as a student of literature — and to uncover the demonstrations my own teaching probably put across to those other students of literature for too many years.

TWENTY-ONE THINGS TEACHERS DEMONSTRATE ABOUT READING

- Reading is difficult, serious business.
- Literature is even more difficult and serious.
- Reading is a performance for an audience of one: the teacher.
- There is one interpretation of a text: the teacher's.
- "Errors" in comprehension or interpretation will not be tolerated.
- Student readers aren't smart or trustworthy enough to choose their own texts.
- Reading requires memorization and mastery of information, terms, conventions, and theories.
- Reading is always followed by a test (and writing mostly serves to test reading — book reports, critical papers, essays, and multiple choice/fill-in-the-blank/short answer variations).
- Reading somehow involves drawing lines, filling in blanks, and circling.
- Readers break whole texts into separate pieces to be read and dissected one fragment at a time.

- It's wrong to become so interested in a text that you read more than the fragment the teacher assigned.
- Reading is a solitary activity you perform as a member of a group.
- Readers in a group may not collaborate; this is cheating.
- Re-reading a book is also cheating; so are skimming, skipping, and looking ahead.
- It's immoral to abandon a book you're not enjoying.
- You learn about literature by listening to teachers talk about it.
- Teachers talk a lot about literature, but teachers don't read.
- Teachers are often bored by the literature they want you to read.
- Reading is a waste of English class time.
- There's another kind of reading, a fun, satisfying kind you can do on your free time or outside of school.
- You can fail English yet still succeed at and love this other kind of reading.

In *Illiterate America* (1985), Jonathan Kozol, citing 1979 Ford Foundation figures, estimates that sixty million Americans are at least functionally illiterate, and quotes U.N. statistics to the effect that the United States ranks as low as forty-ninth in literacy levels among 158 U.N. countries. The latest National Assessment of Educational Progress shows a marked decline in inferential comprehension among secondary-level readers — and a marked lessening in the degree to which kids value and enjoy reading by the time they reach high school. At the same time, scholars note that the level of literacy required to function in American society is steadily increasing. Larry Mikulecky of Indiana University surveyed 107 workers of various kinds and found that 99 percent did "some reading" on the job, with the average 113 minutes a day. Mikulecky also observes that "Up through World War II newspapers were written at about the sixth grade level. Now wire service articles come out at the eleventh grade level, and even sports pages are around ninth or tenth" (Fiske, 1983).

Teachers of English can't help but be concerned. The level of literacy defined as "functional" becomes increasingly more sophisticated, yet in spite of all of our heartfelt, explicit messages, the activities we sponsor and demonstrations we provide are creating too many non-readers — students who either cannot or do not read.

None of us intends this outcome. We enter our classrooms determined to create readers, to do the very best we can at what we know as teachers of literature. But even the most conscientious versions of the standard approach, I believe, demonstrate the twenty-one tacit lessons above. Implicit in the list of demonstrations is our expectation that there's a "proper" way to read; that done properly, reading is as difficult and unnatural an act for humans as swimming is for Atwells. The model of the good adult reader we present is a model few students can — or even want to — emulate.

The good reader our demonstrations call up is a snob straight out of a *New Yorker* cartoon. Ensconced in a leather wing chair in his book-lined study, he's pedantic, punctilious, absolutely dispassionate. He keeps his encounters with books free of messy personal associations and prejudices;

instead he brings to bear a received body of literary criticism and history. The good reader reads no text more colloquial or contemporary than Proust. He finishes every book he starts. He reads every single word. He looks up any word he's not certain of, but only after applying his extensive knowledge of Latin roots, prefixes, suffixes, and rules of word formation. *He is not us.*

Contrary to the portrait of the accomplished adult reader we paint for our kids, we accomplished adult readers don't read this way. I think at heart we're embarrassed about how we do read, and believe if only we can train them properly our students won't inherit our sloppy habits — skipping over or guessing at words we're not sure of, skimming passages when we get bored, abandoning books that don't interest us or are simply too hard. They won't adopt our middlebrow tastes in contemporary popular fiction (or our low-brow tastes for potboilers). They will become good readers. And so we set our priorities for the secondary literature program. Discipline. Standards. Tradition. Mastery. Correctness. And at the center of the curriculum are the Great Works of Literature.

Alan Purves sets different priorities: "At the center of the curriculum are *not* the works of literature . . . but rather the mind as it meets the book. The response" (1972, p. 27). When we invite readers' minds to meet books in our classrooms, we invite the messiness of human response — personal prejudices, personal tastes, personal habits, personal experience. But we also invite personal meaning, and the distinct possibility that our kids will grow up to become a different kind of good reader, an adult for whom reading is a logical, satisfying, life-long habit, someone who just plain loves books and reading. A new set of priorities for the secondary English curriculum emerges. Pleasure. Fluency. Involvement. Appreciation. Initiative. At its center are readers' responses — to the world of the book, to their own world, to the world-wide, literate community of which they become members, to the meanings they make and re-make as they read. If we revise our portrait of the good reader to fit reality, the first thing we might notice is that he isn't so sure of himself or his texts after all. Whenever he opens a book he accepts an invitation to forge and explore new meanings.

Lessons from Writing

In any of its diverse forms, the making of meaning is rarely an orderly or formulaic procedure. Teachers who write as a way of making their own meanings know about disorder. As participants in writing projects and seminars, we've had to level with ourselves and our students about our processes as writers, and we've started to transform our writing curricula accordingly. When we make room for the tentativeness and turbulence of creating written meaning, we and our kids breathe a collective sigh of relief. Writing well isn't a gift God gives to a chosen few. Instead, we provide a powerful demonstration: with enough time to shape and reshape the writing, with topics and audiences we care about and with responses along the way, anyone can write well.

Anyone can read well. Good readers begin to grow when teachers of reading level with ourselves and students about our processes as readers and begin to redefine what good readers do, revising the literature curriculum accordingly. Like writing, reading requires the creation of meaning, this time in collaboration with an author. Like writing, reading becomes meaningful only when it involves the particular response of an individual — one's own ways of perceiving reality through the prism of written language. And, like writing, reading generates its most significant meanings when the reader engages in a process of discovery, weaving and circling among the complex of behaviors that characterizes genuine participation in written language. When we look at our own processes as readers and reflect on appropriate methods for teaching reading, it's hard to justify truncating reading into a lecture-assign-evaluate lockstep, just as reflections on our writing dismantled a similar monolith. For in truth, both writing and reading are written language *processes*.

WRITING AND READING AS PROCESS

Writers and readers REHEARSE, planning and predicting:

- What will I write?
- What will it be like?
- How will it be shaped by my prior experiences as a writer?

- What will I read?
- What will it be like?
- How will it be shaped by my prior experiences as a reader?

Writers and readers DRAFT, discovering meaning:

- Where will these words I am writing take me?
- Where will these words I am reading take me?
  - What surprises, disappointments, problems, questions, and insights will I encounter along the way?

Writers and readers REVISE, reseeing and reseeking meaning:

- Is this what I expected, what I hoped for?
- What do I think of the words on the page?
- What new thoughts do I think because of the words on the page?
- What makes sense? What needs to be changed so sense can be made?

We demonstrate reading as a meaning-seeking process and engage our students minds as real readers' minds engage when we provide in school what real readers need. Just as writing workshop provides what real writers need, extending an invitation to kids' active involvement as writers, so a reading workshop invites their active involvement as readers of others' writing. For the past two years when my classroom wasn't filled with writers at work, it was occupied by readers at work in a reading workshop. Each fall, in addition to establishing my classroom as a place for writing, I've built a new dining room table, one where there's room for all students of every ability to pull up their chairs and join me in a year-long readers' feast.

In reading workshop I expect everyone will read. I expect they'll all discover books they love, that together we'll enter the world of literature, make connections, become captivated, find satisfaction, and learn. I expect these things will happen because just as my sister asked me to avoid suggesting that her son might not learn to swim, I want to provide as few demonstrations as possible that my students might not read, or read easily, or find good books. I hope the literate environment I organize around an imaginary dining room table will demonstrate just the opposite.

I hope our dining room table will serve to develop the habit of reading and, with it, literacy, conjuring up a new and sensible image of a good reader that students can and want to emulate. I hope it places student response in its rightful place — at the head of the table and the heart of the curriculum. And I hope this environment supports reading and readers by providing what readers need. Like writers in the writing workshop, all readers — all learners — need Mary Ellen Giacobbe's three basics of time, ownership, and response.

Time

The most recent National Assessment of Educational Progress reports that American thirteen- and seventeen-year-olds do less reading, especially of fiction, than our nine-year-olds. In a *New York Times* feature about Americans' reading habits (Fiske, 1983), Jan Marsten of the University of Chicago observed that traditionally "there seem to be periods in the life-span during which reading tends to drop off, including adolescence. It would hardly be surprising if people did less reading during periods of such upheaval in their lives."

Secondary teachers know about upheaval in adolescents' lives. First jobs, first cars, first boyfriends and girlfriends are hallmarks of adolescence. So are a preoccupation with peers and participation in junior and senior high's extra-curricular activities. Reading necessarily takes a back seat as teenagers' worlds become impossibly full. A former student of mine anticipated April vacation of her freshman year by saying, "Ms. Atwell, I'm going to read six books this week. All of them are books I've been dying to read since Christmas. I just look at them and feel depressed. There's always something else I've got to do." When reading doesn't happen at school, it's unlikely to happen away from school, which means it's unlikely to happen at all. And we know from John Goodlad that reading isn't happening at school.

Goodlad found that U.S. elementary school students, grades K–6, spend only 6 percent of a typical school day actually reading; our junior high kids devote, on average, less than 3 percent of their time in school to actual reading, and at the high school that figure is less than 2 percent of each school day (1984, p. 107). We need to be concerned about statistics like these for two reasons: because we know readers' fluency is a function of sustained experiences with printed texts (Smith, 1971), and because our students soon enough know from our methodologies that their sustained experiences with printed texts are low-priority concerns of the very institutions empowered to bring them to literacy. The time we don't make for students' independent reading is probably our most harmful demonstration.

I've learned to make time for real reading. Periods of silent, independent reading are perhaps the strongest experience I can provide students to demonstrate the value of literacy. Rather than relegating it to homework status, as a follow-up activity to the teacher's lectures, I make reading the central activity of the literature program. Reading is so important an undertaking that it takes highest priority, commanding extended chunks of time when students can forget jobs, sports, social life, family obligations, and homework for other courses — when they can enter the world of literature and make it their own. And they do, as Jane did consistently.

One morning in the spring Jane darted into my homeroom for a quick visit, talking her usual mile a minute. "Oh, Ms. Atwell. You won't believe this. This weekend we went to Boston and I took along the letter I got from Lois Lowry with her return address and we found her apartment building so I went up the steps and saw her name right there on her mailbox and then I went back down and got in the car again and we drove to Barnes and Noble — have you ever been there? because you should go if you haven't — and I'll never, ever forget it." She took one deep breath. "So now I'm going to read *Autumn Street* which is her latest and then I'll probably read all the Sue Ellen Bridgers and then maybe some poetry."

"You just looked at her name plate?" I asked, trying to backtrack through the maze of Jane's story.

"Yeah, 'cause that was enough really, just to know where she lives so I can imagine her writing there when I read her books."

Jane reads every school day, Monday through Friday. She thinks about her reading when she isn't reading even when she's on vacation. She is a habitual reader.

At the start of eighth grade, Melissa wrote, "I don't like to read because I think reading is boring. I like to do things. I'll read the sports page and comic books but that's it because it's JUST SO BORING." Melissa read every day, Monday through Friday. At first she read because I expected her to. She'd say, "You know, some people hate reading and it's not fair that they should have to read for one whole period every day." I'd answer, "Some people don't like math but they do math. Some people may not like science but they take science. This class is called reading, and people who come in here read. But they get help when they get stuck. I know some great books. I know Amanda's a friend of yours, and she knows some great books. We'll help you find books you love."

By December Melissa read because she loved reading. She carried around the list of books Amanda recommended and crossed off titles one by one as she finished them: *Tiger Eyes, Snowbound, Two for Survival, Pardon Me, You're Stepping on My Eyeball.* Then she moved on to good stories she found on her own: *Rock 'n' Roll Express, Out of Bounds, Where the Red Fern Grows.* At the end of May she wrote in my yearbook, "I just wanted to tell you for the first summer in a *long* time (since about 3rd or 4th grade) I'm going to find a book to read over the summer." Melissa became a habitual seeker after good books, a reader.

Randy was one of my special ed students last year, mainstreamed for writing and reading workshop. He read every school day, and for a long time, that was it: Randy read when and because he had to. Then I nudged him toward S. E. Hinton. He finished *The Outsiders* in a week. "I read it Friday night and Saturday and finished Sunday. I didn't believe how fast I finished this book. You got any more books like this one?" I had more. At the end of eighth grade Randy wrote, "This year I read a lot more books that were thicker than last year. I read *lots* more books then last year, and I have read them at home!" Randy, who entered eighth grade reading at the third grade level, became a habitual reader.

So did Lori, who entered eighth grade a lip reader. Sometimes she went beyond lip moving to reading aloud to herself, word by word. Lori had all the problems of lip readers. She couldn't understand or remember much of what she read, and it was no wonder. Focusing on and pronouncing one word at a time, she read so slowly that often she had forgotten the beginning of a sentence by the time she got to its end. For her, reading was a matter of sounding out all the words on a given page.

From the first week of school Lori read every day for forty-five minutes. Right from the beginning I nudged her hard — to read with her finger on her lips to prevent them moving, to push herself to read faster and increase the number of pages she read each day, to "chunk" meaning, taking in phrases and sentences and not fixing her eyes on every word (Smith, 1984). By the end of May, Lori had read twenty novels. She wrote:

> I can't really believe that I've read that many books this year. At the beginning of the year I just read so that I would pass reading but now I read because it's fun. Now that I've stopped moving my lips it seems like I'm just going right through the books. And you were right. *Taking Terri Mueller* has really picked up and now it's really intresting I'm at the part where she first goes to see her mother and it's really great. And I'm almost done so that will be 21 this year.

The daily time I make for students' independent reading is probably the most questioned of all my classroom practices. I justify with anecdotes, stories about readers like Jane, Melissa, Randy, and Lori, and with hard facts. Last year's eighth graders, including eight special education students, read an average of thirty-five full length works, from Blume to Brontë, Strasser to Steinbeck, Voigt to Verne. Their scores on standardized achievement tests averaged at the seventy-second percentile, up from an average at the fifty-fourth percentile when fully twenty-one percent scored in the bottom quartile; last year, that figure was just two percent. In June, 92 percent of my students indicated that they regularly read at home for pleasure — that they were taking home the books they read during reading workshop — and when I asked how many books they owned, the average figure they gave was 98, up from September's average of 54. (I have no way of knowing whether they did, in fact, own more books by the end of eighth grade. I do know they perceived themselves as owning more, as being the sort of people who acquire and collect libraries.) This is the kind of evidence that begins to convince doubting administrators and parents: children read more, comprehend better, and value books to a greater degree when we let them read.*

If my primary aim as a reading teacher is to let students read, my primary responsibility is to ensure that reading happens, both by establishing expectations for reading class and by creating a reading environment. My expectations are demonstrated in the predictable structure of reading workshop and in the procedures that govern readers' use of workshop time.

Reading workshop too begins with a mini-lesson. We spend five or ten minutes talking about an author — Richard Wright, Robert Frost, Lois Duncan, S. E. Hinton — or a genre. We read and discuss a poem, short story, or opening chapter by Cummings, Updike, Wilbur, Stevens, London, L'Engle, LeGuin, or one of the kids in the class, peeling away layers of the text and coming to meaning together. We focus on writing and reading processes, how we read and reread a text and how authors might have come to write as they did. (Chapter 9 addresses more comprehensively the topic of reading mini-lessons.)

The rest of the period is devoted to independent reading. Students settle back and dive in. I move among them for the first ten minutes or so, asking "How's it going?" and finding out if anyone needs my immediate assistance, and then I sit down and read too, my books and their books. Each day that a reader follows the written guidelines I've established for reading workshop, he or she receives points. Over the course of a quarter, these points can total one hundred (e.g., 2.5 points per day multiplied by 40 days of reading workshop equals 100 points). This figure represents one-third of the quarterly grade in reading. Students who don't follow the rules outlined below on a given day lose points accordingly.

RULES FOR USING READING WORKSHOP TIME

1. Students must read for the entire period.
2. They cannot do homework or read any material for another course. Reading workshop is not a study hall.
3. They must read a book (no magazines or newspapers where text competes with pictures), preferably one that tells a story (e.g., novels, histories and biographies rather than books of lists or facts where readers can't sustain attention, build up speed and fluency, or grow to love good stories.)
4. They must have a book in their possession when the bell rings; this is the main responsibility involved in coming prepared to this class. (Students who need help finding a book or who finish a book during the workshop are obvious exceptions.)
5. They may not talk to or disturb others.
6. They may sit or recline wherever they'd like as long as feet don't go up on furniture and rule #5 is maintained. (A piece of paper taped over the

---

*See Appendix *F* for a copy of the reading survey I administered in September and then again in June, from which I obtained most of these statistics.

window in the classroom door helps cut down on the number of passers-by who require explanations about students lying around with their noses in books.)

7. There are no lavatory or water fountain sign-outs to disturb me or other readers. In an emergency, they may simply slip out and slip back in again as quietly as possible.

8. A student who's absent can make up time and receive points by reading at home, during study hall (with a note from a parent or study hall teacher), or after school.

The environment where these procedures are carried out makes it easy to follow the rules. Except for the mini-lesson that begins reading workshop, there isn't any teacher to listen to and there isn't anything to do but read; the teacher reads too. A carpet on the floor lets readers get comfortable, and noises that distract from books, like talking and the door banging shut, are kept to a minimum.

Once again, if I saw my students only one period each day, for the typical English class that includes both language and literature, I'd continue to make sustained time for reading. I'd schedule three periods per week of writing workshop and two for reading, still giving writing and reading highest priority as English class activities, making as much time as I could for both. Only in regular reading workshops can students gain the experience with printed texts they need to grow to fluency. They can see me and other readers reading. They can get hooked by whole texts and real stories and, finally and most importantly, readers in the reading workshop can choose the books that will hook them. Making time is just one demonstration crucial to developing readers. Another is accommodating readers' own choices of books.

Ownership

I was incredulous when I read *Pride and Prejudice* at age twenty, convinced it couldn't possibly be the same novel I'd suffered through as a high school sophomore. Just last summer I finally gathered my courage and re-read *My Ántonia*, eighteen years after barely passing a multiple-choice test on the novel. My list of reconsidered readings goes on and on: *Anna Karenina*, *The Scarlet Letter*, *Crime and Punishment*, *The Mill on the Floss*, *Hamlet*, *Moby-Dick*, and *The Canterbury Tales* (which I discovered, when I finally got hold of a copy minus the standard high school ellipses, were bawdy).

In his autobiography *Hunger of Memory* Richard Rodriguez has similar stories to tell about the literature he "read" as an adolescent:

One day I came across a newspaper article about the retirement of an English professor at a nearby state college. The article was accompanied by a list of the "hundred most important books of Western Civilization" . . . I clipped out the list and kept it for the several months it took me to read all of the titles. Most books, of course, I barely understood. While reading Plato's *Republic*, for instance, I needed to keep looking at the book jacket comments to remind myself what the text was about. Nevertheless, with the special patience and superstition of a scholarship boy, I looked at every word of the text. And by the time I reached the last word, relieved, I convinced myself that I had read *The Republic*. In a ceremony of great pride, I solemnly crossed Plato off my list (1983, p. 64).

Like Rodriguez, I never read, in any genuine sense of the word, much of the literature on which I fixed any teenage eyes. I was in fact a good reader, but a different reader — a different person — than today. When I was ready for complicated and complex themes and language, those books were there waiting for me to enter and enjoy. That I did go back was in spite of, not because of, my own teachers' spoonfeeding and forcefeeding. I chose to do so. Making the choice was my first step toward understanding and appreciating the literature.

If we want our adolescent students to grow to appreciate literature, another first step is allowing them to exert ownership and choose the literature they will read. Preliminary to that, we might take a giant step as readers ourselves and acknowledge that the term *literature* embraces more than the risk-free, prescribed, junior high canon of second-rate Dickens (*A Tale of Two Cities*), second-rate Steinbeck (*The Red Pony*), second-rate Twain (*The Prince and the Pauper*) and second-rate Hemingway (*The Old Man and the Sea*). The last twenty years have witnessed an explosion in the number of novels and short stories written expressly for young adults, adolescent literature of such breadth and depth no teacher need ever apologize for building a curriculum around kids' responses to their own books. Much of the writing — I'm thinking of Robert Cormier, Lois Lowry, Susan Beth Pfeffer, Madeleine L'Engle, Robert Lipsyte — is exquisite. More importantly, much of the sentiment expressed in contemporary adolescent fiction mirrors and celebrates what Tom Newkirk terms the emerging power — that sense of independence and of self — of the adolescent mind (1985, p. 119). As we adult readers can turn to fiction for portrayals of the universalities of our condition, our students can find their perspectives reflected and explored in a body of fiction of their own, books that can help them grow up, books that can help them love books.

Last year's average of thirty-five books per student grew as much from students' power to choose as from the time I made for them to read. I heard again and again from students of every ability that freedom of choice had turned them into readers. Teresa, who arrived in September calling herself "a hopeless case when it comes to books and reading," wrote in November:

> I've learned more from you already than from any other reading teacher I've had. The way my other reading teachers taught was, you read a story they tell you to read then answer questions at the end. I never learned anything from it. Last year we did that and we also *had* to read books like the *The Prince and the Pauper*, *The Mouse That Roared*, and *The Call of the Wild*. I could never get into those books because we HAD to read them. (Luckily I did get into *Call of the Wild*.) What I'm trying to say is that I'm happy with myself and with what I'm doing, and I'm learning so much about books and authors.

Teresa's authors during eighth grade were among the best writing for adolescents. She chose books by Doris Lund, Lori Boatright, Lois Lowry, Todd Strasser, Susan Beth Pfeffer, Arthur Roth, Jay Bennett, S. E. Hinton, Maia Wojoiechowska, Judy Blume, Paula Danziger, Norma Klein, Harry and Norma Fox Mazer, Lois Duncan, Stella Pevsner, Francine Pascal, and Robert Lipsyte. At the end of eighth grade Teresa and each of the other eighth graders rated all of the books they'd read over the school year. Their rating system, 1–10 points per book, was designed to help me select novels to restock the classroom library. My shopping list appears here as Appendix *G*: a list of all the books rated 9 or 10 by at least three eighth grade readers. A classroom library filled with popular titles serves as an invitation to readers to browse, chat about books, select and be selective. It also provides an important demonstration, showing students that supplying books for them to choose and read — in Don Graves's phrase "surrounding them with literature" (1983, p. 65) — is a high priority of their teacher and school.

Allowing readers to choose also helps their fluency. I heard again and again from readers of every ability that freedom of choice had increased both reading rate and comprehension. For example, Lori wrote:

> I think the reason that I liked *Waiting Games* better than *The Other Side of the Mountain* is that I was more interested in it so it really kept me going like I didn't want it to stop. So I read faster so I could see what was going to happen next, and never moved my lips once.

Suzy, another student who diagnosed herself as a word-by-word reader at the start of the year, also complained, "I guess from what people say reading is a pretty good thing to do, but sometimes I read and I don't know what I read." By May, she had read nineteen novels and wrote, "I really enjoy reading for pleasure. But I hate having books assigned. I just can't get into them as much."

Allowing readers to choose virtually ensures that everyone will "get into" books. Each year by the end of September even the most reluctant readers have found the one good book that begins a turn-around in their attitudes toward reading and abilities as readers. I could never choose one title that would similarly affect seventy eighth graders: this one book doesn't exist (however close S. E. Hinton's *The Outsiders* may come). In short, there is no one book everyone has to have read.

Allowing readers to choose their books can lead to surprises, on occasion mildly unpleasant ones, like books unsuitable to be read in school. When this happens I ask the reader to take the book home, since it's not a book I could defend, not a book worth my risking my job. (In fact I have very few censorship problems because readers are choosing their own texts rather than having them assigned by me.) Most often, the surprises are pleasant, like Danny's discovery of "something different":

> I finished all of the seven Westerns I bought. They were really great, but I'm a little bored with Westerns right now so I'm reading something different. The book is called *Waiting for Godot*. It is a book about a mess of people waiting for one guy and he never shows up! It's a really

weird book and I can't wait to let you see it! It's written in play form and it seems quite funny . . . This Godot might be a very high honored and respected man, or he might be evil and mean. I'm really not sure.

In choosing *Godot*, Danny had found a book he was ready and willing to read. Patrice was ready and willing to sample Shakespeare.

> I finished *Macbeth* today. The reason I decided to read *Macbeth* was because a girl at Skyway Middle School, who I am friends with, read it and really loved it.
>
> I found that the three witches were my favorite characters. Many movies have used take-offs of these characters. *The Beast Master*, a movie I saw on cable, did. They used them differently, but they were used to tell the future.
>
> Macbeth himself was, overall, a very confused guy. His wife made him kill the king, and he was hearing voices that told him to "sleep no more." Putting one of Shakespeare's plays into movie form could almost be as bad as Steven King, because of all the killing and walking around with people's heads.
>
> I truly enjoyed *The Comedy of Errors*. I enjoyed the way the two characters called Dromio spoke. Every time they opened their mouths they spoke in riddles. The overall idea was very good and funny. The reunions were like this: 2 father-son, 3 husband-wife, 2 brother, and 2 owner-slave. There is one wedding. Some of the reunions are *very* technical.

As part of making choices eighth graders discover their own theories about literature. Patrice's remark about "technical" reunions has its roots in a discussion that had taken place about a month before during a reading mini-lesson. We were talking about Hardy's poem "The Man He Killed" and Mike said, "Ms. Atwell, I really don't like this poem. I mean, why couldn't he just say it in regular language?"

Mike had been reading Frost and Wilbur. He loved Cummings. He wasn't asking for colloquial prose when he said "regular language."

I said, "Show me what you mean, Mike," and he read the line, "We should have set us down to wet right many a nipperkin" — a word I'd had to look up the night before and could find only in our *O.E.D.*

I'd made a foolish assumption. I thought my kids knew language changed over time, that English wasn't just American and contemporary. So we talked. Over the next weeks students began collecting and bringing to class examples of prose and poetry from other times to share in mini-lessons. When they hit Shakespeare I made copies of speeches from five of the plays and we looked at how the language differed within the plays, how Romeo and Juliet spoke one way, Macbeth another, and why. We began to puzzle out what makes a tragedy a tragedy and a comedy a comedy. They decided just about everyone dies in a tragedy and a new order begins. In a comedy, almost everyone gets married, reinstated, or reunited. John said, "Yeah, just like on *Love Boat*." Kellie commented that the Capulets and Montagues were a lot like the two squabbling families on her favorite soap opera, *Santa Barbara.* And from there we talked about basic plot conventions through all of literature, and how and where Shakespeare had borrowed his plots. Then they found and read to each other stories from Greek and Roman mythology.

They and I were collaborating as theorists, discovering, testing, and acting on literary principles. As readers, eighth graders discovered that literature is accessible; that literature is reading, and reading is sensible, interesting, and fun. This kind of collaboration is the final key to reading workshop's success. Readers need time and ownership, but they also need help deciding what they'll choose to do with the time at their disposal. Readers need response.

Response

In chapter one, I described my dining room table as a literate environment. The table is a forum where readers — my husband and I and our friends — engage in congenial talk about books, authors, reading, and writing. It was a forum I knew I had to try to recreate in my classroom, giving students similar opportunities for literary talk with the teacher.

I think opportunities to respond, to engage in literary talk with the teacher, are crucial. It is not enough for schools simply to make time and space for independent reading. For too many kids, sustained silent reading programs are little more than a nice break in the day's routine. With nothing happening before or after the reading, the context in which readers read doesn't support or extend their interests. As Donald Fry observes, the teacher needs to keep the ball rolling, "to be resourceful and responsive to what (the student) does in order to maintain that interest and allow that process to bring about change and not stagnate" (1985, p. 29).

Recreating my dining room table, being resourceful and responsive to what seventy-five individual readers were doing, presented problems of logistics. Class size averages twenty-five, so one-to-one reading conferences during the workshop allowed students to do little more than provide quick plot synopses of their books. There wasn't enough time or teacher to go around. And I discovered that even when the opportunity arose for an extended discussion between a student and me, readers had real difficulty moving beyond telling what happens. In talking with me they rarely analyzed or critiqued what they'd read or articulated what they liked or valued, a phenomenon also observed by Applebee (1978), and Whitehead (1977). I spent reading conference time trying to stay awake through retellings of novels I came to know too well.

At the time I was struggling to orchestrate meaningful discussions with readers, Dixie Goswami, my teacher at Bread Loaf, pointed me toward Jana Staton's dialogue journal research (1980, 1982). Staton studied the written dialogues that a sixth grade teacher sustains over every school year with each of her students, letters written back and forth in a bound journal. In these dialogue journals I recognized what I'd been looking for: a way all seventy-five eighth graders might pull up their chairs and join me at my dining room table. The following September I gave each reader a folder with a sheaf of lined paper and a letter from me inviting them to write back clipped inside.

I initiated written dialogues about literature because I had some hunches about the combined possibilities of writing as a way of reflecting on reading, and teacher-learner correspondence as a way of extending and enriching reflection through collaboration. I suspected kids' written responses to books would go deeper than their talk; that writing would give them time to consider their thinking and that thoughts captured would spark new insights. I also suspected that a written exchange between two readers, student and adult expert, would move readers even deeper inside written texts, with the give and take of the dialogue helping them to consider and develop their thoughts. Finally, I believed this special context — a teacher initiating and inviting first-draft chat — would provide a way for me to be responsive to every reader as well as creating a specific occasion for them to write and reflect: a genuine and genuinely interested audience who was going to write back.

The dialogue journals between my kids and me confirmed my hunches. Over each of the last two years we've exchanged thousands of pages of letters. In our correspondence we've gone far beyond plot synopses and traditional teacher's manual issues such as genre, theme, and character to give accounts of our processes as readers, to speculate on authors' processes as writers, to suggest revisions in what we've read, to see connections between a published author's work and our own writing, to see connections between books and our own lives, and to engage in some serious, and not so serious literary gossip.

For example, this is an exchange with Jennipher. We're calling each other "Robert" here because one week we happened to read or talk about four works by various authors with that name. Jenn decided we'd substantially increase our chances of becoming published authors if we were white males named Robert, so she changed our names.

5/2/84

Ms. A. Robert,

Just to see what Anne Frank was going through was miserable. Her "growing up" with the same people every day. I think she got to know them a lot better than she would have if they weren't in hiding, her mother especially. That sudden change, going into hiding, must have been hard.

It amazed me how much more they went downstairs in the book.* And it seems so much bigger in the book. It also told a lot more of her feelings, right up until the end. It must have come suddenly — to see police come in and arrest them.

I'm going to read some Robert Frost poetry now.

J. J. Robert

P.S. I think she would have been a writer.

---

*Jennipher had also read the Broadway stage play script of *The Diary of Anne Frank* by Albert Hackett and Frances Goodrich.

5/3/84

Dear J. J. R.,

I don't have any doubt — if she'd survived, she would have been a writer all her life. Her prose style is so lively, and her insights are so deep. And she loved to write.

We've talked about how movies alter (often for the worse) the books on which they're based. Plays can't help but do the same. All that inner stuff — reflections, dreams, thoughts and feelings — doesn't easily translate into stage action, although Hackett and Goodrich tried with Anne's between-act voice-overs.

If you're hungry for more information on Anne, please borrow my copy of Ernst Schnabel's *Anne Frank: Portrait in Courage* when Tom Apollonio returns it to me.

Ms. A. Robert

Jenn wrote to me again the day after I'd returned from an out-of-state conference. My lesson plan had called for the sub to read aloud as the mini-lesson and kids were thrown by the difference in read-aloud styles.

5/10/84

Ms. A. Robert,

We *missed* you! You get used to people's voice. The switch is hard for me.

Robert Frost's poems are really good. "The Witch of Cöos" seemed to me some where between Stephen King and Ray Bradbury. Kind of weird, huh? I heard someone quote (kind of!) one of his poems. It was on "People's Court," (Dumb Show) and there was a fight about a fence. In the end the guy came out of the courtroom and was talking to the reporter. He said something like, "This goes to show — good fences don't make good neighbors." I almost freaked out.

Back to the books.

J. J. Robert

5/10/84

Dear J. J. R.,

They quoted Frost on "People's Court?" (You WATCHED "People's Court"?)

I need an aspirin.

N. A. R.

All of this is first draft writing, unpolished and unrevised. Creating and maintaining a literary relationship with each student is one of my primary goals as a reading teacher, and the informality and spontaneity of notes passed in class help achieve that goal. When revision appears in a student's half of the dialogue, it's more likely to occur as a change in thinking over time as evidenced in a chronology of letters. For example, Justine was reading John Irving, whom she knew from her mother "is supposed to be a really good writer." Justine wasn't so certain. In excerpts below from four letters written over three weeks, she explores and revises her thoughts about narrative voice, character development, and her own criteria for qualities of good writing.

4/6/83

As I'm reading *Garp* I'm wondering why Irving didn't write it in first person. I want to know more about what Garp is feeling and thinking. Right now I picture him as a short, muscular writer who just thinks about books and sex. I want to know more.

4/13/83

John Irving must be an excellent writer to keep people entranced for *600* pages!
But why did he choose third person narrative?

4/25/83

The only part I found sad in *Hotel New Hampshire* was when Egg and Mother died. And that was way in the end. The plot to destroy the opera with a bomb seemed as if Irving just threw it in there.
I guess Irving's a good writer but his style is not my favorite. (I was trying to explain this to my mother the other night and she didn't understand.) His characters are so . . . cold (is that the word I want?) They were interesting books to read but I like S. E. Hinton or L'Engle or Tyler better.

4/27/83

I told my mom about what I thought about Irving and L'Engle. She said that maybe Irving's characters are more realistic and harder to swallow. No! The thing I like about Anne Tyler's books is the people's personalities. They are so unique but "I expect I could pass (them) on the street and not know (them)." And she writes third person!

Some of Justine's knowledge of literature — in this case, her reference to narrative voice — indisputably grows from my talk in mini-lessons. There are some useful bits of literary information I know and want to share with my kids. But I limit that talk to five- or ten-minute whole-class meetings so that it may be of most use to readers, providing a taste or an invitation rather than a dissection or dissertation.

Most of Justine's knowledge of literature grows from her own experiences as a reader of literature, of Irving, Hinton, L'Engle, Tyler and many others, and from opportunities to talk with other readers, such as her mom, and with me in the pages of our reading journal. Although there's no talking out loud during the reading workshop, there's plenty of talking on paper. We use the workshop time not only to read but also to write and pass notes about our reading, conferring in a special way. In this chapter I've only touched on the uses of dialogue journals as an approach to conferring about reading; the following chapter explores them in depth, detailing how we use them and to what effect.

Fitting the three keys of time, ownership, and response together once again creates a new big picture of what's possible in a junior high literature program — the possibility of widespread fluency, of deep involvement, of pleasure and appreciation and growth. A workshop approach offers all kids unlimited possibilities as readers. And, in turn, the demonstrations that surround readers in the workshop lead to the recognition and realization of their potentialities. In each day's workshop they see the uses of literacy. They see reading as a whole, sense-making activity, and written texts as open books — wide open to kids' opinions, questions, and interpretations. They see all students' rights as literate human beings and they see around them a community of readers in action. Before their eyes in the midst of their community, they see a new model of The Good Reader emerge.

Jennipher/Robert could and did emulate that new model. In her final letter to me she connected Frost's poem "Nothing Gold Can Stay," about the evanescence of dawn and all of nature's creations, with Hinton's novel *The Outsiders*, in which the young narrator recollects Frost's lines at a turning point in his life, with her own world — a world that is changed because J. J. Robert is a reader.

6/8/84

Dear Ms. A. Robert,

I finished *Autum Street*. It was excellent how Lowry told it from her childhood view of things, her feelings and then how she was back in the present in the end.

Sunday morning was special. The cats were under my bed at 4:15 doing something, I don't know how they got upstairs. I took them down and looked out the window. Low and behold, sunrise! But no, it did not rise. All I could see was a golden strip across the sky. I pulled up a chair and put my feet up. I said "Nothing Gold Can Stay" in my mind without stumbling and found how Ponyboy could have felt in *The Outsiders*. After fifteen minutes when the sun didn't appear I went back to bed feeling new.

We're really going to miss you.

See you sometime.

J. J. Robert

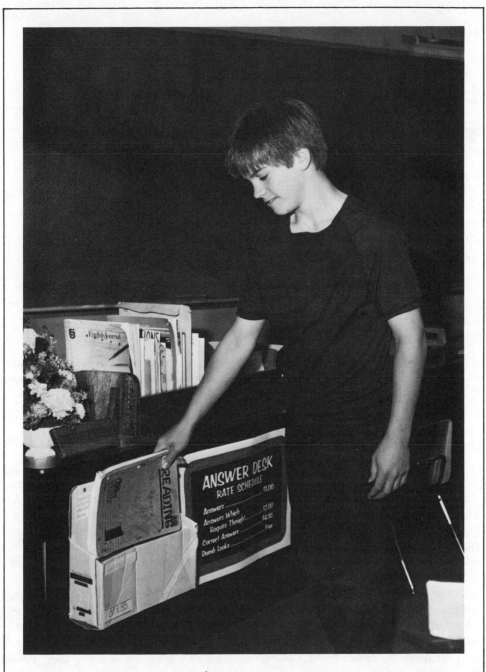

Mike delivers a letter about literature to Ms. A.

CHAPTER 8

Building a Dining Room Table, Part II: Responding to Readers and Reading

"Literature is no one's private ground, literature is common ground; let us trespass freely and fearlessly and find our own way for ourselves."
Virginia Woolf

1/6/84

Dear Ms. A,

I finished King's *Different Seasons*. Two of the stories were good ones. "Apt Pupil" and "The Body" were well written but the other two I didn't like. All of these stories were shorter than novels but longer than short stories. I looked it up and it's called a "novella."

Bean

Somewhere in the dark recesses of my memory the term *novella* lay buried. Bean's letter called it out into the light and reminded me of favorite novellas — *Good-bye Columbus* and *The Death of Ivan Illyich*. Bean's note also showed me again the kind of initiative kids will take to uncover new information when motivated to pursue their own interests. And I was reminded, once again, how our dialogue journals are a two-way street. From two years of eighth graders' letters to me, I've learned a lot about adolescent readers' interests and concerns. I've learned the value and necessity of allowing kids to read as real readers do, choosing, skimming, skipping, and abandoning. Maybe the hardest lesson of all, I've learned how to respond authoritatively to what readers are trying to do without coming across like a teacher's guide or a test. Instead, I can affirm, challenge, gossip, joke, argue, recommend, and provide information a reader needs. I can also offer some well-placed "nudges."

Through our dialogue journals my students learned, too, about the world of written texts — what good writers do, what good readers do, how readers talk, what books are for and how kids can get in on it. When I asked eighth graders to be specific about their literary knowledge, to spend a few days reading through our letters and making categories of the kinds of things we talked about, they named over 150 literary topics, including how authors wrote — how they began and concluded books, developed characters, used dialogue, selected a narrative voice, pointed themes, structured chapters, followed or overthrew formulas and conventions. We also talked about authors — their lives, their other books, the ways they researched their subjects, their latest reviews. We talked about concepts of genre: what makes a novel a novel and a short story a short story; how poetry differs from prose and how we classify fiction, non-fiction, and all their various modes. We talked about reader's process — when we skimmed, skipped, and abandoned books and how we made these decisions; when and why we re-read; how we planned and predicted and revised in our heads the ways books should have been written; how we learned to read and what we were learning about ourselves as readers. We made and followed up on recommendations. We gossiped about the world of publishing, about editors, agents, advances, royalties, remaindering, how and when hardcovers become paperbacks and books become films. We noted format — jacket copy, cover illustrations, copyright dates, type size, and length. We made connections between published authors' styles and subjects and those of our own writing. And we made connections between books and our own lives. In Appendix *H* I've given a complete listing of our dialogue journal topics.

This, finally, is the greatest of all the benefits of letters about literature: the range of talk in which we engage in school is much the same as the genuine literary gossip at my dining room table. This chapter features eighth grade readers' responses on a sampling of subjects, illustrating how written dialogues about literature can work to open up texts to young readers and compel reflection. It also presents principles for responding to kids' letters; introduces a new wrinkle, student-to-student exchanges about literature; and spells out procedures for initiating and maintaining dialogue journals and evaluating reading.

Literary Gossip: Kinds of Talk About Books

In their letters readers most often connect stories about others' lives to their own feelings and experiences. Although this response to literature isn't often encouraged or accommodated in school, I think it's one of the surest signs of a reader's involvement. For example, Jon responded personally, and pretty intensely, to the loyalty and love among roommates in *The Lords of Discipline*.

Pat Conroy puts four boys in a room, changes them into men, and then puts them against the world. But there is a traitor amongst them, which is a startling blow because there is so much love in that room. That is another thing that I liked. Conroy put an incredible amount of feeling in this book. The roommates love each other an incredible amount. When the main character exposes a secret organization, you have an immense feeling of joy for that character because he succeeded in doing the right thing; he put himself against men in power and he won. I just can't stop thinking about how much love there was floating in that room. It isn't like they are gay, they just care an incredible amount for each other, and Conroy illustrates this excellently. Normally I would have dropped a book like this, but this book has changed my way of thinking. I don't think that one boy caring for another boy is weird now.

Jon's personal connections with books ran the gamut. Here, in the same week, he connected fiction and life as only an eighth grader could.

I have an uncanny experence to tell you about. I was going up to Sugarloaf/USA and I took *Live and Let Die* with me. I came back on Sunday (I went up on Friday), the book finished. On Sunday, *Live and Let Die* was on ABC-TV!! I really couldn't believe it!!

Students also connected literature and real life by responding to the specific information authors presented via fictional narratives. They learned some things about the world around them through stories:

I finished *Goodbye Paperdoll.* It is a great book. It's very informative and I think helps alot in understanding anorexia nervosa, like *Deenie* taught me about scoliosis. (This was one book I really enjoyed the ending. It wasn't your typical, everythings all better, she gains thirty pounds type of ending.)

Their dialogue journals elicited another kind of personal connection that I'd never observed in eighth grade readers. In their letters they began to reflect on themselves as readers, to become conscious of and articulate how they learned to read, their reading rituals, and their processes as readers, the ways they went about reading and thinking about what they'd read:

I just can't remember how I got to like reading so much. It might be that way because of my mother always reading to me until I was in fourth grade.

When I read it's a special time for me to be alone. I sit on my bed with a pillow leaning against the wall and another one on my lap so I don't have to hold my arms up. I get completely relaxed. Also, after I finish reading, I just sit for a while thinking about the book . . . The only thing that bothers me is when I get a phone call or if it's time for dinner and I'm right in the middle of a good book. I try to get the interruption over with so I can get back to reading. How about you?

When I pick up a mystery novel, after examining all of the characters, from the leading lady to the gardiner, I make a logical asumption of who I think did the dasterdly deed, and many times I'm rite, like in King's novel I'm reading now, I asume something like "Boy! CHRISTINE's gonna get them!" and usualy it happens, so thats why I like King's work, because I can have a say in the ending. King I feel is trying to have people asume, and that's what makes him so great. What do you think?

Dear Theo was a collection of letters written by Vinsent Van Gogh to his brother, and it tells me many things I didn't know about him. He was a gifted artist who led a mostly terrible life . . . The letters were arrainged in the days he sent them. I picked the ones I wanted to read by skimming down the pages.

This is my second reading of *Conan the Warrior*. And this time it was different to me! I read things I missed or didn't think much about the first time when I mostly wanted to see how Conan was going to live through the danger.

I've sort of noticed "trends" or "cycles" in my reading. Right now I'm in a Paula Danziger "cycle." At the beginning of the year I was in a Science Fiction "cycle."

I just finished *Accident* . . . The only thing is that at the end I don't think she would of (in real life) been as calm as she was about having a limp, but theirs lots of things I still wonder about like — (1) Will she have a limp? (2) Will Adam and Mike be friends? (3) Will Adam ever go to Harvard? (4) Will Jenny change her mind and go with Adam?

While I was reading this book (*About David*) I could imagine what David looked like. I could picture the town, the houses, the school, everything. Like in *The Language of Goldfish* at the end they let you think what is going to happen. I like that, it makes me part of that book. You have to let the reader do some of the writing. Let them be a part of the book their reading. That way they will like the book more.

Advice to authors and comments on how authors wrote — their processes and styles — is probably the most frequent response eighth graders make in their letters. I often wonder if this would still be the case without writing workshop, the other half of the junior high language arts program. As authors themselves, eighth graders make choices and have a lot to say about the choices professional authors have made. The excerpts below — touching on character development, credibility, subtlety, authority, titles, suspense, and use of language, description and conventions — show students' emerging criteria for good writing.

The only problem I found with *Hitchhikers Guide to the Galaxy* was that I think he could have developed the characters a little more. I didn't care about them as much as in some of the other books I've read. I think its humor is the only thing that makes this book work.

Everyone in this book (*An X-Rated Romance*) was too, too childish. The dialogue was bizarre and the plot was barely okay. I mean some kids develop crushes on their teachers but don't do things like trying to seduce them. Also the part about the camera, when Emily came out with it around her neck and her mother was too dumb to suspect, sheesh!

I think that some of Auel's situations were a bit silly. One thing that bugged me was how Ayla discovered things, like building a fire with flint, riding Whinney, etc. You knew exactly what she was going to do next. When she gets on Whinney you just know that's going to lead to riding her, then using her to chase animals, then to hunt. She makes it so obvious! (Do you understand what I'm trying to say?)

By the end of the story you got the reason why the author wrote this piece, like the book was only written to show An Important Lesson About Life and the author just fitted the rest in. NOT EXACTLY SUBTLE.

Glendon Swarthout is really good. He was probably writing about some of the things that he and his friends did. He probly went through alot of problems like the kids in this book. I think it is important that authors as well as kids write from their own experiences because they know just what to write. Especially their true feelings and thoughts.

I just finished the sequel to *The Cat Ate My Gymsuit*, you know, *There's a Bat in Bunk Five*. I think the titles of both of these books were stupid. They have nothing to do with the major plot, and I was sort of lost by how the title and story differed. I don't think Danziger wanted me to spend time being confused by that.

After what seemed like ten million years (but it was only a month) I finished *The Chancellor Manuscript*. This has been the only Ludlum that I have been disapointed with. It seemed to me that it just dragged on and on forever. There were also some pretty disgusting parts in it too. It's like your on a train travelling at a certain speed. With all the other Ludlums, the train would speed up as you got toward the end of the book (or destination). With *The C. Mans.*, you stayed at the same speed throughout all the book and when you got to the end, you stopped dead. Usually, when you reach the end, you are travelling ten times faster and when you reach the end you have to rest to catch your breath. Do you see what I mean? I'm not going to drop Ludlum, but I will most certainly hope that the next one I read will be better.

One thing I like about Pfeffer's writing is the way she ends her chapters. If you look through you'll notice the short, one-sentence paragraphs. This really adds a lot of force to what she's saying.

There is one thing I don't like about Adams' writing. I would just be getting to a really exciting part (of *Shardik*) and he would stop and give this long metaphore and I was so anxious to find out what happens I would skim it. Adams is a very descriptive writer, and I think he sometimes gets carried away.

I love the way King puts thoughts in italics and parenthesis, and sometimes runs all the thoughts together into one sentence. It gives you a feeling of what's running through a persons mind. Have you noticed him doing this?

Part of kids' education as reader-writers was sorting out such issues as genre, formula, and point of view. Sandy used her dialogue journal to articulate the differences between gothic romances and novels, both of which she was reading and enjoying but for different reasons.

My analysis of a love story is: a book with a simple plot, not much you have to go by, and the same book as alot of others only the title is changed.

A novel is: a book which one enjoys reading because of an interesting, different plot. A book where characters are different and each has a quality (whether good or bad): themselves. A book you don't know the ending to just by reading the first couple of chapters. Something that has substance, that you can grip onto rather than fall through. A surprise ending. Also, not a book that has between 100 and 150 pages so that you can zip through. Maybe, something longer, with a theme that keeps you interested.

I've shed most of my anxieties about adolescents' attraction to formulaic fiction over the last two years because I saw readers passing through this stage of their histories as readers in the pages of their journals. Amanda discovered the formula of her once-beloved teen mysteries, and Jenn discovered the Sweet Dreams recipe.

This book was alot like a Nancy Drew's. I saw them (Susan Sand mysteries) in a magazine and the ad said "Getting tired of Nancy Drew's from your mother's time?" There almost exacly alike. And Every Single Nancy Drew is The SAME. When I was reading them alot, I could tell exactly when things would happen like when she would be captured near the end ect. ect. ect. It drove me crazy. These weren't that bad, but if I read them alot it probably would be. The girls are *so* perfect. Then the author makes them have dead parents or something so it won't be so perfect, but the girls don't even care. It's dumb.

I have read many, probably just about all, "Sweet Dreams" and "Wildfire" series. It used to be all I ever read. As you keep on reading so many I realized that basically they're all the same. I'm quite surprised with myself lately. I haven't been reading any. During this time, I've read other books I enjoy more. Stories with more of a plot than, a boy and a girl fall in love, have some problems, and at the end get together again. They are so boring. My mother is happy I'm getting over my love stories and into interesting novels. Although I don't know why, she usually reads Harlequins.

A big piece of their growing dissatisfaction with formulaic fiction grew from a growing awareness of narration and point of view. They wanted to believe in, trust, and feel close to a central character, especially if that character was also the narrator.

I really like a book that tells alot of description about the person who is telling the story. It makes it easier to relate and have feelings towards them. It also helps to know what the characters are feeling. During this story, Leslie never mentioned her feelings about what was happening to her and the way she looked. I needed more of a person from Leslie.

I've decided I like a book that has a one person view. *Killing Mr. Griffin* could have been better if a character involved told the story from his or her view. I like a book with more feelings; I like to know what a character is thinking rather than just his or her actions.

I think this is going to be my last which-way book. When your reading this your thinking to your self during the whole book that this would never happen. But when your reading a novel you picture your self in the person's spot that your reading about and in this book you can't unless you really have a wild imagination.

As the school year and correspondence progress, students have more to say on an ever greater range of literary topics: the length of a chapter, what makes a main character a main character, copyrights, jacket copy, type size, leads, and conclusions. When they gain experience and reflect on that experience, a new diversity of issues affects how readers approach and perceive written texts.

I hate the way they just picked a picture for the cover. You can *tell* it's no one in the story. Isn't an illustrator supposed to read the book he's illustrating?

I've decided I prefer paperbacks. One of the things I don't like about hardcovers is that when I'm reading it the cover sometimes gets in the way and I have to take it off to concentrate on reading.

Alot of times I've noticed that by the title of the book that it's going to be a good one. Like the two books I'm going to read. One is called *White Fang* which sounds exciting and the other one is *Me and Fat Glenda* which sounds hilarious.

It used to be that I'd go into the library and just close my eyes and grab a book. A thing I've noticed is how I've gotten fussy. It's not just that I know what I like, I know authors I like. Now I ask for Cormier or Hinton or Myers or for some author like them.

By the way, did you watch *Watership Down* on TV? I saw some of it and thought it was rather disappointing. I didn't like the comical beginning and they shortened the exciting parts so much that they lost all their excitement. I don't think they'll every make a movie anywhere close to the quality of the book. (Is it possible to make a movie close to the quality of any good book?)

Do you like the Boss's song "Glory Days?" I always think of Updike and Rabbit.

Many of their letters about good books were letters of recommendation, sometimes in the form of advice to pass on to other readers in other classes, sometimes in the form of warnings:

Another book I read over the weekend was a book by Farley Mowat, called *The Barrens*. I thought it was a very, very good book. I would encourage you to take a look at it. It was about two hundred pages long and I liked it so much I read it all in under two hours. I don't exactly know if that is good timing or not; I just know that it was a very good book.

I recommend the series starting with *A Wrinkle in Time*, by Madeleine L'Engle, to Jenny, if she hasn't already read them. But they are a little different from *A Ring of Endless Light.* They're a little more fantasized, but excellent. If she's already read those, she could try *The Arm of the Starfish* which is more like a good guy, bad guy book. But it has some characters in it. The best one to read after *A Ring of . . .* is *Moon by Night*. It has Vicky Austin in it, *A Ring of Endless Light* is its sequel. But you can still read the second one first.

I also read *Flowers in the Attic*. I don't know if you've read it or not, but if you haven't "don't." I don't think it's a book you would like. I don't think you would like any of the characters.

The responses eighth graders most often wanted from me were answers to their questions. These were the letters that brought me the most satisfaction: when my students asked me to teach them. They asked for my recommendations of good books — funny, scary, or sad stories, or a book like one just finished, or other books by a particular author or on a particular topic. They asked for information, about how books are published, about the length of time it takes for a hardcover to be released as a paperback, about various genres, about strategies like skimming and speed reading, about conventions like epigraphs, epilogues, flashbacks and foreshadows. They asked for my theories about why authors had written in particular ways. And they did a lot of comparing notes, wondering if I'd noticed or experienced something they had in their reading.

I esspecialy like "Crosbey Dream", one of the stories in here. That was about the best even though the others were right up there too. I wish there were more of these books around. I looked at Edgar Alan Poe's book and said "Forget this!" It was too hard. I know I've asked this before but, do you know of any other short horror tales?

In two books I've read latley (*Heads You Win, Tails I Loose* and *Dinky Hocker Shoots Smack*) they've talked about "A Street Car Named Diseree" or something like that. What is it, a play, a movie or a book? I think it was a play but I'm not sure. Is it in a book (or even a script)? Do you have any ideas on how I could get it / Who is the author, ect.? It sounds like I might like it. It's supposed to be funny isn't it?

Bell Jar ended so abruptly when I wanted a more flowing ending. Do you know what I mean? I guess I wanted a fairy tale ending. After I read the biography in the back about Plath my happy feelings about the recovery of the character soured. "The bell jar descended again" and Plath succeeded in killing herself. Well, maybe Esther did too. How are you supposed to read an autobiographical book? If Plath died can Esther live on?

Writing Back

Over the last two years I've had to re-learn my role as reading teacher. I've had to put a stop to teacher talk, to spitting out questions like a computer and lecturing my kids about what they're supposed to see and appreciate in the literature they read. There is no one set of questions to ask every reader; there are, instead, individual readers with their own strategies, questions, tastes, and styles. There is no one correct way to approach or interpret a text; there are, instead, individual readers with an incredible range of prior knowledge and experience. Through the dialogue journals I've discovered alternative ways a junior high English teacher can talk to students about literature. The letters I write to readers are personal and contextual. That is, what I say in my half of the dialogue journal comes from my knowledge of how the student reads and thinks, of what the student knows. Response grows both from what I've learned about a reader and how I hope to move the reader's thinking.

As I've learned to respond specifically and personally, I've also discovered some general principles of writing back. The first is not to respond too personally. Toby Fulwiler reminds teachers that "journals exist somewhere on a continuum between diaries and class notebooks . . . Like the diary, the journal is written in the first person; like the class notebook, the journal focuses on academic subjects the writer would like to learn more about" (1980). Our dialogue journals focus on the academic subjects under consideration in my course: books, authors, reading, and writing. I'm not a counselor, and the purpose of the letters is not to invite students' personal problems or offer counsel.

Neither is the purpose of the letters to test writing. Again, the dialogue journals were conceived as first-draft chat, not polished pieces of writing. I make no corrections on students' letters, but I do comment if I'm having trouble reading them.

Neither is the purpose of the letters to test reading. Students' most perfunctory letters were responses to letters of mine that read like a teacher's manual, bombarding them with questions. One good, thoughtful question is more than enough. I received my most interesting letters when I responded as a curious human being, asking a question about something I really wanted to know, but also when I leveled with students about my own experiences, tastes, and opinions as a reader, sharing freely and frankly, agreeing and disagreeing.

Most often, my one good, thoughtful question to eighth grade readers is, "What do you think of the writing, of how this author has written?" Answering this question takes kids inside the text where they can actively engage, evaluating and analyzing, rather than synopsizing the plot, peering in at some great distance from outside the book. Don Murray recently said that in writing workshops we're also teaching our students to be readers. Writers in a workshop are probably the most analytical of all readers, both of their own and others' emerging texts. I think the reverse also holds true. In reading workshop, I'm also teaching students to be writers. As readers in a workshop I'm hoping they'll go beyond plot, stop letting the story happen to them, and start making decisions about what is and isn't working in pieces of their reading, this other kind of emerging text.

At the start of the school year Libby's letters to me stayed on the outside of written texts. She gave daily blow-by-blow accounts of plot, of what characters were up to, as in this letter about June Foley's *Love by Any Other Name*.

9/11

Dear Ms. Atwell,

Billie is getting restricted because of Bubba and his friends mostly, and partly herself. First she got restricted for being late. And then she got restricted for sitting with Bubba's friends (and a day before they got a lecture on food fights) and a girl (a friend of hers) brought in a table cloth, wine glasses, china plate ware, napkins, champagne, for them and the table! And so they all got detention for a week! But why would they get a detention, because of the champagne? Probably.

> Your friend,
> Libby

P.S. Have a nice day!

Every time I wrote back to Libby I wrote back about the author, using the author's name and speculating about why he or she had decided to have characters behave as they did. My response to the letter above is typical:

9/11

Dear Libby,

Well, I do think champagne is a little bit much for a cafeteria lunch, but it's a good example for what Foley is trying to do here. Can you see how she's trying to show how far and foolishly Billie is willing to go to be in with the in crowd? (And can you guess what's going to happen to Billie by the novel's end, how Foley is going to have Billie end up? I can see it coming.)

> Ms. A

I nudged right through the first two months of school, modeling author talk like crazy, and by the end of October Libby had begun to come inside.

10/24

Dear Ms. Atwell,

I have started reading *That Was Then This Is Now* by S. E. Hinton. It is a pretty good book! I didn't know that she had Ponyboy Curtis in the book as a character. That surprised me! I like the way she writes. It's like you are there in the book. You can picture what it is like and stuff.

> Sincerely,
> Libby

P.S. Have a nice day!

10/24/85

Dear Lib,

I know just what you mean. Hinton puts us inside the characters. She tells so much about what they're thinking and feeling that we see things through their eyes and feel with their hearts. In *The Outsiders*, with Ponyboy as her narrator, she really puts us there, in the book.

I loved it that Pony showed up in *That Was Then . . .* It was like an in-joke. You had to know *The Outsiders* to pick up on the reference: sort of like, be a member of the Hinton Club.

Ms. A

P.S. I'll be really anxious to know what you think of how Hinton decided to conclude this one. She shook me up but I think she was right.

My role as correspondent strikes a balance between experienced reader, mentor, and teacher responsible to her adolescent students. This means sharing what I've learned about reading, offering my advice and expertise, and nudging — sometimes hard — when I think a student needs it. Dan needed a nudge to set aside a book he plainly wasn't enjoying.

Dear Dan,

Is *Watership Down* feeling too long to you? You seem to be making little progress. It's okay — it's more than okay — to abandon a book that you're not enjoying. I know I recommended *W.D.* to you, but that doesn't obligate you to finish it. If it's getting boring, please put it back. Does this make sense?

Ms. A

Dear Ms. A,

Yes, I think it does make sense. Yes, even though I liked *Watership Down* it got too long for me and I was getting pretty discouraged. I put it back and got this other book I really liked by Farly Mowat, *Never Cry Wolf.*

Thanks.

Dan

Lance wrote to me for clarification about the conclusion of Hinton's *Rumble Fish.* He didn't understand why Motorcycle Boy freed the zoo animals and the fighting fish at the novel's end.

Dear Lance,

When Motorcycle Boy frees the animals, you have to figure — because of the strength and intelligence of his character — that he's doing it for a reason. To him the animals represent something else, someone he can't set free of cages and walls. Can you begin to figure what the animals and piranha might represent to him?

Ms. A

Ms. A,

Yes, I think he thinks about himself and the other boys in the gang as trapped in a cage, a cage of fights and puzzlement. A cage that men build around themselves and even Motorcycle Boy with all his brains is stuck inside it . . .

Sandy was similarly confused about the conclusion of Robert O'Brien's *for Zachariah*:

Dear Ms. Atwell,

I'm trying to decide whether or not this book was too deep and whether or not it was written for kids my age. I'm trying to think if maybe there was something there, like the answers to my questions and I just didn't realize it. I was really disappointed by the ending. I felt she gave up what was rightfully hers. I felt she could have had more guts. Also, I didn't like, to me, an unanswered ending.

Sandy

Dear Sandy,

I often think: is there something wrong with me or something wrong with this book? This most often happens when I read something I didn't entirely understand. Sometimes I'm tempted to write to an author and say, "Would you mind revising this? I don't get it the way you've done it here," or "I don't like how it came out."

I did like how *Z* came out — the fact that it didn't become a futuristic version of Adam and Eve. The girl and the man didn't live happily ever after because they couldn't. Even those two people couldn't live amicably; the man had to initiate his own, private war after the big one had managed to wipe out (probably) the rest of the world. To me the novel was about human nature, about how our basic instincts lead us to suspicion and competition rather than harmony and cooperation. I think O'Brien is essentially pessimistic, like Wm. Golding's *Lord of the Flies*, but although I'm interested in this theme I don't think I agree with him.

Ms. A.

Ms. Atwell,

I agree with you. I'm awfully glad they didn't make the story out to be a happily-ever-after book because life isn't like that. Also they get boring after reading so many of them.

The book was different from any other book I've read and I decided finally that I liked that. I liked the change. Your statement makes alot of sense to me. I guess I really didn't try to look at what they were getting at until now. Your opinions helped me a little more to understand parts.

Sandy

Some of my responses supply background information, filling readers in about an author's life or sources, gossiping about how a book came to be, as in these dialogues with Bean and Kristen.

3/26/84

Dear Ms. Atwell,

One Fat Summer was good. I really like it a lot. I wouldn't turn my light off last night until I finished it. I liked the way Robert Lipsyte had Bobby imagining things while mowing the lawn ("Captain Marks of the Third Cavalry! We must avenge those lawns!") because I think everyone does that but won't admit it for fear people will make fun of them. (I do it.) I don't know if I will read *The Contender* because I'm afraid it won't be as good. That happens with me a lot. I pick up a book by a certain author and it's his or her best one, and then I'm disappointed in his next book.

Beano

3/27/84

Dear Bean,

Lipsyte's *The Contender* is a very different book, set in an urban ghetto and focused on pro boxing. Lipsyte was also a sports reporter for *The New York Times* and really knows his stuff.

He has also, however, written two sequels to *One Fat Summer*, each of them better than the last, I think: *Summer Rules* and *Summer Boy*. I have both of them in my library.

Ms. A

P.S. I think Bobby Marks is so realistic—sometimes embarrassingly so— because Robert Lipsyte drew on his own life, as little Bobby Lipsyte, to create the *Summer* series.

*   *   *   *   *

1/18/84

Dear Ms. A,

I've just finished Lois Duncan's *A Gift of Magic*. It was really good. You know what? I have a little bit of E.S.P. myself. I used to have it a wicked lot when I was little. (My mother told me from experiences with me.) But now I get it only once in a while.

But the book's really good. It sounds like it could happen in real life, too, except when Brendon & Greg made the boat and it floated. I really don't think that could happen.

Kristen

1/18/84

Dear Kristen,

In a speech she gave at the NCTE convention in Denver, Duncan said she gets hundreds of letters from kids who've read *A Gift of Magic* who also experienced astral projections; that, like you, these kids seemed to gradually lose their gift as they matured. Duncan based the novel on research into children's E.S.P. conducted at Stanford University in California. If you're interested in following up on this, you might want to write to her for more information, or for the name of the Stanford study.

Ms. A.

Some of my letters confirm and extend. Lilias was another Lois Duncan fan. We conferred in her dialogue journal about a phenomenon common among readers of fiction: empathizing so deeply that we project ourselves right into the story.

10/9/85

Dear Ms. Atwell,

I read many chapters of *Daughters of Eve* over the weekend at my babysitting jobs while they napped or went to bed.

The part in the book when the Daughters of Eve are having a meeting, you start believing that men are enemys and you yourself start believing that you hate men. But when you close the book you have to say to yourself, "This is only a book. Not all men act like that," so the anger that book filled you up with won't be taken out on the next male that's in your sight.

My favorite Duncan book is *Down a Dark Hall* which I read last year. What's yours?

Lilias

10/10/85

Dear Lily,

I know what you mean. Sometimes a writer creates such a mood that a novel can spin us completely out of our real world and into the world of his or her fiction. It can take a conscious effort to tell the difference and come back to reality. I'm reading *Good-bye Paper Doll*, a novel about a girl with anorexia nervosa, and feeling thin and hungry. Then I look down. Lily, I may be hungry but I'm definitely not anorexic.

My favorite Duncan is *Chapters: My Growth as a Writer.* I also liked *Down a Dark Hall* and *Summer of Fear.*

Ms. A.

Finally, some of my letters contain more explicit nudges as in these three excerpts dealing with, respectively, "Choose Your Own Adventure" books, a student whose first letters consisted of plot synopses, and a reader who complained about a change I made in his seat assignment during reading workshop.

These "Which Way?" books are driving me crazy. I'm using the term "book" loosely. I hated the one I read. It was just arbitrary — the characters never developed, nothing built toward anything with any logic, and my involvement was minimal and artificial compared with the way I get involved with a good main character. I came away feeling as if I'd spent thirty minutes reading the backs of cereal boxes. I bought a couple of books last week I think you'd like. One is *Friends Till the End* by Todd Strasser. It's in the classroom library if you'd like to give it a try — a good and surprising story with a main character who's a decent, interesting, funny guy. I think you'd like him.

*   *   *   *   *

By the way, your letter was little book-reportish, mostly recounting what happened in this book. You've got to keep me in mind, Kellie. If you're writing about a book I've already read, it's a little boring for me to read an account of the plot. And if it's a book I haven't read, it's pretty exasperating because you've told me the outcome and ruined the story for me. Do you see what I mean? I'm mostly interested in your reactions: what you liked, didn't like and why; what you think; what you wonder about.

*   *   *   *   *

You can't sit on the floor any more because you read less when you sit on the floor. I've been worried that you haven't finished a book in well over a month now. I want you to read a lot and get better at reading – and pass this course, too. Your chances of accomplishing these things are better if you work in your seat.

Student-to-Student Dialogues

One January afternoon Jane and Arelitsa were passing notes in the back of my room during writing workshop. I asked, "What are you two doing back there?" and Jane answered, "Oh, Ms. Atwell. You'll be interested in this." She was right.

One of my students' favorite poems is Robert Frost's "Nothing Gold Can Stay." They like it because it appears in S. E. Hinton's *The Outsiders* as the novel's leitmotif, and they like it because it deals with the evanescence of youth and beauty. Sometimes they see themselves as golden, fated to join the jaded world of adults just as dawn inevitably "goes down to day." Arelitsa was absent the day we'd talked about "Nothing Gold Can Stay" as the reading mini-lesson. Because kids had requested I leave it on the board so they could memorize it, the poem was still up there when Arelee returned to school. The notes she and Jane were passing were about the poem and what it meant to them, two exuberant thirteen-year-olds gossiping about poetry and forging meaning together.

Jane,

Whoops.

~~What~~ Umm, did you guys talk about that poem on the board a while ago. I think I missed it. Could you PLEASE tell me what it meant and what she said about it. I really love that poem wicked. I got to know more about it.

Okay?

Arelitsa Kazakos

Dear Arelitsa,

She said it was like an apple was growing. (That apple story) First the bud is gold, then it has a blossom and the first and second lines of the poem was about how the bud on the tree can't stay gold. And the third and fourth lines are about how the blossom on the apple tree blooms. The fifth line is about how the leafs blow away in and hour. And the rest of the poem is about how the blossom turns into an apple.

Jane

Jane,

I don't get why it becomes an apple? Thats good. So how could it be (Nothing gold can stay).

Also did she say anything about what it meant in real life. Ya know? WRITE.

Arelitsa

Arelitsa,

It becomes an apple after the blossom is gone. And I don't know how the poem ends for the apple but the last line means you can't stay young for the rest of your life. And then it meant for Johnny and Ponyboy that they couldn't go back home to do all the things they did before like look at the stars because Johnny killed Bob.

Jane

Jane, But I don't get only so an hour? Im so confused with the poem that I'll probably ask Ms A.

Arelitsa,

Arelitsa,

I don't know about the hour part. But about the gold part meant that they don't do the things like they did before Johnny killed Bob. It meant that Ponyboy and Johnny couldn't act like 14 and 16 they had to act like adults.

Jane

So this whole poem is about how great it is to be a kid?

Arelitsa

Not really but it's about how you have to go on with your life.

Jane

Clearly there were more audiences for dining room table talk than the teacher. It was time to change again. Jane and Arelitsa put their letters on overheads and I shared them with my classes in the next day's reading mini-lesson, opening the door to students' exchanges about literature. For the remainder of the school year readers could write to me and to each other. About a quarter of the kids wrote regularly to friends and occasionally to me, another quarter chose to write exclusively to me, and the rest regularly moved back and forth between me and friends.

Suzy fell into this last category. She wrote the letter on the next page at home; it's addressed to Hilary, who sits next to Suzy in class, and concerns a novel Hilary loaned Suzy, *Mr. and Mrs. BoJo Jones*, about a teenage shotgun marriage. In conferring with her friend, Suzy critiqued the novel's lead and conclusion, connected the experiences of the characters with her own life, predicted while she was reading what would happen, and made plans to re-read the book.

Hilary,

It's about 12:00 (midnight). I just finished *Mr. and Mrs. Bo Jo Jones*. It was the best book I've ever read in my life.

The book was a slow start and got to be a little boring at times. But the end was so fast and different. I loved it! I cried so much. Did you? (I hope so, 'cause I'll feel quite embarrassed about what I'm going to say!)

I didn't cry until right when the Doctor and BoJo came in to say the baby was dead. It was strange?! I felt so sorry for her (even though it's fiction) for having that happen. Then at the Coffee Pot when they said it was quits I was so mad! I knew they were just getting to be very much in love, but thought it probably would be best. I knew for some reason that something good was going to happen when they met at the apartment.

When they sat down and talked and realized they wanted each other but couldn't face it until their decision, it was great. I cryed then too 'cause I was so happy for them! It was great how they went ahead three years and said how it was going. The book was great! I'd recommend it to anyone.

I almost forgot. Did you stop to think if that was you or someone you knew? I did and it seemed so terrible. I thought what if that happened, if I'd do the same. That's not how I wanted to say it, but good enough.

Suzy

By contrast, there were Brad and Lawrence. Both basketball players, both typically macho eighth grade boys, they rejected out of hand my invitation to write to friends. Brad said, "Only girls pass notes." After a month or so of watching classmates writing to each other, they changed their tune and decided they'd like to give it a try. The excerpts below are from Brad's log. Lawrence is also writing about his reading in his own log, in letters to Jody. Brad's book is Terry Brooks's *The Elsfstones of Shannara.* (Brad is "Drum" and Lawrence is "Durf.")

2/29/84

Durf,

The book I'm reading is starting to get better. Mike Thib. said it was one of those fantasy books. Even if it is why should he care, right? He's not reading it. I am. How's *Tuned Out* coming?

The Drum

Drum,

I don't think Tib has the right to call it a fantasy book. If he's not reading it he shouldn't say anything even it if is. I've heard a lot about that book from Chad and he said it was a very good book. And *Tuned Out* is coming along good. It just started to pick up.

Durf

3/6/84

Durf,

Hows it going? I mean the book you know, *Tuned Out*? My book is starting to get excellent. This man the elves haven't seen for a long time comes to seem them. The elves were looking for some place called Safehold. All along the man said he would look in their history. Well, when he got to the castle he was attacked and he shot this blue flame from his fingers and killed all the demons. Isn't that excellent!

The Drum

3/20/84

Durrrfee,

How much more do you have to go on *Tuned Out*? Don't even ask how many I've got. The only time I seem to read is when I'm in class. I don't get much done. Ms. Atwell just said I should read a little before I go to bed.

See ya later Durrrfee.

*   *   *   *   *

It's a good idea. You should start reading before you go to bed. Oh yeah I only have a little left on *Tuned Out.*

Durfee,

How do you like the name Durrrfee? I sort of like it. Do you read at home? I don't get a chance to. My life is too exciting.

Drum

Drum,

How do you like the name Drum? I think it has a good beat to it. I don't read too much at home because I live my life, not read it.

Durf

3/27/84

Durf,

How much more do you have to go on *Tuned Out*? I broke the 200 mark a couple of days ago. I got about 380 more to go. After I finish this one I'll probably read one of her new ones. Don't you think she's got a nice selection?

Drum

P.S. The book I'm reading, you know *Elfstones of Shannara*? It's an excellent book! I think it would make an excellent movie. I just read a part where Valeman and an elven girl were getting chased by Demon wolves and Valeman and the elven girl jumped over a river called: Silver River, and a light from out of the sky shot down and rescued them from the Demon wolves. It's *excellent*. Maybe I'll let you borrow it sometime?

Drum

Brad and Lawrence wrote this last exchange, below, the week they returned to school from April vacation.

4/23/84

Durf,

I finally finished my book. Boy did that take me a long time. But I was determined to read the whole thing. So how's your book coming? I'm going to read *The Divorce Express*. Ms. Atwell recommended it. I imagine it's pretty good.

Brad,

I'm almost finished with *Hoops* and it's a great book. After this I'm going to read a 3 to 4 hundred pg. book. I read the back and it seems to be good. When did you finish the *Elfstones*?

Durf

Durf,

What is the name of the book you're going to read? What's it about? Oh, yeah. I finished *Elfstones* this Friday on the way home from Gardiner.

Drum

In other words, for all his posturing about how exciting his life was without wasting time reading, Brad spent his April vacation in Gardiner reading and finishing *The Elfstones of Shannara*.

In June, I asked my kids to conduct a small piece of research: to categorize their student-to-student talk so we could compare it with our categories of student-to-teacher talk. Each student read through the letters in his or her log and described what was there. This is a chunk of Brad's summary of his correspondence with Lawrence:

> I've talked about what we was reading, telling them whether we think they'd like it or not. We also asked them if they have any recommendations. We talked about how a book starts off, if it starts off interesting but gets worse or if it starts off bad but gets better. I would also tell them how it started, then when I got to a good part I would stop and leave them in suspince. We would talk about some characters in the book. We would also have writing names like Eel One and Eel Two, Al, Gos, and Child #1 and Child #2. We would sometimes just write to each other if we found a good part in a book and we would talk about it. We would also tell how we felt about a certain book, if we liked it or not. Once we was talking about a book and I gave it away. You know he said he was almost done with the book and you say, "Oh do you remember when so and so got burnt?" And he says, "No I haven't got to that part yet." You feel so stupid. We would also talk about how the day's going for you, boring or if its excellent. This day is going real s-l-o-w. We would talk about how my friend couldn't read real long books because they bored him. We would talk about the only time we seemed to read is when we're in class. I've gotten over that problem. I think Lawrence has too. We talked about how Ms. Atwell has a nice selection of books and how she knows exactly what you would like to read. We would talk about this special book I was reading. It was called *The Elfstones of Shannara*. How a kid in our grade said it was just a fantasy book and how we said it wasn't up to him to say anything like that because he wasn't reading it so why should he care? Personally I loved it. We talked about a special part in this book. Oh heck, I'll tell you too, OK? This man that the elves haven't seen for a long time . . .

Clearly, the ways eighth graders write to each other are different from the ways they write to me — not better or worse, but different, in some of the same ways peers' talk just naturally differs from talk with the teacher. For example, right from the start I saw that mechanics were less careful. Kids automatically and unconsciously adjust handwriting, spelling, and punctuation to a different audience's expectations. These letters look like notes passed in class.

There's more description of affect in kids' letters to each other. They write about crying, laughing out loud, gasping in amazement, grinding their teeth in anger. The question they most frequently ask each other in their logs begins, "How did you feel when . . . ?" There's also more description of characters and of plot, more sharing of "the good parts" as in Brad's and Suzy's letters excerpted here. When students write to each other they ask more questions about what to read and make and follow-up on more recommendations. As a matter of course they trust each other's advice more than mine, however widely and sympathetically I've read their books. And they're much more playful, joking with and teasing each other as students never could with a teacher. Their dialogues with each other provide another way social relationships can be put to work in the classroom. Finally, my students wrote more and longer letters than when I was their sole audience. They like to talk to their friends, and I like to enable them to go even deeper into the literary life by talking with their friends about their books.

There's no guarantee that readers' letters to each other won't occasionally get out of hand, or that they'll stay confined to literary topics. When correspondence exceeds reasonable boundaries either one of the correspondents puts on the brakes or I'll intervene. For example, in this exchange with Heather, Mike finally puts on the brakes. Answering Heather's letters is taking too much time away from his book.

10/2

Mike,

Chow. How is your book going? Oh, mines really good. It's *Divorce Express*. I love the main character. Her name is Phoebe. She is really cool. What it's about is her parents are divorced and she stays with her father durning the week and her mother every weekend. Times are really tuff for her. She doesn't really like switching towns every weekend. But she knows it makes her parents happy so she does it any way. Finally she has made a friend. Now things are going pretty good for her. I love the book.

Sincerely,
Heather M.

10/8/85

Dear Heath,

The *Divorce Express* sounds like a good book.

I am reading a mystery by Jay Bennett called *The Dangling Witness*. It's about this kid who witnesses a murder and the murderer finds out. If he tells anyone, the murderer will kill him. So he can't do anything about it. The characters and plot are real good. Lots of suspence. Jay Bennet is a good author. By the way, how's your nose? I broke mine a year ago. Your lucky. I had rings around my eyes for a couple of weeks after. Well, gotta go.

How

10/8/85

Mike,

My nose is fine. I reading a book called *Class Pictures*. It's good. The plot is about two girls who tell me there whole friendship from kindergarten up. It's really good. Sorry about your nose. At least it looks normal.

Heath

10/8/85

Dear Heather,

Class Pictures sounds good. My book keeps getting better and better. What's your favorite book you've read this year? Have you read any good supernatural or mysteries?

How

10/8/85

Mike,

I have read some really good books this year. I think you should read *Haunted.* It is my favorite book. Or try *The Spectator.* Kelli said it was good.

You wouldn't like the book *Class Pictures.* It's a girls book.

Heath

10/8/85

Dear Heather,

I read *Haunted* last year. It was good. I finished it in two days. It was one of the best ones I read. Kelli told me *The Spectre* was good too. I'll probably read it soon.

I hate to be mean but I don't have any another other way to put it. DON'T WRITE BACK AGAIN THIS PERIOD!!!

Sincerely,
Mike

Since journals are stored in a box in the classroom and since readers continue to write to me, too, I know what and how students are writing to each other and can step in if letters are consistently inappropriate. Dan and Kevin, for example, started out in September exchanging some information and some insults.

9/85

Dear (Tramp) Kevin,

This book I am reading *Gullivers Travels* is getting better! Gulliver the adventurer was just attacked by a giant creature! Sort of like me to you. The big man is probably 30 feet tall while Gullivers is about 6 feet tall. How is your book going? I hope it takes you two years to finish it. Ha! Ha! What is it called? What is your main characters name!

I'm thinking about reading the *Earthsea Trilogy.* Jon says it's great. Or I might read that series that you're on. Give me your opinion on the series. Thanks vegetable.

Sincerely, Yeah! alright! Yahoo! excellent!
Dan #1

Dear (Doilly) Dan,

It sounds as though you aren't actually reading the book but are remembering it from the cartoon movie they had on cable last year.

My books main characters name is Garion although through circumstances he is now called Belgarion. I guess that's where they got the name *The Belgariad* for the series. In my opinion you should read this series (although words like to, it and we are awfully tough for you.)

Are you sure your brain can handle all this information in one letter?

> Unsincerely,
> Kevin

By the beginning of November insults had overwhelmed information ("My dog is better looking than you *when* your hair is brushed." "Oh yeah? Concerning your hair, have you ever seen a Medusa?"), and I intervened. In a letter to Dan I asked him to talk about books more and trade taunts less and reminded him literary talk was the journal's ultimate purpose. He and Kev complied, and were still able to maintain some of the playfulness of their previous exchanges.

> 11/4/85

Kev,

How is *The Enchanter End Game* going? I'm beginning to get more interested in my book. It's beginning to get more exciting. Anyhow I haven't been having to much trouble understanding the book. (*The Lord of the Ring*). Any trouble I have had would be understanding some of the words he says, like unintelligible.

After I finish this I'm going to read some of Mike's *Twilight* books, then I will probably go back to the series.

Ms. A. says I have to stop insulting people so much instead of telling about my books.

I hope you enjoyed this letter.

> Dan

Dan,

Let's have a peace treaty. (Letters only!)

What is your new book about anyway? Mine is going well although Ms. A. says I should read more at home.

> Kev

Kev,

Sign the peace treaty.

I Kevin Ames will write letters of books and books only in my log and in Dans log.

My book is about this guy named Frodo Baggens . . .

Procedures for Dialogue Journals

It took me a while and some major revisions to get straight the mechanics of dialogue journals — who would write when, where we would store the journals, how letters would be delivered. Our current system works pretty well. I ask each reader on the first day of school to buy a spiralbound notebook, one that will mostly stay in the classroom and will be used exclusively for reading. I specify spiralbound because the journal should be sturdy and permanent, should function as a book in which we can turn and number pages, and should contain enough pieces of paper for nine months of correspondence.

When all the notebooks are in we alphabetize each class's set and then number these on the outside cover so they'll be easy to file and retrieve. I provide boxes in which each group stores their journals, and once they've shelved the boxes I deliver to each reader a copy of my first letter of the school year, spelling out the notebook's purposes and procedures:

Dear Readers,

Your notebook is a place for you, me, and your friends to talk this year about books, reading, authors, and writing. You'll be chatting about literature in letters to me and friends; we'll write letters back to you. All our letters will stay here together, arranged chronologically, as a record of the thinking, learning, and reading we did together.

In your letters talk with us about what you've read. Tell what you noticed. Tell what you thought and felt and why. Tell what you liked and didn't and why. Tell how you read and why. Tell what these books said and meant to you. Ask questions or for help. And write back about our ideas, feelings, experiences, and questions.

As a bare minimum for passing this course you must write at least one letter a week in your own lit. log. I should be the recipient of a letter from you at least once every two weeks. These are only minimum requirements; you may pass a literary letter as often as you wish.

When you write to me, put your lit. log in the mailbox attached to my desk. When you write to a friend, give your log to that friend. When a friend gives you his or her log, you must answer within twenty-four hours. After you've written back, file your friend's log, correctly by number, in your class's box on the shelf. You may not lose or damage another's log. Unless a log is being written in, it should be on file in the box.

You may write letters and respond to letters both during and outside reading workshop.

Please date your letters in the upper right-hand corner. Please number the pages of the notebook, as in a book. Please mention the title of the book you're talking about and, since the proper way to indicate the title of a book is to capitalize and underline it (e.g., Tiger Eyes or The Hobbit), please capitalize and underline the titles of books to which you make reference.

Finally, enter the title and author of each book you finish this year on the log sheet I'll tape inside the back cover of your notebook. This record will serve you as a quick reference.

Your collection of letters will provide one third of your grade in reading. Follow the procedures outlined above, write often and a lot, and correspond about your thoughts on literature with involvement and care, and you'll do well.

I can't wait for your letters. I can't wait to learn from you, learn with you, and help you learn more.

Yours,
Ms. Atwell

My letter doesn't leave much to chance. Although I know it will take kids a while to get the hang of it, the system is in place from the beginning, as are my expectations. Our letters are my vehicle for teaching and theirs for learning. Without a regular, frequent exchange of responses, reading workshop is little more than a study hall. Very few students ignore the minimum requirement, especially after the first quarter's grades are figured and they see, finally, that I'm serious: the letters are more than a nice thing one might do. Readers date their letters, among other reasons, so we have a record of when they wrote to whom.

Another kind of simple record students keep appears in the back of each journal, in the form of a reading log. Kids list three items: the title of each book they finish, its author, and the date on which they finished it. These log sheets are valuable because they provide an easy reference for me, readers, and parents, showing what each reader has accomplished, pointing trends or cycles, and serving later on as the basis for the mass book rating we do at the end of each school year in preparation for re-stocking the class library.

Kids write and answer letters both during the workshop and in study halls and after school. This means that at any given time in the reading workshop some students will be reading, some will be writing letters in their own journals, some will be answering letters in others' journals, and some will be retrieving or delivering these notebooks. All of this happens silently. The twenty-four-hour rule about writing back ensures that journals written in outside of class are back in the room in time for the next day's workshop, if the reader should need it.

I write some of my responses in the workshop, alternating writing with reading my own book, and some after school. I love to read and respond to their letters. It never seems a chore. I never know what I'll find when I turn to the last letter. I remember suffering through piles of junior high book reports, the dullest writing I've ever read. By contrast, kids' letters are a constant source of surprise, pleasure, and stimulation. And what they replaced — book reports, worksheets, quizzes, and tests — ate up more of my time than keeping up with my seventy-five correspondents ever will. Best of all, our letters allow me to be on the inside, too, to become another reader in the workshop.

Evaluating Reading in Conference

As in writing workshop, my system for grading students' progress in reading should match what I've been asking of them in each day's workshop. One thing I ask is that they read every day and follow the rules for using reading time. I also ask that they write at least a letter a week in their literary journals and go beyond plot to analyze and evaluate what they've read.

Finally, I ask that they exhibit growth over time in the areas my teaching of reading stresses — fluency, speed and pacing, risk-taking, personal involvement, recognizing good writing and what authors do, making use of prior knowledge, predicting, critiquing, establishing criteria for selecting and abandoning, and so on.

Therefore, one-third of a student's grade in reading is the total number of points accumulated over a quarter's reading workshops, according to the procedures outlined in the previous chapter. Another third of a reader's grade is contributed by the literary journal, where I look for frequency and depth of response. The final third is represented by the degree of progress each student makes toward a few individual goals established in collaboration with me at the beginning of each quarter. For, as in writing workshop, I hold nine-week evaluation conferences with each reader. The mark I record on report cards is the average of these three grades; in the first quarter, when we haven't yet established individual goals, I figure grades by averaging just points and journal.

Our reading evaluation conferences proceed along the same lines as those for writing. I ask questions and record students' answers, then we evaluate progress toward old goals and set new ones. In interviewing readers I model my basic questions on those I ask when evaluating writing. "What does someone have to do in order to be a good reader?" is a question that gets at kids' changing notions of reading process. "What's the best book you read this quarter and what makes it best?" reveals their criteria for good writing. And "What do you want to do as a reader during the next nine weeks?" helps them consider their own strengths and needs. To these I add the one or two research questions I'm interested in pursuing that quarter. In each class I review and post a copy of the questions I'll be asking a week or so in advance of conferences, so readers may begin planning their responses. During reading workshop the following week I don't read or write letters but meet briefly with each reader.

I bring to each conference a copy of my interview questions, a half slip of paper on which I've written the one or two goals I've already established for the reader, and a blank slip on which the student can copy down the goals for his or her records after the conference. I ask my interview questions, write down and talk about their answers, add the goal or goals they come up with to my half slip of paper, and discuss what I've already written there. As in conferring about objectives for writing workshop, about half the time the goals they suggest for themselves are identical to those I'd come up with the night before. There are few evaluation "surprises" in a process approach because day to day students and teachers are so closely in touch and in tune.

The nature of the goals I set reflects my understandings of reading, for which I'm greatly indebted to Frank Smith (1971, 1984), and my knowledge of each reader. Over the past quarter objectives have included:

- Read more at home: at least _____ evenings a week for half an hour or so before you go to sleep.
- Read with your finger on your mouth to prevent your lips moving and slowing down your reading rate.
- Read as fast as you can, trying to see "chunks" instead of one word at a time and trying to read for the meaning of the story.

- Get out of the habit of using a card or bookmark to underline your reading because it checks peripheral vision and slows you down.
- Don't stick with a book you're not enjoying. Give the author (*some number of pages or chapters*) and if you aren't happy with the writing, abandon the book.
- When you get to an uninteresting section of text, skim or skip it.
- In looking for good books, follow up on the names of authors whose works you've liked.
- In looking for good books, ask for and follow up on recommendations from me and from friends.
- In your journal, synopsize plot less and analyze writing more: tell what you think of how the book is written, of what the author did.
- Try at least one book that represents a different kind of writing than you've been reading.
- Remember to bring a book to class with you.
- Remember to write regularly in your journal: once a week, and to me at least every two weeks.

I would never include as goals either "Read X number of books," or "Write X number of pages in your journal." The first goal tells kids to select books based on how long (or short) they are, rather than how well they're written or how compelling their subjects. No reader could choose *Dune* or *The Lord of the Rings* or *And the Ladies of the Club* under those circumstances. It's time spent reading at school and at home that I value, not numbers of books completed. The second goal tells kids to churn out verbiage and practically guarantees tedious — and easy — plot synopses. I'm interested in carrying on regular, genuine exchanges of ideas, not plowing through book reports.

In the end, my goals and expectations are higher than any mandated by a standard junior high literature curriculum. I expect every student will take books as seriously as I do and will confer about reading with the same passion and pleasure as fills my dining room most evenings. But I also back up my expectations by inviting kids' participation just as sensibly and generously as I can, so that literature can truly become, for these eighth graders, Virginia Woolf's "common ground." Dialogue journals play an important role in encouraging students to pull up their chairs — to become readers, enter the world of written texts, and make it their own. They allow me to respond, pointedly and personally, to what my students are doing. Dialogue journals allow me to teach every reader.

Kim was one of my students last year. Classified as a slow, low-comprehending reader, she'd spent years in remedial reading programs. In my letters I nudged Kim hard to use alternative reading strategies, abandon books she didn't enjoy, and try novels her friends and I knew were great stories. Kim read twenty-one books that year and showed three years' growth on the standardized reading test our school administers each spring. Most significantly, Kim knew and could describe her growth to fluency and her right to a place at the dining room table.

Dear Ms. A,

I just finished *E.T.* and again I really liked it, the only problem was my mind kept racing ahead. The part I like best is the last chapter, when everything starts to get going. Excitement builds and at the same time your getting everyones (including animals) thoughts and feelings. It's great.

I have changed so much as a reader this year. I think I changed as I read but also when you were talking to me at the beginning of the year. "When you read you should take the words in groups not one at a time." You said, "And don't go back, just keep reading. Don't read over and over what you've just read." And also you encouraged me. "Keep reading, but don't read a book you don't like. Find one you do and read it as fast as you can." And I also found with your help some books that I couldn't believe how much I liked. Thanks, Ms. A.

Yours,
Kim, A Reader

Missy adds a new poet to her personal anthology of favorite poems.

CHAPTER 9

Reading Mini-Lessons

"'Tis the good reader that makes the good book."
Emerson

Brendan was the first person I saw Monday morning. He stood in the
school's front lobby. "Hey, you're back," he announced. "Ms. A., I wish you
could've heard that guy's mini-lessons. He couldn't read. I mean, he read at
us, not to us."

"Are you a born complainer or what?" I teased.

"Well, it's true. I am glad you're back." Brendan headed outside. I went
upstairs to my classroom.

"Ms. Atwell! We missed you. Geesum, the sub was awful." It was
Michelle, coming downstairs.

"What do you mean?" I asked. I know the man who had come in for
me. He is not an awful sub.

Michelle replied, "You should've heard him read to us. That poem on
Friday — it was supposed to be a sad poem, right?"

"Right. 'Country Dog.'"

"Well, no one cried. Some of the guys even laughed. You've got to read
it again today, okay?" I promised I would and moved on. By the time I un-
locked the door to my room, six eighth graders had stopped me to welcome
me back from the 'flu. They had missed me. Or rather, they had missed one
part of me.

Each day's reading workshop begins with a mini-lesson, and some days
the mini-lesson is a read-aloud. I think the kids had missed more than a familiar sound at the start of Friday's class. They missed my reader's voice, the
part of me that chooses, loves, and lives literature. It's personal voice that
gives me my authority in reading workshop, just as my own writing conveys
authority in writing workshop. More importantly, I think that because this
voice reflects my particular interests and strengths, it allows kids to discover
their own literary idiosyncracies. When my brand of literacy sparks theirs,
kids too may become active readers, involved readers, obsessed readers — in
short, they may live truly literate lives.

There is no canon of teacher-proof reading mini-lessons that will create obsessed eighth grade readers. There is, instead, the eighth grade teacher's voice — what each of us loves of literature, adolescent and adult — and what we know of our students' needs. These are the lessons we can teach well. I can teach the poem "Country Dog," as I did that Monday morning by popular demand, so well that kids will cry. I like the poem. I don't like many of the selections in my old literature anthology, and I know I didn't teach them well. Don Graves advises teachers to discover what we love of literature, to draw on our personal tastes and talents in the classroom:

> Teachers have their own ways of surrounding the children with literature. They surround the children according to their own interests, whether it is choral speaking, story telling, role playing, informal drama, or story reading. Teachers have different strengths and backgrounds that can be used to enrich their presentation of literature in the classroom. But the provision of literature is not a passive event for children. At every turn the teacher seeks to have children live the literature (1983, p. 75).

"Living the literature" becomes possible for students when teachers live the literature, too. In this chapter I'll describe some of the reading mini-lessons I've conducted based on my particular strengths and background, and what I've seen kids need to know of literature and reading process. I don't mean to prescribe. I tell what I do by way of suggesting lessons others might develop in drawing on what they know of literature and students. When I looked back over three years of reading mini-lessons I found three categories of presentations. Some days I present procedural information, talking about how the workshop works and how students function in a readers' workshop. Sometimes I discuss literature, introducing literary elements, authors, and genres. And sometimes I teach skills, sharing practices that will allow students to read according to their own intentions and teaching kids what good readers do.

Procedures of Reading Workshop

At the start of the school year most reading mini-lessons describe procedures and routines of the workshop, acquainting kids with their roles and mine just as I do in early writing mini-lessons. As with writing, there are fewer and fewer procedural mini-lessons as we get further into the year and kids learn the ropes of the workshop.

My first reading mini-lesson, however, is preceded by a quick piece of research. Before I say anything about the reading program I conduct a survey that will give me some idea of where kids stand as readers — what they know, think, and do. Appendix *F* is a copy of the survey. Kids' answers show me where to begin. For example, if few students can name favorite writers I'll plan mini-lessons introducing some of my and eighth graders' favorite authors of adolescent literature. If kids mostly respond to my question about how they decide which books to read by referring to cover designs, I'll begin soon to share other ways they can go about finding good books. The survey results give me my first insights into what kids know and need to know. I'll ask them to take this same survey again at the end of May. Then I'll return both to each student and see what sense individuals will make of any changes in their responses. Every year the changes are amazing — in the number of books owned and read, in time spent reading at home for pleasure, in knowledge of how and why good readers read. This simple research tool reveals a lot about how a year of reading workshop affects eighth grade readers.

The same first day of school, after the survey, we talk about general expectations for reading workshop. In chapter seven I listed procedures for using reading time and assessing points. I give a copy of this information to each reader, explain and clarify the guidelines, and tell why my reading program is a readers' workshop — what I've learned about reading that makes me believe that kids' choosing their own books and reading every day is the way to create good readers. I also tell everyone to buy a spiralbound notebook that will stay in the classroom and be used exclusively for reading, and I allow three days for notebooks to be purchased. Finally, everyone has homework. For tomorrow they'll each need a book for our first reading workshop. For the rest of the class they and I browse in the classroom library, talking about, choosing, and signing out paperbacks.

In chapter eight I reproduced the letter I write to students inviting them to correspond with me and their friends in reading journals. On the second day of school, as the reading mini-lesson, I give everyone a copy of the letter and explain journal procedures. Because the directions are so complicated I'm particularly aware during this presentation that I'm providing background, not definitive instructions. In the opening minutes of other reading workshops I'll explain again when kids do the actual writing, how often they have to write and to whom, where the journals are kept and how they're to be filed, how letters are delivered, why it's necessary to date the correspondence, and what to talk about when writing.

What to talk about when writing is the next logical mini-lesson. The information is important at this point because readers will start corresponding the following day. I review the second paragraph of my letter to the group — "tell what you noticed; what you thought, felt and why; what you liked, didn't and why," etc. Then for the past two years I showed what I meant on the overhead projector, reproducing a half-dozen exchanges between previous years' students and between students and me. Nothing I'd told kids about the letters had nearly the same effect as their reading other students' words — now they could see what I meant. Sharing with students how other students have talked about books circumvents the worst problem connected with the letters — book report plot synopses. For teachers thinking of asking students to keep dialogue journals about reading, a good place to start might be making and showing transparencies of some of the eighth graders' letters in chapters seven and eight so your students, too, can see what you mean.

At the start of the next day's reading class everyone should have a spiralbound notebook. We put a numbered sticker on the front of each journal indicating the order in which journals will be filed in each class's box. On the inside front cover kids staple a copy of my initial letter to them about journal procedures. On the inside back cover they staple a "Reading Log" sheet. The log sheet features three columns, headed "Title of Book," "Author," and "Date Finished," with lines for listing. In a mini-lesson I tell how and why they're to use the list:

> This year you'll be reading a lot. One thing readers often do is to keep track of their reading, to make a record of the books and authors they've encountered. For one thing, it gives a terrific sense of accomplishment to look through a year's record of your reading, to see what you've done in black and white. But listing books also helps you spot trends in your reading — what kinds of books you like at different points in your history as an eighth grader. And listing authors helps when you've particularly liked a book. Because you have the author's name in your records, you can look for other good books by that author. Finally, it's interesting to see how long it takes to read certain books and whether the rate at which you read picks up through the year because you're reading so much or finding more books you like.
>
> Each time you finish a book, from now until June, record the title, author, and date you finished the book on the Reading Log sheet. It's that simple. If you fill the sheet, there's a folder full of extras on the shelf next to the journal box. Staple the new sheet under the old one so the log shows the chronology of your reading. At the end of the year I'll ask you to go through your voluminous lists and rate what you've read. Over the summer I'll buy the books you like to re-stock the classroom library for next year's eighth graders.
>
> Any questions or comments?

Choosing books to read during the workshop is another procedural topic. At the start of one class during the first weeks of school I'll distribute copies of my latest list of favorite adolescent fiction (Appendix *G*). We update the list each year from students' reading log sheets. In June readers rate every book they read, 1–10, and I note the clear favorites, ones that received a rating of nine or ten from at least three kids. These are the titles I order for the classroom library, the ones I list for students' reference. In a mini-lesson in September I explain how the list was derived — that these are last year's favorites — and ask each reader to tuck a copy of the list inside the reading journal. Through the year, as readers get stuck for books, this is one source of options.

Another procedural mini-lesson describes a second source for good books. After kids complete their reading surveys on the first day of school I compile their answers to the question, "What kinds of books do you like to read?" Among other things, the question gets at entering eighth graders' concepts of genre. I list each genre they come up with at the top of a piece of colored tag: "Sad Love Stories," "Dog Stories," "Books About People Dying," "Kids in Ghettos," "Kids' Real Life Problems," "Fantasy/Adventure," "Funny Books," "Westerns," and so on. Then I file the tagboard in a folder marked "Recommended Books by Category." In the mini-lesson I show kids the folder, read each heading, and invite them to please list for others the good books they know about or encounter in any of the categories. We keep the "Recommended Books" folder on the shelf next to the journal boxes.

Kids add to it and consult it all year long. The lists are easy to use and, because the genres are of students' own devising, they are especially relevant and helpful.

Students' survey responses also tell me that the classroom library isn't their only source for good books. Many of my kids have small libraries of their own. In the fall I present a mini-lesson about the pleasures of owning books, about what precious possessions good books can be, and tell where good books can be bought locally and where adolescent fiction is shelved in each bookstore. In another mini-lesson I talk about borrowing books from friends. Susan Stires, Boothbay's primary resource room teacher, leaves novels in my mailbox at school. She calls me at night when she's looking for a novel she thinks Toby and I might have. I encourage kids to develop their own novel networks by listing somewhere in their logs the titles and authors of books they own so their correspondents can browse and ask to borrow, or to post a list of the contents of their personal libraries on the classroom bulletin board.

Throughout the year, as I receive monthly flyers, I'll also present mini-lessons on commercial school book club offerings. I describe the books I think would be worth buying and owning and give kids a week to bring in orders and money. The advantages of book clubs continue to be their comparatively low prices on paperbacks and the bonus points teachers receive toward free books for the classroom library. (The disadvantage, more so every year, is that fewer and fewer book club offerings are books. Last year my three reading classes, confronted with posters, Mad Libs, and sticker books, ordered nothing from about half the monthly flyers.)

Other procedural mini-lessons are explanations of the classroom library and how it works. I own about eight hundred paperbacks stored in counter-top bookcases the local parents' club built for my room. There's no system to the filing — the last way I want to spend my time is sorting and shelving books. The sign-out system, too, is the least elaborate I could come up with. When I buy a new book I print my last name in magic marker across the top of the spine and add it to the library. If a lost book gets found, the chances are pretty good my name will be prominent enough for the finder to return it. When a book is borrowed, the student writes his or her name, the title, and the date on a classroom library sign-out sheet taped to the counter where the bookcases rest, and where I also keep a pen on a chain. The reader draws a line through this information when returning a book to the shelves. I tell kids how to sign out a book, how I've made it as easy a system as I can for all concerned, and stress the need to bring back borrowed books. The only way others will have books to borrow is if readers use the system. The classroom library we start with in September has to last all year.

I still lose a lot of books. I decided to accept the situation — that paperback novels will disappear no matter what the system — and spend as little fruitless time as possible administering the library and running around after missing books.

Finally, five procedural mini-lessons deal with evaluation. In September I explain the grading system for reading workshop, how ranks are one-third independent reading points, one-third reading journal, and one-third progress made toward individual goals. Then, near the close of each of the four rank periods, I take five minutes to let kids know what will happen during the upcoming evaluation conference and what they need to do to prepare — what questions they should be thinking about.

The bulk of procedural information I share in September and October mini-lessons covers the same kind of ground I tried to cover in other years during the first week of school — basic information I'd then have to re-teach all year long. In mini-lessons students get a quick shot of one particular kind of information and a chance to ask questions when I've finished. They still don't "get" everything the first time through, but the mini-lesson provides a more practical forum for introducing expectations and guidelines. There's less overload, a better sense of how and why things work, and greater student independence earlier on.

Literature

The term "literature" embraces mini-lesson topics that deal with what we read and what we know about what we read. They include different genres, authors, and elements of literary works. In literature mini-lessons I do one of three things. I read aloud and talk about a short work — a poem, essay, scene, myth, or short story. I tell about an author and read an excerpt from the author's work. Or I present information or ask kids to gather information about literature and how it works.

The ways literature works range from the language itself to literary devices, techniques, and publishing conventions. For instance, I take five minutes at the beginning of a reading workshop to ask kids, "Who's the main character of the book you're reading? How do you know?" Together we'll figure out what makes a main character a main character — how the author talks more about the person but also how the author shows the person's point of view, takes us inside the character's heart and mind, and describes some problem or change the character experiences. The main character is someone for us to be with, a crucial fixture in a work of fiction. And we'll talk about what often happens when we don't like or aren't interested in the main character — how, with no one to be with, we'd sooner not be in the book at all. Another literary element I discuss in mini-lessons is narrative voice:

> One thing I notice about novels is who's telling the story. Sometimes it's a first person narrator. That means an "I" is telling us the story of what happened to him or her. Be careful. In fiction, the "I" isn't the author. The "I" is a persona the author creates to tell the story. Like in *The Outsiders*, S. E. Hinton created Ponyboy Curtis to tell the story Hinton wanted to tell, and in *The Adventures of Huckleberry Finn*, Twain the writer uses Huck the character as the voice of the book to tell about the adventures Twain dreams up for Huck and Tom. First person narrators are limited in that they can only describe what they personally see, hear, and know — they can't get into the other characters' minds and tell what's going on there. But they can take you and

keep you right in the heart of a character, as M. E. Kerr does in *Gentle-hands* with Buddy, and Paula Danziger did with Phoebe in *The Divorce Express*.

Other times authors use third person narration. This is when a voice that's telling the story isn't the voice of anyone in the book. It's the voice that tells "She did this," or "He felt that." In *A Swiftly Tilting Planet*, someone is narrating the story but it isn't a character in the novel. It's what's called an omniscient narrator. Omniscient means all-knowing. An omniscient narrator can see into different characters' minds, as the narrator in *A Swiftly Tilting Planet* can tell what both Meg and Charles Wallace are thinking. In a novel like *Clan of the Cave Bear* you pretty much have to have a third person narrator. It wouldn't be very believable to have Ayla the prehistoric woman narrating a novel.

Finally, there's a new, weird trend in fiction — a second person narrator. If first person is I, and third person is he/she, second person is you. I just read a second person novel by Jay McInerney called *Bright Lights, Big City* and the whole story is told, "You get up in the morning and you think this. Then you do this and you say this." As I said, it's strange — you feel as if you've had more than enough after just a few chapters.

Today when you read, notice which narrative voice the author chose, and think for a minute about why the author might have decided on this approach.

Any comments or questions?

Other literary conventions come up in other reading lessons. One day I'll discuss plot by way of teaching about formulaic fiction: books that feature predictable characters in predictable situations with predictable outcomes. At the same time I recognize the appeal of formula, of such series as *Twilight* mysteries and *Sweet Dreams* romances, of Westerns and *Nancy Drews*. The familiarity of the genre makes reading easy, something that should be a main goal of teachers of reading. Because basic literary elements of plot, motivation, and theme are so blatant, so much larger than life, adolescents can see and respond to these elements more easily than in more sophisticated works of fiction. I've learned to nudge kids toward other kinds of literature, in mini-lessons and in journal correspondence, and I've learned to be patient. The summer between my seventh and eighth grade years I read eighteen *Trixie Beldon* mysteries that I bought in a supermarket. By the end of the summer I was all Trixied out and ready for something different. My mother had the good sense to understand I needed to read *Trixie Beldon* at age thirteen and that the need would pass, just as every other phase of childhood eventually ends.

In another day's mini-lesson I discuss titles and leads — the ways authors bring us into their works — and ask volunteers to read aloud ways their authors decided to begin. I also discuss prologues and epilogues and how they serve authors' ends. In the first months of school I think eighth graders would prefer that every novel they read conclude with an epilogue. Ambiguous endings drive them wild when they seriously begin to read fiction, and when they seriously begin to write fiction, prologues and epilogues often show up in their manuscripts. They want to know and show everything about everything.

Kids take equal pleasure in sequels and trilogies. They experience the instant comfort of old friends — of not having to acquaint themselves with new main characters — and they're able to learn even more about the lives of characters they already care about. In mini-lessons I'll discuss sequels — how *That Was Then, This Is Now* is not a sequel to *The Outsiders* even though it's Hinton's second novel and Ponyboy Curtis makes a cameo appearance; how I think the sequel, *There's a Bat in Bunk Five*, is superior to Danziger's first book about Marcy, *The Cat Ate My Gymsuit*; how for me Cynthia Voigt's books about Dicey don't constitute a trilogy because although *Dicey's Song* is a sequel to *The Homecoming*, *Solitary Blue* introduces and focuses on a new main character. I'll talk about trilogies — Tolkien's *Middle Earth* and Terry Brooks's *Shannara*, Ursula K. LeGuin's *Earthsea Trilogy*, Robert Lipsyte's three novels about Bobby Marks, and the science fiction trilogy by Madeleine L'Engle that begins with *A Wrinkle in Time.*

A Wrinkle in Time was the first novel I read where I was aware of theme, although I didn't know the word then. I did know that L'Engle was writing about good and evil, about each person's responsibility to fight evil and strive to be a force for good in the world. It bowled me over back in sixth grade to discover a novel could do more than tell a story. Now I introduce the idea of theme in mini-lessons by telling the story of my experience reading *A Wrinkle in Time*, and define theme simply as what is shown to us about life and living through what happens to the people in a story. Theme is a new concept for adolescents. For some it's difficult because it requires a level of abstraction beyond plot and character: the understanding that there's more going on than what's going on. Whenever I mention a fictional work in a mini-lesson I describe it by theme as well as plot, introducing new books by way of the ideas they engender:

> I finished a novel last night that I wanted you to know about. It's called *Hanging Out with CiCi* by Francine Pascal. Mindy made me read it, and I'm so glad I did. Pascal had me laughing out loud, something I almost never do as a reader.
>
> *Hanging Out with CiCi* is about the generation gap, about how hard it is for kids and parents to understand each other, even though all parents were kids once and most kids will be parents some day. This girl, Victoria, goes back in time and meets her own, strict mother as a teenager — and her mother is this rowdy troublemaker who gets Victoria in trouble, too. She can't believe that this CiCi kid is her mother, Cecelia. I thought it was a much better, funnier look at the gap between parents and kids than *Freaky Friday.*
>
> By the way, if you read Fran Arrick's *Tunnel Vision* or *Steffie Can't Come Out to Play*, novels about teen suicide and prostitution, Fran Arrick and Francine Pascal are the same person. I don't know which is the pseudonym, but she seems to write her dark, serious novels as Arrick and her lighter stuff — comedies and romances — as Pascal.

My First Love and Other Disasters is another Pascal you should know about. It's a realistic look at the choices you have to make when you fall in love, and it's funny.

The conventions of publishing, such as authors' pseudonyms and why they use them, are topics ripe for literary mini-lessons, which also include copyrights, copyright dates as a quick way to know when the book you're reading was written, numbers of reprintings as an indication of a book's popularity, paperback rights, how and when hardcovers become paperbacks, jacket copy and cover illustrations, royalties and agents, how novels are adapted for film as screenplays, and how something called a "novelization" is an adaptation of an original screenplay as a book. Readers who know how books are published make better choices. They're more confident, less intimidated by libraries and bookstores. They have inside information that dispels the mystique of Literature.

Inside information about authors benefits readers too. Every fall at least half the eighth grade readers I survey can't name a favorite author. Others list obvious choices — Beverly Cleary and Judy Blume. They need introductions to authors who write well for adolescents. Once a reader knows a name, he or she can look for books by that author, the best kind of educated guess someone in search of a good book can make.

On different days I give brief introductions to different authors. I get a lot of my information on authors from their publishers. Dell/Laurel-Leaf and Avon, for example, offer free flyers on their writers that feature both about-the-author information and interviews. In a mini-lesson on Todd Strasser I read parts of the Strasser flyer and then a few good pages from his *Rock 'n' Roll Nights*. To introduce Paula Danziger I read aloud the funny first chapter of *The Divorce Express* and then excerpts from a Dell flyer featuring Danziger's comments on writing the book, and I show copies of Danziger's other novels. I read aloud the first pages of Susan Beth Pfeffer novels. And so on. I have a fat folder of biographical material from publishers on Lois Duncan, Nat Hentoff, Jay Bennett, M. E. Kerr, S. E. Hinton, Arthur Roth, the Mazers, Robert Cormier, Paul Zindel, and other authors of contemporary adolescent fiction. I also have copies of their novels to show readers, from which I read excerpts selected and rehearsed beforehand.

I usually talk about authors' lives when I introduce the individual short works I read in genre mini-lessons. When I was an undergraduate one of my methods instructors told us never to give kids biographical information about writers, that it bored kids and took away from the impact of the work. As it turned out, this couldn't be further from the truth. Kids who write like to know about the lives and intentions of the writers they read. When I introduce tall tales I tell what I know about the life and methods of Ellis Credle, who collected Blue Ridge Mountain stories, and Marshall Dodge of Maine's *Bert and I* tales. Then I read aloud Credle's "The Man Who Rode the Bear" over several days' mini-lessons, and play Dodge's recording of "Harry Whitfield's Trip." In that week's writing workshop three or four writers will try their hands at a Maine tall tale of their own, gathering ideas by talking with their grandparents and mimmicking Dodge's version of a Down East accent.

Parody is another genre mini-lesson, one especially appropriate to eighth graders for whom caricature is a way of life. I collect examples of imitations I think kids will recognize. Whenever Russell Baker parodies politicians' or journalists' talk in his *New York Times* column, I clip it. Diane White's *Boston Globe* columns often parody books about popular culture. Veronica Geng's book *Partners*, a collection of her *New Yorker* pieces, is a great source of nonsensical pokes at serious writing. The poet Paul Dehn parodies nursery rhymes; his little Miss Muffet is frightened "to *bits*" by an H-bomb. Eighth graders' favorite parodist is Woody Allen. They like his versions of two-minute mysteries and mythological creatures in *Without Feathers*, and the U.F.O. sighting reports in *Side Effects.* Finally, I have a folder of eighth graders' parodies — Janet's "'Twas the Day Before Christmas," Jenn's version of the principal's weekly newsletter to parents, B.J.'s poem about school titled "Nothing Dull Can Stay (I Hope)," Tim's script for an Anacin commercial. Each year the parodies read aloud in reading workshop inspire kids to write parodies in writing workshop. Each year I have a bigger and better collection from which I can draw in showing what happens when authors borrow a style and then twist the theme.

I also read aloud short stories, pieces I like and think eighth graders will like too. They include Paul Gallico's "The Snow Goose," Jack London's "To Build a Fire," Truman Capote's "A Christmas Memory," selections from Robert Cormier's *Eight Stories*, "Flowers for Algernon" by Daniel Keyes and stories by F. Scott Fitzgerald, Alice Munro, Shirley Jackson, J. D. Salinger, John Updike, O. Henry, Raymond Carver, Margaret Atwood, Richard Wright, John Cheever, and Kurt Vonnegut, Jr. In the September reading surveys, typically about ninety percent of eighth graders say they like being read to. For a long time I'd thought of oral reading as something primary level teachers did to entertain little kids; I assumed that as kids grew they left behind the pleasure of listening to stories. From the survey and then from their responses to my readings I learned this wasn't so. Eighth graders — all of us — are enthralled by a good read-aloud. More importantly, read-alouds led many kids to borrow the books I shared and to look for other works by those authors, to go beyond listening to a more active and personal involvement with texts. Charlotte Huck (1986) recently said it's a mistake for educators to regard reading aloud as mere entertainment, that it is essential to readers' growth. Hearing good literature brings it to life, fills the classroom with an author's words, and provides kids one more avenue for loving books.

Reading aloud is a skill unto itself and takes constant practice. I'm still learning. Kids need opportunities to learn, too. In the spring my students organized a shared reading day with Judy Burgess' first grade class. Each first grader and each eighth grader selected one of his or her own pieces of writing and one professionally published selection to read aloud to a partner from the other grade. One Friday morning they settled themselves in pairs, in corners and under desks, and read and talked about the manuscripts they'd chosen. For the eighth graders Friday morning came at the end of a week of intense preparation. They spent some of that time picking the texts they would read, and they spent much time practicing reading them aloud.

In one morning's mini-lesson I asked kids to do a quick observation of me as an oral reader. As I read Shel Silverstein's poem "Little Abigail and the Beautiful Pony," they were to note anything I did that made for an effective reading. Afterward I compiled their observations on an overhead and added a couple of pointers I'd learned about oral interpretation. Students used the final list as a guide in preparing their readings. I think it's a useful guide for teachers as well.

TIPS FOR READING ALOUD

1. Read the selection at least once to yourself beforehand. Decide how you will read it. You may want to skip over difficult sections or long descriptions, or shorten a work that's too long to read in the time you have.
2. Don't begin reading until listeners are ready, until they've settled in and are looking at you.
3. Read to them, not at them. Make eye contact as often as you can. (Practice helps.)
4. Keep your reading rate slower than conversation. Avoid a tendency to speed up.
5. Pause often, before and after parts you want to stress, to let things sink in.
6. Speak in a voice loud enough to reach every corner of the room.
7. Change your voice for the story's different characters, becoming each character.
8. Change your voice for the story's different moods: anger, sorrow, happiness, etc.
9. Change volume: louder then softer, as appropriate.
10. Use facial expressions: smile, frown, gasp, show surprise, anger, suspense, etc.
11. Involve listeners. Ask them what they think will happen next.
12. Talk about and show any illustrations.
13. Make sure it's a book, poem, or story you really like.
14. Decide not to be embarrassed and give it everything you've got.

Greek mythology is another genre I read aloud and talk about in mini-lessons. In the old days when I was covering a curriculum I spent two weeks on mythology, all period each day. I still spend two weeks on myths; now I present what particularly interests me and what I think kids would enjoy knowing, rather than drilling and testing the life out of these tales. What interests me and what I think kids should understand is simply this. Classical myths are wonderful stories, and distinctive, too, in that they have inspired so many different kinds of great art, including the literature we read today. Furthermore, they were the ancient Greeks' sacred explanations for how the world worked. So we begin with the Greek creation myth in one mini-lesson and then look at the immortal to mortal chain of being, from the mating of

Heaven and Earth that produced the Titans all the way down to demi-gods, heroes, and us. On another day I give kids a list of the thirty or so most important Greek divinities, a kind of playbill to which they can refer once the stories begin. Then I read my favorite myths — how the seasons came to be, Icarus and Daedalus, Pygmalion and Galatea, Perseus and Medusa, Hercules and Atlas. Last year one eighth grader, Danny, was so knowledgeable and enthusiastic about classical and Norse mythology he prepared and presented mini-lessons of his own.

When I approached mythology in mini-lessons, something happened that I never saw during my two-week literature unit. Readers started borrowing my collections of myths and asking the librarian if they could borrow hers, and during reading workshop about a half-dozen kids in each class continued reading mythology on their own.

Reading mini-lessons have also allowed me to introduce literature I never would have considered appropriate for heterogeneous groupings of eighth graders. Shakespeare, for example, whose works could not be taught in whole to whole groups of eighth graders, was a hit as a series of mini-lessons. I chose four of my favorite scenes and speeches, ones I thought kids would enjoy and understand, and a couple of the sonnets. Over five days I talked about Shakespeare, of what little we know of his life for a writer considered the most important who ever lived, and discussed the kinds of plays he wrote and their differences. Each day I told the story of one of the plays and then gave kids copies of, read aloud, and discussed a speech or scene from the play — Hamlet's soliloquy, the balcony scene from *Romeo and Juliet*, the quality of mercy speech from *Merchant of Venice*, Jaques' seven ages of man speech from *As You Like It*. On their own initiative groups of students in two classes used the reading time that followed the mini-lesson to go off to an empty classroom and rehearse scenes they later performed for their classes. During the next two weeks I could hear kids in the hall between classes speaking to each other in what they thought passed for Elizabethan dialect, and when an eighth grade girl hosted a VCR party the movie she showed was Zefferelli's *Romeo and Juliet*. Again, the mini-lessons had served their purpose, giving kids a taste of the pleasures of a particular genre and whetting their appetites for more.

Finally, the heart of my literature mini-lessons are presentations of poetry. Other than fiction, poetry is the genre I read most often and love best. In reading mini-lessons I get to share some of my favorite poets. Sometimes my kids love them, too; sometimes they don't. Some of the most successful mini-lessons happen when readers tell why they don't like what, when they make and defend judgments. Poetry requires personal response more so than any other genre, because a poem is such an intensely personal response to the world.

In preparing poetry mini-lessons I either choose several favorite works by a particular poet or works by various poets that address a particular topic or theme. I make at least a class set of clean xerox copies of each poem so eighth graders may see what the poems I'm reading look like. I collect these sheets at the end of the mini-lesson and file them in labeled construction paper pockets tacked to one of the bulletin boards. Through the school year kids are free to take copies of the poems they like once they're filed. In effect, students create their own individual poetry anthologies. They leave eighth grade owning a collection of their favorite poems.

Individual poets whose works I teach in mini-lessons include Peter Meinke, Charles Simic, Langston Hughes, Richard Wilbur, E. E. Cummings, Theodore Roethke, Robert Frost, Marge Piercy, Shel Silverstein, William Carlos Williams, Margaret Atwood, and Emily Dickinson. They are among my favorite poets; theirs are the poems I can teach with genuine pleasure.

When I introduce a particular poet's works, I tell a little about the poet's life and the general themes of his or her poetry during the first mini-lesson and read aloud a short poem from one of the poetry sheets. Over the next few days I read aloud and talk about other poems. I tell how I read each poem — the first and second and third times through — and what I found each time I returned to peel away new layers of language and imagery. One day a student, Brendan, said that reading a poem was like peeling the layers of an onion. We can peel one layer of meaning or many and still have a poem — just so long as we don't peel away to nothing, dissecting the poem to death. In a letter to me in her reading log, Sybil discussed the joys of peeling onions.

Ms. Atwell,

Since you are the only one I know who enjoys poetry as much as I do if not more I'm going to write to you. I'm really getting into poetry now. I don't know why but I am. I've gotten to the point where I read a poem, stop, read it over, and then try to understand the author's point of view. Even then I may read the poem over. I have even memorized some of the poems I enjoy because I love to always have a poem to say to myself. They are also fun to bore my mother with.

I'm glad that I'm reading poetry now. It gives me a chance to relax, unlike in a book where you normally have to read 100 pages to finally get the idea. In a poem it's not all spelled out for you. Like you said, you've gotta peel away at the onion. That's what I've started to do with poetry. I've got a new saying, "Never base a poem by your first reading." I made that up a few days ago. And like you said in today's mini-lesson, about when you read "Boy at the Window" but didn't know the author was Richard Wilbur you said it was bad because it was about a kid and a snowman. Sometimes I really feel like that. I haven't read many poems yet but I intend on reading a lot more before the end of school. From what I have read I think Paul Dehn is one of my favorites. He writes funny poems that have a lot of meaning. I also like the poem "Sonic Boom" by John Updike. It has a special meaning to me I can't put my finger on, but I think it's my favorite poem. What's yours?

Your faithful onion peeler,
Sybil

I tell kids how I read — and mis-read — to teach them how readers of poetry approach poems. Students need to know that teachers return to a work again and again in order to discover the meanings we glibly present to our classes, and that much of the pleasure of poetry is in returning to savor and ponder. (A couple of years ago, when I was still glibly presenting neat explications, a kid looked at the poem I was about to gloss and asked, "Couldn't you just mark the lines with the hidden meanings?")

I also tell kids how I read to show them how I connect poetry with my life. Good poetry calls up memories and images; in turn, good poetry is called up by scenes and occasions of real life. Things I see and experience often make me think of particular poems. Because I live in rural New England, the poet whose works come to my mind more than any other is Robert Frost. When I take a walk, I see some of what Frost saw. When I present Frost mini-lessons, I tell what his poems enable me to see that I would otherwise miss. My first Frost mini-lesson, after introducing the poet, ends with "Dust of Snow."

> This is a great, short Frost poem. It's easy to memorize. It's the first Frost I ever committed to memory. I'm going to ask you to do a couple of choral readings at the end of class, and I'll leave it on the board for a couple of days. I like owning this poem, having it in my mind. You may want to own it too.
>
> When we first moved to Maine we lived in a big old house in East Boothbay. The house was surrounded by firs. One morning in the middle of the winter we woke up to find two feet of new snow and no announcement that school was cancelled. I was not a happy person. Every winter we lived in the house in East Boothbay I managed to put my car off the road at least twice on the way to school.
>
> Anyway, I was heading out the back door in a miserable mood to shovel out my car when up above in one of the firs two sparrows started to tussle in the branches. I looked up just as they kicked down a dusting of snow. It covered my face and hair, and I had to laugh — at their antics and at my bad mood. And I thought of Frost's "Dust of Snow."

(After reading the poem:)

> This poem is about as romantic as Frost ever gets about nature. Although he's thought of as a nature poet, and uses the natural world to help us reflect on human life, he warns us in his poetry not to make the mistake of believing the natural world notices or cares about man. Another Frost poem we'll read, "The Need To Be Versed in Country Things," is a strong warning that no matter what happens to us, nature goes on. The best we can expect from nature is an occasional "dust of snow" that distracts us from the business of life. Maybe the next time a gorgeous sunset or a particularly pretty cast of light on the water or something pleasing in the natural world lifts your mood for a minute, you'll think of "Dust of Snow."

Then, on other days, I read to them and talk about "The Road Not Taken," "Nothing Gold Can Stay," "Country Things," "The Pasture," which we also try as a choral reading, and "Stopping by Woods on a Snowy Evening." Brendan's onion analogy is especially appropriate in glossing "Stopping by Woods." For that day's mini-lesson I take to school my little daughter's book-length version of the poem, illustrated by Susan Jeffers (Dutton).

> I remember the first few times I read this poem. I was in sixth grade and I thought it was a nice story about stopping on the way from one place to some place else to enjoy a pretty scene. Let me read it to you as a story and show the illustrations from this book my baby loaned me.
>
> The next times I read "Stopping by Woods" were in a high school English class. I read it then as a poem about wanting to be closer to nature. The speaker wanted to stay, to become part of this lovely natural world, but life, with all its responsibilities, beckoned.
>
> Then in college I read "Stopping by Woods" again. My teacher presented the critic John Ciardi's interpretation of the poem — that it's a contemplation of suicide, that the sleep the speaker desires is death. This was the deepest layer of the onion I penetrated.
>
> Finally, a couple of summers ago at Bread Loaf I dealt with the outermost layer of the onion. In fact, it wasn't even a layer. It's the crinkly brown skin that covers the layers. Do you know the song "Hernando's Hideaway"? Well, at Bread Loaf I learned you can sing "Stopping by Woods" to the tune of "Hernando's Hideaway." It goes something like this . . . .

My discussion of "Nothing Gold Can Stay" centers on its inclusion in S. E. Hinton's novel *The Outsiders.* Ponyboy Curtis recites the poem at a point in the novel after his friend Johnny has killed another boy in self-defense, and they've run away to the country to hide.

> Let's take a look at this poem from S. E. Hinton's perspective. She puts "Nothing Gold Can Stay" in Ponyboy's mind at a particular moment in *The Outsiders*, after Johnny has killed Bob. Why? What's she getting at? Let's take away some layers, try to uncover Frost's meaning, and then come back to the question. Last night, when I read and reread "Nothing Gold Can Stay," this is what I came up with.
>
> Frost begins in his typical style by comparing with nature. In spring the first signs of life to appear on the trees aren't green leaves; they're gold buds. This gold color is nature's "hardest to hold" because it only lasts a short while. The gold buds quickly pass.
>
> Next the tree blossoms. But these early leaves, these flowers, only last a short time, too. In Frost's metaphor, they only last an hour — he's stressing how quickly this beauty goes.
>
> Then leaves give way to leaves. The mature leaves of summer take over, fade, and die. And then Frost switches gears and compares this natural process with the end of the Garden of Eden. When Adam and Eve sinned they lost Paradise. They lost their first, innocent beauty and were banished from Eden. And then Frost switches gears again, and brings in a new comparison. This loss is like the way every beautiful dawn, all fresh and new, soon becomes just regular, normal day. And altogether we see that innocent beauty — the "goldness" of young, new life — can't last.

In *The Outsiders*, Pony himself isn't sure why he thinks of this poem at this moment. I think it's because it's a poem about the end of innocence, the impermanence of young beauty. "Gold" symbolizes this evanescent beauty. When Johnny kills Bob, his "golden" days are suddenly ended. He's thrown into a hard, brutal world. If you read *The Outsiders* you'll see how Hinton makes the theme of this poem one of the major themes of the novel.

Any questions or comments?

I bought twelve paperback copies of *Robert Frost's Poems* and added them to the classroom library. After the Frost mini-lessons they were in constant circulation. He is unquestionably my eighth graders' favorite poet. Another favorite is E. E. Cummings, whose poetry pocket I have to re-stock until June. In mini-lessons we read "who are you, little i," which they read as a response to "Nothing Gold Can Stay," "in Just-spring," "anyone lived in a pretty how town," and "Buffalo Bill's defunct" — their very favorite because of its piercing sarcasm, I think, and because they're so taken with the word "defunct" which shows up all over the place in their compositions. Last year Nikos, an eighth grader, made his first visit to the town library. He checked out three books: *No Thanks* and *73 Poems* by E. E. Cummings, and a critical study of Cummings' poetry by Barry Marks. Nikos said, "You've got to love this guy's poetry. The layers are unbelievable."

Mini-lesson poems grouped by theme include sports poems, poems of protest and social commentary, and metaphors. Sports poems kids and I have liked are John Updike's "Ex-Basketball Player," A. E. Housman's "To an Athlete Dying Young," "The Double-Play," by Robert Wallace, "The Base Stealer" by Robert Francis, "Foul Shot" by Edwin Hooey, and three sports poems by three former eighth graders. Protest poems are Hardy's "The Man He Killed," Michael Casey's "Bummer" from his Vietnam collection *Obscenities*, May Swenson's "Southbound on the Freeway," "Richard Cory" in both the E. A. Robinson and Paul Simon versions, and again, works by eighth graders.

After I introduce the concept of metaphor in a mini-lesson I give kids copies of poems that consist of extended metaphors but delete their titles, and ask readers to get together and try to name the poems. I use "Steam Shovel" by Charles Malam, "The Toaster" by William Jay Smith, "Fireworks" by Babette Deutsch, "Daffodils" by May Swenson, and two or three extended metaphors by eighth graders; for example, Jon Dunton's "Sun":

> There it is waiting
> right before me — as if in thin air.
> It's over here.
> No — over there.
> Can't you see?
> It's everywhere.
> It's up, up so high
> it seems to enjoy every edge of the sky.
> Some days it's lost
> and some days it's there but very soft.

Low then high then low,
it comes and it goes.
It's nature's light show.

I photocopy and save much of my students' writing. When kids take their permanent folders home in June I have my own folder of their work, filed according to genre, subject, or theme. All of the genre mini-lessons feature examples of eighth graders' writing — because I want to narrow the gap between professionally published authors and my students, because they can learn from good examples of peers' works, but mostly because they write so well. I want to own their poetry, too. In turn, the student writing I share in literature mini-lessons in reading workshop inspires more good student writing in writing workshop that I can add to my files.

Most of the professionally published poetry I teach can be found in collections of individual poets' works. Some are drawn from anthologies of poetry. For teachers looking for a few good poetry anthologies for themselves and their classrooms I recommend: *Reflections on a Gift of Watermelon Pickle*, Stephen Dunning, editor (Scholastic); *Writing Poems*, Robert Wallace, editor (Little Brown); *Pictures That Storm Inside My Head*, Richard Peck, editor (Avon); *Go With the Poem*, Lilian Moore, editor (McGraw-Hill); *The Voice That Is Great Within Us*, Hayden Carruth, editor (Bantam); *Contemporary American Poetry*, Donald Hall, editor (Penguin), and five wonderful collections edited by Paul Janeczko. They are *Postcard Poems*, *Don't Forget to Fly*, *Poetspeak: In Their Words*, *About Their Work*, and *Strings: A Gathering of Family Poems*, all Bradbury Press publications, and *The Crystal Image*, a Dell paperback.

At the end of the last school year, Sybil, my faithful onion peeler, initiated a special project. One day in May she asked, "When do we get to do mini-lessons of our favorite poems? We own your favorites. Don't you want to own ours?"

Of course I did. At the beginning of each reading class the next day students scheduled themselves to present poetry mini-lessons over the following days and weeks. Each chose a favorite work, one I hadn't yet read to them, and each planned what they would say to introduce the poem, how they would read it, and what they'd say afterward in peeling away to meaning. Finally, each was responsible for getting a clean copy of the poem to me at least a day in advance so I could make a class set. Kelli, the first student in her class to present, was giddy with nerves that day. "Ms. Atwell," she wanted to know, "how old were you when you did your first mini-lesson?"

The range of poetry they chose to read astonished me. Sarah read a poem her grandmother had written. Some students — Janet, Kelli, Lilias, Steve, and Brian — chose their own best poems. Heather, Mary Jo, and Jenn presented favorite poems by classmates and previous years' eighth graders; they found kids' verse in current and former class poetry magazines shelved in the classroom library. And others read professionally published poetry. Chris read Poe's "Annabel Lee." Trevor read "The Sleeping Giant" by Donald Hall. Alice read Robert Service's "The Cremation of Sam McGee." Sybil read her favorite, Updike's "Sonic Boom." Missy read Emily Dickinson, Allan read

Eve Merriam, Kevin read John Masefield, Dan read Shel Silverstein, Jamie and Keith read Robert Frost, and Nikos, of course, read E. E. Cummings.

Skills

I'm using the word *skills* to describe the things good readers do, my notions of which were formed by Frank Smith's work, particularly *Reading Without Nonsense* (1984). I think it's the most important book written about the act of reading; it's the one text every junior high English teacher should own. Smith cuts straight through the maze of skills and methods invented by textbook publishers — vocabulary and paragraph development, literal comprehension, inferential comprehension, phonics rules, dictionary skills, sequencing, finding the main idea, locating supporting details, and on and on. Instead, he tells about the nature of reading, arguing that what teachers need is not more methodology but an understanding of reading itself and of what competent readers do.

Competent readers, for example, do not depend on phonics, which is the reading method most frequently taught in U.S. schools. When good readers, adults and children, meet a word we don't recognize we most often react by skipping over it. As a second alternative we guess at the word's meaning. The last least preferred reaction is to sound the word out. Phonics is the last choice because phonics "is the least efficient choice" (1984, p. 66). Yet phonics is the method we mostly teach. In fact, guessing is the most efficient way to read and learn to read. Smith calls it "informed guessing" — making reasonable guesses from a relatively small set of possibilities. The set is small because what readers already know about written language helps us make predictions about new information, and because of the redundancy of written language — the way structures repeat themselves in printed texts.

To briefly summarize, Smith says knowledge about how texts work is stored in our "long term memories." When we read we employ "short term memory" which helps us attend to the immediate present. Smith compares short term memory to a bottleneck. Elements from our reading go through this memory bottleneck to be organized and stored permanently in long term memory. Unfortunately, short term memory has a capacity for only about six or seven items at a time, and only one element makes it through short term memory to become established in long term memory about every five seconds. Competent readers are those who get the most information possible through the bottleneck; they do this by picking up the largest units of information possible: six or seven chunks of meaning rather than six or seven words or letters. Competent readers make good use of the information already stored in long term memory to help make guesses about new information coming in (Smith, Chap. 3).

What all this means for students in our classrooms is that much of the advice we give readers is wrong. Telling readers to slow down, be careful, avoid mistakes, and re-read what they don't understand makes them victims of short term memory. The result is short term memory overload and failure to remember much of anything that was read. Kids need advice that approximates what good readers really do. I advise my kids in reading mini-lessons.

My mini-lessons that address skill issues amount to a year-long introduction to Frank Smith's psycholinguistic model. Through the fall I explain and demonstrate Smith's theory, and through the remainder of the school year I show kids ways to put his theory into practice. Some of these lessons involve unteaching "skills" learned from other teachers. For example, in a mini-lesson I'll show kids what happens when they use a card or a pencil to underline a line as they're reading — how peripheral vision is checked and "chunking" meaning is no longer possible. In another mini-lesson I'll talk with kids about how lip-reading and vocalizing are bad habits because they slow down the reading rate and force the reader to see single words instead of chunks of meaning. On one day I'll ask kids to time themselves silently reading a page from their books and then to read the same page aloud, timing themselves again. It usually takes at least twice as long to complete the oral reading, because the eye is so much faster than the mouth (the average person speaks at the rate of about 200 words per minute while a fast reader reads about 450 w.p.m.) and because we don't stop to look at every word on a page. In fact, Smith estimates that a competent reader attends to only a fifth or less of the visual information on the page (1984, p. 62). I'll also unteach regressing — going back over material already read in an attempt to comprehend it. Habitual regression decreases rather than increases comprehension. In slowly going back over material a reader overloads short term memory and makes memorization virtually impossible. Speeding up increases comprehension because it increases concentration; speed also diminishes distractions. I urge kids to forge ahead and to count on the built-in redundancy of texts to help them straighten things out.

Speed rarely gets readers into trouble. When it does, it's sometimes on a text specifically designed to trap fluent readers. Tests of hidden assumptions, for example, are designed to take advantage of competent readers' strategies. In one mini-lesson I'll give kids a series of trick questions I've collected over the years. The next day I'll go over the test with them and talk about why good readers do poorly — for the most part, because their long term memories switch into gear and automatically supply information that's not there on the page or isn't appropriate to the situation. Below are ten trick questions. Answers and explanations of how the questions deceive good readers appear at the end of this chapter.

TEN QUESTIONS

1. Two men played chess. They played five games, and each man won three. How do you explain this?
2. Answer this question within five seconds and do not return to check your answer: How many animals of each species did Moses take aboard the ark with him? (Note: the questions is *not* how many pairs, but how many animals.)
3. An archaeologist reported that he had discovered two gold coins in the desert near Jerusalem dated 439 B.C. Many of his fellow scientists refused to take his claim seriously. Why?

4. If you have only one match and you entered a room to start a kerosene lamp, an oil heater, and a wood burning stove, which would you light first, and why?

5. Here is a question on international law: if an *international* airliner crashed exactly on the U.S.-Mexican border, where would they be required by law to bury the survivors?

6. Some months have thirty days; some have thirty-one. How many have twenty-eight?

7. A farmer had seventeen sheep; all but nine died. How many are left?

8. You have a dime in an empty wine bottle. The bottle is corked. Your job is to get the dime out of the bottle without taking the cork out. You must do this without damaging the bottle in any way. How do you do it?

9. Explain the following true boast: "In my bedroom, the nearest lamp that I usually keep turned on is 12 feet away from my bed. Alone in the room, without using wires, strings, or any other aids or contraptions, I can turn out the light on that lamp and get into bed before the room is dark."

10. Memorize the phrases below. As soon as you do this, turn the paper over and write them at the top of the back of this page. Do not look at the phrases once you have turned this page over.

PARIS   ONCE
IN THE   IN A
THE SPRING   A LIFETIME

BIRD   SLOW
IN THE   MEN AT
THE HAND   AT WORK

In other skill mini-lessons I'll stress the importance of reading as much as possible as fast as possible. This is the way to beat the bottleneck. I teach simple speed reading techniques such as skimming, scanning, and skipping. Kids need to know that speed readers aren't gifted. They've trained themselves to relax, to stop their eyes less frequently, and to see more with each stop. And they've trained themselves to be flexible, to adjust their speed to the kind of material being read. For instance, fluent readers know when to skim — when looking for the answer to a specific question, reviewing material that's familiar to them, deciding whether they're interested in reading a text. Effective skimming is mostly a matter of knowing that key information can usually be found in the first and last sentences of a paragraph.

I don't teach formal study skills. When I was a high school student I rebelled against SQ3R, PQ4R, REQUEST, and all the other kid-proof reading procedures because they made reading tedious. I had my own system. In a course Mary Ellen Giacobbe and I recently taught we asked our students, forty teachers, to describe their systems. Not one used any of the formal study procedures they taught their students. They had their own systems, too. When I asked, "What efficient strategies do you employ when you read for information?" they named the same techniques the good readers in my eighth grade classes identify each year when I survey them: "I look to see how long it will be." "I do a quick skim of the whole thing." "I read the conclusion first." "I read the forward or introduction." "I read all the subheadings." "I look at the pictures or charts." "I close the book when I'm done and write what I remember or think is important in my notebook." These, then, are the strategies I teach in reading mini-lessons — the real strategies that good readers come up with to help themselves learn from printed texts. From this repertoire each reader can begin to develop his or her own system.

The week before eighth graders take standardized tests in reading I present mini-lessons that help them understand the conventions of standardized tests. Students who understand how such assessments work are more confident going into the test situation and they have practical techniques at their disposal once they begin the test:

> One thing you should know about standardized achievement tests in reading is that there are just four basic kinds of questions. There's one group of questions that asks for the best title, best topic sentence, main idea, or general idea. Whatever the terminology, these are all getting at one thing: what the passage is mostly about. Then there are the inference questions. These are meanings that are implied by the passage, rather than directly spelled out. Often, it's just plain common sense. There are always detail questions. These are the ones that ask for specific information you can look up in the passage. Finally, they'll often ask for the meaning of a word in context, that is, what a word means in the sentence or passage in which it appears. I have about a half dozen typical passages and sets of questions, the kind you're sure to find on the test next week. Let's take a look at the questions and see what the testmaker was trying to get at in each one.

Students and I look at selections and questions from an old S.R.A. reading kit. On another day I'll distribute copies of and talk about some general procedures for reading the passages and answering the questions, procedures kids developed and found useful in previous years:

1. Read the first couple of sentences, the last couple of sentences, and the questions. You'll get an idea of what you'll be reading and what you'll be asked to know.
2. Then read the passage, looking for answers to the questions — the general idea, details, and so on.
3. When you answer the questions, start by eliminating the alternatives that show the least merit. Then re-read the question and the remaining answers.
4. Return to the selection whenever you need to, using a skimming/scanning approach.
5. When a question asks for the meaning of a word, read the whole sentence or passage in which the word appears. You're not being tested on whether you already know a word but on whether you can figure out its meaning by using the words around it as clues.

6. Avoid spending too much time perfectly coloring the dots. One big, deliberate mark is enough.

Finally, many reading lessons address larger issues of reading process: the conscious decisions readers make every day about how, where, and when they'll read. I encourage reading in bed at night as a tranquil way to end the day. I discuss the importance of re-reading good books — how it isn't cheating or a waste of time to return to a favorite. I'm convinced that re-reading is one sign of a good reader, and I'm depressed when I talk to English teachers who can't name a book they've read more than once for pleasure. (In fact, the book English teachers most often name when they have re-read for pleasure is *Gone with the Wind*, the kind of good, trashy read many deny their students.) And I talk about abandoning books. Many of the students who don't like to read when they start eighth grade have never put aside a book they weren't enjoying. They stuck through to the bitter end every time, and they need permission — and a nudge — to abandon books that don't please them. In a mini-lesson I describe my criteria for abandoning a book and ask students to describe theirs. I tell how long I give a book to get good — usually no more than a few pages — and ask students to tell how long they allow. Eighth graders need to know there are too many good books out there waiting to be read to waste time on a book that doesn't satisfy.

At the beginning of this chapter I stressed that the lessons I can teach well are based on what I love of literature and know of my kids' needs as readers. Some students won't trust that there is such a thing as a good book. Their experience of literature is so limited they don't yet know what they like to read. I know that for some a lack of experience with books will have led to a lack of fluency. For them reading will be awkward and slow. Some students will come from homes where reading is as natural as breathing; others will have grown up without books and without adults who love books.

I also know eighth graders' typical strengths as readers and can build on what they already know and do. Most can "decode" with some degree of competence; they don't have to be taught how to read. Most are on the threshold of analytic reading, ready to go beyond plot to deeper meanings. Eighth grade readers, all readers, have an innate desire for meaning. Eighth grade readers are also willing to experiment, and they're still uninhibited enough to be openly enthusiastic when their enthusiasm is warranted. They delight in quality. When they recognize that something is good, they acknowledge it. And they are generous. When something is good, they're more than willing to recommend it to others. In reading lessons teachers can model and celebrate all the qualities of good readers, and more. We can show the happiest lesson of all — how the voice of the good reader interacts with printed texts to create the good book.

ANSWERS TO TEN QUESTIONS

1. The two men didn't play the games with each other. Long term memory supplies an assumption: if two men played chess they are each other's opponents.
2. Moses didn't build the ark. Noah did. Experience as readers tells us to assume that test questions always provide correct information.
3. The date "B.C." couldn't have been used before Christ: how could someone have foreseen the future date of Christ's birth? Our eyes have learned to skim over a commonplace like "B.C." without stopping to consider what it stands for.
4. You'd light the match first. Long term memory automatically fills in the "missing" information that the match is already lit.
5. Survivors cannot be buried. Our experience with printed texts tells us to pay special attention to words in italics, to focus there. The stress on the word *international* shifts focus off the crucial word, survivors.
6. All of them. Here long term memory inserts a word: "only."
7. Nine. Our prior experience with math word problems tells us we should expect to perform an arithmetical computation, in this case, subtraction.
8. Push the cork into the bottle and shake the dime out. Prior knowledge tells us that corks are for pulling out of bottles, not pushing in.
9. He does it in the daytime. Again, long term memory supplies "missing" information.
10. Paris in *the the* Spring. Bird in *the the* hand. Once in *a a* lifetime. Slow men *at at* work. Good readers see a chunk of meaning, not separate words.

Connecting Reading and Writing

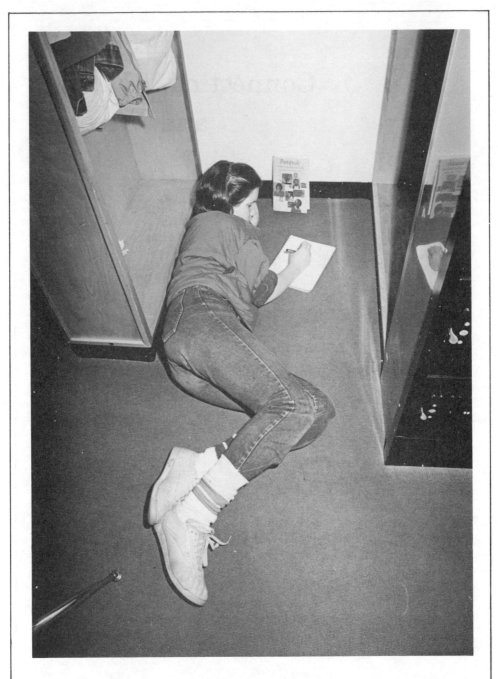
Sybil, the poet and reader of poetry, in reading workshop

CHAPTER 10

Learning to Write
from Other Writers

"The mystique of authorship is removed that children may find the beauty and depth of information contained in literature itself. It is removed that children might learn to think and experience the joys of authorship for themselves."

Donald Graves

Hilary waved her hand at me from her seat at the back of the classroom. I picked up my conference chair and carried it over to her desk. "What's up?" I asked as I settled in.

"Could you edit this for me? I need it for tonight." I asked Hilary what she had and she replied, "It's a poem for my mom and dad for their anniversary. I sort of got the idea from that poem of yours, you know, the one you wrote for your mother."

"I know the one," I responded. "Hilary, have you been borrowing again?" She blushed and laughed. Hilary had been borrowing all year from the best — Robert Wallace, Robert Frost, E. E. Cummings. It was an honor to be included in their company. Hilary read me her poem. She had taken off on the theme of my poem, an apology to my mother for bad times I'd given her as a teenager, and gone well beyond it. My poem came first, but Hilary's was the truer explanation of adolescence. They both appear below.

For Mom

You've always been my mother.
I've always been your daughter.
We're wedded to each other
By birth and blood and time.

And I know that time has changed us,
Tugging our love back and forth.
And I know that I once blamed us
For my wildness, doubts, and tears.

But the tears were part of growing up,
The doubts a part of knowing me,
And the wildness? It was showing up
My mother's ways and love and dreams.

These days, my dreams are all my own.
My ways, more sane, come from my heart.
But I grew to myself through the love you've shown,
My dearest friend and mother.

You've always been my mother.
I've always been your daughter.
We're wedded to each other
By love and dreams and time.

N.A.

*   *   *

We promise according to our hopes,
and perform according to our fears.

LA ROCHEFOUCAULD

Promises

I've made you many promises.
Some, I have not kept.
It's just that some I could not keep.
I'm sorry if you wept.

Some of those, I could not keep.
Some I had to break.
You may not have agreed with me,
But it was my decision to make.

I'm growing up.
I can't stay young.
My adolescent song
Will never go unsung.

So think of me with laughter
When my eyes are filled with tears.
Think of all the fun we've had
Throughout these fourteen years.

I hope you know how I feel.
It's a word I cannot say.
Maybe in time it will come forth
On some unexpected day.

I just want to thank you
For all that you've done—
For adding a daughter
Along to your son.

HILARY SMITH

I never asked Hilary to relate her writing to her reading, nor sponsored exercises calling on kids to make writing-reading connections. It happens naturally, inevitably, in workshop settings. In writing workshop conferences and mini-lessons we talk about what authors do. In reading workshop conferences (the journals) and mini-lessons we talk about what authors do. It doesn't take very long for students to begin to bring knowledge and expertise from one area to the other — to view literacy as both considering and trying what authors do.

In reading workshop students come to look at texts from the inside, from a writer's point of view (Newkirk, 1982, p. 113). They criticize and analyze what they read, suggest revisions, and select and reject. A few days after a September writing conference with me where we talked about her lead, about how to go about grabbing a reader's attention, Heather wrote to me in her reading journal, "I'm trying to decide what book I'll read next, *Gentlehands* or *Solitary Blue.* I'm deciding by reading the leads to see what one grabs me most."

In writing workshop students come to look at their own texts from the outside, from a reader's point of view. They criticize and analyze what they've written, suggest revisions, and select and reject. A few days after a September reading mini-lesson where I read the beginnings of *One Fat Summer, A Ring of Endless Light,* and *That Was Then, This Is Now,* giving kids a taste of Lipsyte, L'Engle, and Hinton, Alan asked me in writing workshop to respond to his lead. He said, "I think my lead is fouled up. It doesn't really attract my attention like the books you read to us. I'm trying to tell too much about the whole camp. Maybe I should just begin with the lecture by the Detroit Pistons' coach. That way people will get some good stuff right from the start, like in *One Fat Summer.*"

Heather brought first-hand knowledge of writing to her reading. Alan adopted and revised another writer's style. And Hilary adopted and revised another writer's intentions. The culture surrounding them provided grist for their literary mills. They knew they could borrow meaning (Blackburn, 1984) to forge their own.

Half-way through the school year, all of Hilary's eighth grade classmates identified themselves as literary borrowers. In January's writing evaluation conferences I asked, "As a writer, do you think you learn from other authors' writing — from what you read?" Every eighth grader said yes. And then each answered my two follow-up questions: "If so, who has influenced your writing? What kinds of things do you do differently in your own writing because of the author(s)?"

Kids named three kinds of literary influences. The professional authors they mentioned included S. E. Hinton, Susan Beth Pfeffer, Francine Pascal, Paula Danziger, Lois Lowry, Frank Bonham, Lois Duncan, Robert Lipsyte, Lloyd Alexander, C. S. Lewis, David Eddings, Madeleine L'Engle, Theodore Taylor, Arthur Roth, Lew Dietz, Wilson Rawls, Jim Kjelgaard, Donald Clayton Porter, Stephen King, Marshall Dodge, Charlie Daniels, Robert Frost, E. E. Cummings, and Theodore Roethke.

They also mentioned other students who had influenced their writing — Julie, Brian, Bean, Arelitsa, Jake, Sabrina, *The BRES Reporter,* previous years' eighth graders whose pieces I'd shared in mini-lessons, and pieces read in group share sessions. They also mentioned me, talking about things they tried to do as writers because I'd tried them and shared my attempts.

In addition, every eighth grader was able to name specific things other authors had inspired them to try. Their borrowings took three forms. Students borrowed genres, trying a new mode after reading another author's writing. They borrowed topics or themes, as Hilary's poem thematically piggybacked on mine. And they borrowed techniques, adopting a new style because of a way another writer had written. In this chapter I'll share pieces of student writing they identified as owing debts to other authors, and explore in turn each of the three kinds of elements students borrowed. Along the way I'll discuss some implications of the connections kids made between their writing and reading.

Borrowing Mode

Amanda came over to where I was sitting in reading workshop, carrying a book. "Have you seen this?" she whispered, and held up a copy of Mary Bolte's *Haunted New England.* I shook my head and asked, "Is it any good?"

"It's pretty good," she replied. "It's all true-to-life ghost stories — real legends and stuff about New England ghosts. She even did the Bucksport foot."

"The what?" I asked.

"It's this gravestone in a cemetery in Bucksport. I saw it last summer. There's the shape of a foot and a calf that appears on the stone, and no matter what they do to remove it, the foot keeps coming back." I wondered what the story was behind the phenomenon, and Amanda said she didn't think there was one. She promised to lend me the book when she'd finished it and returned to her seat. Thirty seconds later she was back.

"I'd like to write a ghost story," she said. "I've never written one, but I'd like to make up a story to explain the Bucksport foot." I said I thought it would be an interesting thing to try, and for the next two weeks Amanda crafted her own legend, "The Tale of the Bucksport Foot."

THE TALE OF THE BUCKSPORT FOOT

"Grandma, please tell us," my sister Emily begged. "You promised!"

"Well . . ." Grandma stopped rocking and looked at Bump with a wondering glance.

"Oh, go ahead," our grandfather stated.

"Oh, neat," Emily said. "It'll be even better with the power out because of the storm. That's always the best time for stories."

We seated ourselves around Grandma and Bumps in front of their big fireplace, munching on apples and readying ourselves to listen to a local legend.

"Well," Grandma started, "your great-great uncle, Harris Buck, had always been great friends with Abigail Abbott and Benjamin Livingston. As children they were always together and could seldom be separated. As they grew up, none of the three ever made other friends; they just stayed together.

"When they were in their early twenties, Benjamin left Bucksport for a year and came back with a new bride, Mary. The foursome spent some time together, but Harris and Abigail, sensing that their friendship with Benjamin was fading, saw more and more of each other. Within a few months, Harris had proposed to Abigail."

Here, Grandma paused in her tale to watch as Bumps put another log on the fire. He caught her eye as he straightened up, and winked. Grandma smiled a small smile, then went on.

"Their engagement dragged on and on, and Harris made no effort to set a marriage date. In fact, after a while he seemed to have lost interest in Abigail, and looked more often to see a new woman in town, Jane Winslow. Abigail took a while in realizing it. Finally, Harris told her he didn't think they should see each other anymore.

"A few months later, in the winter of 1882, Harris hosted a party at his house. Abigail, who hadn't been invited, was walking by his house and heard the music and excitement. She stopped and looked in the window to see dancing couples, platters of food, and Harris — Harris with Jane as his hostess. Without thinking, Abigail barged in. The music stopped as people looked up, amazed.

"'Harris,' Abigail wailed.

"'Abigail, what's the matter? Have you hurt yourself?' Jane rushed to her worriedly.

"'I want to see Harris,' she wailed again.

"'What's the matter?' the shocked Harris asked.

"'Why didn't you invite me?' she questioned, her eyes blazing.

"'Abigail . . .' Harris replied, shrugging his shoulders. 'It's over.'

"'Please,' she begged as he led her to the door.

"'Abigail, listen. It's *over*,' he repeated sternly. As he opened the door, she stepped out.

"'Wait, Harris. Wa . . .' Abigail pleaded, and she put her foot in the door. Harris didn't hear her, or didn't want to hear her. He closed the door on her.

"'Ahhhh!' Abigail screamed. The party-goers gasped as Harris opened the door slowly. Abigail looked at him with furious eyes. Then she slowly cast her eyes down, looked at her partly severed foot and mangled calf, and screamed in pure, pathetic agony.

"'You'll pay, Harris Buck,' she managed to get out in vehement screams. 'God help me, you'll have to pay for this for the rest of your life, and . . . and . . .' Abigail laughed a terrifying laugh and stumbled into the shadows.

"Well," Grandma sighed. "Everyone was soon enough leaving that party, plainly dispirited. They told Harris not to worry about things, but of course he did.

"In ten days, Abigail Abbott was dead. She had gotten a severe infection in her leg. After that, Harris didn't seem to be himself. He was desolate and watchful. Finally, he confided in Benjamin. Harris had been having horrifying nightmares and the grim feeling that someone was ceaselessly watching him.

"And so, as the months wore on, Harris became heavy-hearted and suspicious. He seemed to be receding into a shell. No one saw him but Benjamin. Benjamin took care of his food and firewood for a time, until the day came that Harris wouldn't open the door for even Benjamin.

"One year after the party, Benjamin had a strange feeling something was wrong, and stopped to see Harris. Benjamin opened the gate and walked up the flagstone walk. When he got to the door, he had a strong urge to look down. His eyes glanced down at the piercing whiteness of the untouched snow — untouched that is, except for one bloody footprint. Benjamin was seized with panic and in horror flung open the door and looked into the dimness. He took a step forward and tripped. Looking down to see what had caused him to lose his balance, he saw Harris, dead, his eyes wide open as if he were seeing something more horrendously terrifying than anyone had ever witnessed. And all around him were bloody footprints."

Emily shivered and bit into her apple. I came and knelt close to Grandma's chair. She put her arm around me and came to the end of her tale.

"Harris was buried, of course, but not before they found out what had killed him: heart failure.

"The next day the town was in a frantic commotion. There was an imprint of a human foot and calf on Harris' six-foot-high gravestone. The footprint looked etched in. Benjamin tried to wash it off, but after hours of scrubbing it had faded only a bit.

"The next day, however, the foot was as dark as ever. People tried to sand it off Harris' gravestone. Sometimes the foot seemed to come off but it was always there, the next morning, dark as ever."

Here, Grandma leaned back and looked at Emily and me expectantly.

"Wow!" Emily said. "That's *weird.*"

"Have they got the foot's imprint off yet?" I wondered aloud.

"They have, several times, in the last ten years or so. In fact, they've even put up a *new* gravestone. But the foot continues to come back."

"If you girls want, I'll take you down to see old Buck's grave," Bumps offered, with a twinkle in his eye.

Emily and I looked at each other. Then I looked past her out the window, into the dark storm. My eyes met hers and we shivered simultaneously.

"Maybe some other time, Bump," Emily managed to get out, before she shivered again.

AMANDA CRAFTS

Amanda borrowed a few facts from Mary Bolte's account of the gravestone in Bucksport, Maine, and she borrowed a new genre, a ghost story. She is one of numbers of eighth graders who each year write a kind of writing they've read. Julie wrote poetry because she read Kelli's poems. Billy wrote fantasy/adventure stories because he read Lloyd Alexander and C. S. Lewis. Brendan's writing was affected by his friend Bean's: "Bean's humor and stuff really influenced me. I'm writing a lot of satire and parody now because of him." Carol and Luanne wrote a fifteen-page short story, their first fiction, that owed much to novelist Paula Danziger's breezy, first-person style. Their "Weekend Romance" made the rounds of just about every teen magazine in America and garnered just as many rejection slips. It began:

WEEKEND ROMANCE

Luanne Bradley and Carol Creaser

"Mandy! Mandy! Over here!" I could see my cousin, her blonde hair shining, approaching among the crowd waiting to board the next plane.

"Cheylenne! It's so good to see you!" she squealed as she made her way through the mob. We hugged and I asked her where Aunt Donna was.

"She's out in the car. Oh, this is going to be such an excellent weekend. They aren't even going to be home for the party. Isn't that great?"

"Wild! Now, how about my luggage?" Mandy grabbed my elbow and steered me toward the baggage area. "So tell me more about this gorgeous Russ Dalton you've been going with, huh?" I had my eyes glued to the rollers that conveyed the luggage. My mother had warned me about guys who steal people's bags. Sometimes I think my mom is kind of paranoid.

"In detail?" Mandy asked.

"In total detail." I was getting very nervous about my stuff.

"Oh! He's tall, muscular, sweet, blue-eyed, se-----."

"There it is!"

"What? What?" Mandy looked around wildly.

"My luggage!" I laughed nervously. I hoped that I didn't sound too re-lieved, because she might start assuming I was the overly-cautious type. I had four bags. I knew it was a little much, but I never knew what to expect at one of my cousin's parties. Between the two of us we managed to drag them through the airport parking lot to Mandy's family's big station wagon.

"What took you two so long?" My aunt looked annoyed with us. (Wait'll she sees the house on Sunday, I thought to myself.) "Oh, I'm sorry Cheylenne. It's just that Mandy can be so darned slow sometimes when I'm in a rush. So, how have you been?"

"Okay, I guess."

"Good. And Nancy?" (That's my mom.)

"Fine, fine."

"Good. Mandy, put those in the back seat. And off we go!"

As the car lurched off onto the road, a 747 was landing. Or was it a DC-107? A 727? Who cares? All I knew was that this was going to be one heck of a weekend.

My aunt, uncle, and cousin's house always had this cottage smell to it. I've noticed it ever since I was little. They live on Penopee Lake, in New

Jersey. I live in New York, and my mother had absolutely insisted that I go by plane. I'd suggested the bus and she nearly went out of her head. She thinks a bus gets hijacked every time it leaves the station.

My aunt flopped on the couch and sighed, "Mandy, take the bags up to your room. Cheylenne can unpack later, after I leave. Oh, and would you mind bringing my luggage down while you're up there?" Mandy put her arms out like a robot and headed toward the stairs. I laughed and asked Aunt Donna when she was leaving.

"Whenever your better-late-than-never uncle gets home. He must be caught up in the traffic."

"So, are you going to be at the cottage for the whole weekend?" I asked.

"Yes, we plan to. The mountains in Vermont are so beautiful this time of year."

"I hope you two have fun."

"Yes, I'm sure we will. And thank you for keeping Mandy company while we're gone."

I saw Mandy coming down the stairs with two suitcases. I noticed that she had changed into designer jeans and a light blue blouse. The blouse really brought out the color of her eyes. She looked good. But for what? I knew something was up, so I asked, "Where are you going?"

"Oh! Didn't I tell you? We're going on a double date. And of course, you don't know him, but you will. Don't worry. He's really nice. And Mom . . . we'll come home right after the movie. They won't stay long . . . and you and Dad have a good weekend."

"Wait a second! Movies? A blind date? What is this anyway?" I was upset. Who was Mandy to make my decisions for me? Before Mandy could respond to my questions, Aunt Donna asked us if we wanted something to eat. And again Mandy answered for me.

"No thanks, Mom. We're probably going to stop and get hamburgers at Joe's. Well? Cheylenne, why don't you go upstairs and get ready?"

Suzy and Hilary also collaborated as writers, with each other and with Down East humorist Marshall Dodge. After a series of tall tale mini-lessons in reading workshop, they wrote "Moose Alert" together in writing workshop, and credited Dodge with inspiring the piece.

MOOSE ALERT

I were a clammin' down by the shore one day. When I was bent over, two feet spread, I looked out an' saw the fog a rollin' in as fast as you could blink. I picked up my hoe and stuck it in my clam hod, to join my winnin' total of one clam.

Well, I set off a hoppin' and a skippin' toward home. The fog were a gettin' thick as molasses, and' gettin' thicka still.

I'd been walkin' for quite some time now. I stopped, thinkin' I'd heard somethin'. Then I hears . . . Mmrr!

Right then, I knew I'd met up with a moose! The hair on my head were standin' straight as a needle. I started a prayin' as I were a walkin' down the path towards home. I knew for sure that ole moose was gonna get me.

As I were walkin', I noticed the ole moose were a followin' me. I felt some glad when I saw a dim light up ahead. Home.

"Martha," I yelled. "Git my shotgun! I got a moose out here!"

Martha handed me my shotgun.

I turned around, aiming the gun carefully so as to have to use only one shot to kill it. That there moose looked even bigga now that the fog was slowly liftin'. I'd just put my finger on the trigga when a strong breeze came up, an' the last of the fog lifted.

And there stood my best milker Bessie, with a look on her face I'll never forget.

SUZY MADDOCKS and HILARY SMITH

In our January evaluation conference, when I asked B.J. who his literary influence was, he said, "You, mostly. That piece you wrote based on living with your grandfather? Where you did it third person as a short story? I'm trying that now. I'm taking something that happened to me when I was a kid and fictionalizing it, doing it about a boy without any name, like yours. But I've got an S. E. Hinton lead and conclusion, like in *The Outsiders*. You'll see what I mean."

I did. Here are my story and B.J.'s. His won first prize in a short story competition sponsored by *The Coastal Journal*. In it, as Hinton did in *The Outsiders*, B.J. brings his piece full circle. The end of the piece repeats the beginning, except for one lovely line.

MAG'S HOUSE

She moved into her grandfather's house when her grandmother died. His children, floundering in their grief over Mag's death, put off decisions about more permanent arrangements. So she left her parents' house, her room, her pictures and old toys, her souvenirs and narrow bed. She slept at his house now in the big bed in the front bedroom, and woke at seven every morning to make breakfast for the old man she didn't know.

He was lame and couldn't hear well; could especially not hear her. He was too vain to wear his hearing aid. She was too afraid of him to shout, so she hardly spoke at all. She lived with him because she loved him. She loved him because he was Mag's husband.

The house they lived in smelled like Mag. Her plants were dying in the window boxes, and the kitchen curtains still hung rigid with starch from her iron. The drawers where the girl kept her clothes held tiny mesh bags of lilac sachet. Crochetted antimacassars covered the backs and arms of the stuffed chairs and davenport. They never talked about her grandmother.

She had stayed here before. In those days, Mag's guest, she slept on the davenport, and her grandmother always eased the awkwardness between the bad mannered old man and his granddaughter — between the bad mannered old man and everyone. Now the girl spent her time trying not to displease him. His frozen blue eyes, always on her, were as critical of her as the rest of the world. However much she grew he always seemed forbiddingly big.

He spent most of his day in a chair by the kitchen window, watching the road and the field beyond it. At four o'clock, a cane in each hand, he made his slow way to the pigeon coop. He scooped and mixed grains then fed and watered, whistling and cooing at his racers the whole time. Then he settled on an old canvas folding chair in the corner of the coop, checked birds' band numbers, and made rows of precise germanic marks in his record books.

By six o'clock he was back at his place in the dusky kitchen and she was cooking his dinner. She ran his kitchen with clumsy fingers and heavy breathing. While he waited for his food he watched her, his huge hands folding and unfolding themselves in his lap. When it came time to eat even he seemed to feel the strain as they faced each other across the table with nothing to say except, "Would you like anything more? Grampa,WOULD YOU LIKE ANYTHING MORE?"

She learned to eat quickly and to pretend fascination with the food on her plate and the view from the kitchen window. She longed to read but didn't dare. When she thought he was finished she cleared the table and poured tea that was always too weak. The rest of the night they looked at television, the set turned to a volume that rattled plates.

The fourth week a package came for him in the afternoon mail. She carried its weight with both hands across the street and up the driveway, knowing he'd be watching every step. He was at the kitchen table, ready with his letter opener, when she came in. Her eyes still smarting from the October wind, she watched him cut each string, set it aside, and unwrap layers of brown paper. Finally he lifted the lid off the box.

Inside lay a trophy bigger than any of the others, topped with the brass-plated figure of a pigeon. Beneath was a plaque engraved with his name, the name of the race, and the name of the bird. Mag.

"Oh, Grampa," she said, her voice whining in her ears. "That's really pretty."

The look that passed over her as he turned to hide his eyes held no love — not even recognition. The look said, "Who are you? What are you doing here?" Then he pushed himself to his feet with his canes, set the trophy on top of the refrigerator, and slumped against it, his face pressed against the cool enamel.

"She's dead," he cried. "Mag's dead. Mag's dead. Mag's dead."

N.A.

A NEW BEGINNING

He had to move; he didn't have any other choice. He had to make new friends in a strange place. He had to live with his father; he had to start all over again: new school, new friends, new life.

Why did he have to make this change? Why? He couldn't understand it. He had friends. He had a school. He had a bike like everyone else's. What was wrong with him? But then, lying there in his bed in his small, dark room, he remembered. He'd had a bad fight with his mother the night before. It was to the point where he couldn't live with, eat with, dream or even think of his mother anymore. He had told her he wanted to live with his father.

Thinking about this he walked outside, feeling numb all over and cold. He walked up the worn, familiar trail to the house of Joe, his best friend. At the bottom of Joe's steps he asked himself, "What will it be like with no best friend?" He started up the steps and knocked on the door. Fran, one of Joe's older sisters, came to the door and yelled, "Joe, your queer friend is here!"

"Shut up, Fran," he screamed at her.

"Shut up, yourself," she screamed back.

"Can't argue with that," he thought with respect.

Joe finally came outside, looking kind of pale. "What the heck's your problem, man? I told you on the phone I was sick!"

"I know, I know, but I've gotta talk to ya."

"All right," he said. "What about?"

"Well, see, I'm going to be moving to live with my father tomorrow."

"How come?"

"Had a bad fight with my mom last night."

"What about?"

"Good question. I don't even know myself."

"Well, let's talk about it over an ice cream and a couple of video games," Joe said.

"You're on," he replied.

An hour and a half later he was back in his house, lounging on the couch watching "Adam-12." "Dinner's ready," his mom said in a tired voice. He knew he should've let it go right then and there, but he didn't.

"I'll be there when I'm ready," he said in a sarcastic voice.

Then it happened: his mom broke down and started crying. "Why can't you just do what you're asked?" Those were the last words they spoke to each other through dinner and the rest of the evening. After watching a couple of shows he walked to his room to pack. Then he got some milk and a couple of Oreos and called Joe.

"Just called to say good-bye," he said when Joe finally reached the phone.

"Yeah, well, the best way to do it is fast and at the same time."

"Bye!"

"Bye!" they said simultaneously.

All he heard was the dial tone. He hung up and went to bed.

He woke up early the next morning, loaded his stuff in the car, and took one good, last look at the house. Boy, I'm going to miss this place, he thought to himself. He'd lived on the island his whole life. It was the only home he knew.

His mom got in without a word, then drove down to the car ferry, paid the deck-hand, and drove on. "I don't dare say anything to mom," he thought. "What if I say the wrong thing?" They finally docked in Portland and he rode down one of the waterfront alleys to the main street, then onto the highway.

"I think you'll like it staying with your father," his mom said cheerfully, breaking the silence.

"It all depends," he replied. "What if . . . what if I don't make any new friends?" he asked worriedly. And with that, he fell asleep.

He woke up, startled, as the worn tires ran upon the rocky dirt driveway.

"Are we here?" he asked, looking around.

"Yes, we are."

"Oh. What time is it?" he asked.

"Three o'clock," she replied.

"Mom," he said hesitantly, "I still love you, you know."

"I love you, too," she answered. "But . . ."

She didn't finish. Just then they looked up to see his father with a smile on his face that stretched from ear to ear. He waved eagerly at his dad.

"So," his dad said as they got out, "how was the trip up here?"

"Pretty good," his mom replied.

"Well, let's get unpacked," his dad urged.

When they had finally removed all the boxes of his belongings to his new room, his mom gave his arm a squeeze. "Well, son," she said, "I've got to be going now."

"Okay," he replied. He gave her a kiss on the cheek and said goodbye. Then his mom got in her car and drove up the curvy, narrow drive. He watched her car until it disappeared.

"Well," his dad said, "after you get your room squared away, we'll put up the new basketball hoop I just bought."

"Hey, great!" he replied enthusiastically, and ran to his room to start putting his things away. When he'd finished, he walked outside to find his father.

"Dad? Dad?"

"Rahh!" He came up behind the boy and gave him the biggest hug he'd ever had. "Wow! You're heavy," his father said jokingly, pretending to gasp for breath.

"No, I'm not!" he laughed. "Can we put up the new basketball hoop?"

"Sure. Let's go do it now."

"All right."

After an hour or so they had the rim up and were about to fasten the net. "Can we shoot a round after we get the net up?" he asked.

"Sure thing," his dad agreed.

Once the net was attached, he ran to get the basketball. He came back, shot, and missed. That was the beginning of a two-hour period of shooting baskets. Finally they were so tired they both sat down and took a rest.

"What time does the bus come by this way in the morning?" he asked in a tired voice, idly twirling the ball between his palms.

"About . . . um . . . say, uh, how about you just go up there at about twenty after seven, just to be safe?" his dad replied.

"Sure thing," he said, repeating the line his father had used. It was getting dark so he threw the basketball into the garage and went into the house for supper. He finished eating quickly, then reported he was going to bed in order to get an early rise.

"Goodnight!" his dad said.

"Goodnight."

He couldn't get to sleep that night he was so full of thoughts. He'd had to move; he hadn't had any other choice. He had to make new friends in a strange place. He had to live with his father; he had to start all over again: new school, new friends, new life.

He was scared. He was excited. Finally, he was asleep.

B.J. SHERMAN

These diverse pieces of writing show how readers internalize the conventions and structures of particular literary forms. Their knowledge of genre is more subtle and more accurate than the definitions and distinctions I used to make kids memorize. I remember asking students to graph the short stories in the literature anthology, each work rising to its inevitable "climax or highpoint of the action," and then to create their own short stories with similar "rising action" and "falling action." I remember writing on the blackboard "the characteristics of a novel" — I think there were six — and testing kids on my simplistic formulations: every novel has a setting: the time and place of the action. My dictums were no substitute for first-hand knowledge of genre, of how different kinds of writing work for writers and for readers.

These diverse pieces also have in common the literary environment in which they were written. In mini-lessons, conferences, the pages of their reading journals, our class magazines, and on the shelves of the classroom library, I teach about genre every day. The modes available to writers become evident through pointed demonstrations, nudges, and the good variety of literature available to eighth graders in their classroom.

Borrowing Topic and Theme

Lance's most serious problem as a writer was coming up with topics. He was often stumped and abandoned many pieces of writing because he didn't care enough about the subjects he chose. When he did find a subject he cared about, most often it was borrowed from a friend. That is, Lance listened hard to pieces read in conferences and group share. He listened in order to respond — he was a helpful, specific responder — but also to discover what sense he might be able to make for himself of the other writer's subject. On at least two occasions that he identified Lance borrowed from me after responding to my writing. He borrowed the idea of writing a serious piece about his grandfather from my piece "Mag's House." Like B.J., he took just what he needed, then created something entirely his own. Lance wrote "Sad and Solemn" for his grandfather for Father's Day.

Sad and Solemn

Sad and solemn the man walks up to me, reminding me of the past, what happened, where it has all gone. But that was the story of his whole life. He's always been like that. With a physically weak self but a strong heart he keeps on top of things, always on the go and never really slowing down.

Having the experience of six years in the Army, he knows most everything. And I'm proud of him for that. He lives by himself in an apartment. I stay with him sometimes. I don't want him to just waste away.

Now that his wife is dead, things have changed for him. Really changed. I feel badly for him at times. I want to go up and tell him that but . . . I can't. He's too sensitive to hear it. He walks around talking to himself now, telling me, "She was a good woman, a *real* good woman," and then he starts to cry.

"It'll be all right," I say back. Even though he can't hear too well, he knows what I am thinking, and he knows that I care for him a lot.

Sad and solemn the man walks up to me with tears in his eyes and says, "You're my grandson and you'll always be my grandson," and he hugs me.

LANCE DADALEARES

On another occasion Lance borrowed from me long after he was my student. When he was still in eighth grade much of the poetry I shared, including my poem "Death Cup," made Lance angry. He didn't like ambiguity. He especially didn't like peeling away layers of onion. Lance had to "get" a poem on the first reading, and he did not get "Death Cup." "So what are these death cups?" he said. "What do you mean by deadly umbrellas? Who are the strangers in cars, anyway?"

Death Cup

When I was
small,
poison toadstools grew along the creek banks —
little deadly umbrellas.
One of our dangerous games
was touching them —
one finger gently prodding a toadcap on a dare.
We knew about them from our mothers,
like we knew about
yellow jackets and matches,
strange dogs,
and strangers in cars.

Well, I grew
but the death cups grew, too —
big, deadly umbrellas now,
in clouds of color
nature has never seen.
These colors charge the air.
They burn.

Strangers in cars own the world now.
Each sits,
one finger gently prodding a button,
and says
Dare you,
dare you.

N.A.

A year later Lance walked over from the high school one afternoon for a quick visit. He said, "You know that poem of yours, about the mushrooms?"

It took me a minute. "Yes. What about it?"

"I finally figured it out. It's about nuclear war and mushroom clouds, about how the world should be a safe place once you're an adult, and it isn't," he explained. I agreed that was one of the themes. Lance took a folded piece of paper from his pocket and put it on my desk. "Read this," he instructed. "It's my poem about nuclear war. I got the idea from you."

A Leaf Then Falls

The moon shone dimly.
The sun would barely rise.
The day's air rose repulsive
Toward the radical skies.

A second passes.
The earth revolves.
Minutes strewn forth.
A leaf then falls.

The streets are vacant.
People head for shelter.
The anarchy and mess —
All is helter-skelter.

An hour passes.
The earth revolves.
Days strewn forth.
A leaf then falls.

The city begins to tremble.
Mushrooms all around.
The shock from the blast
Leaves craters in the ground.

A week passes.
The earth revolves.
Months strewn forth.
A leaf then falls.

Fires engulf the earth.
The city remains to shake.
The tragedy is endless.
Quake gives off to quake.

A month passes.
The earth revolves.
Years strewn forth.
And no leaves fall.

The moon shone dimly.
The sun would barely rise.
The tears had long subsided
In man's forgotten eyes.

LANCE DADALEARES

Reading "Death Cup" and "A Leaf Then Falls," or "Mag's House" and "Sad and Solemn" without any background, one might be hard put to see the direct relationship Lance claims. The connections are in his head — for instance, the thinking he did over many months about my poem, about the possibility of nuclear holocaust, and about ways to shape his thoughts as poetry. In fact many of the connections kids described between what they read and wrote were so subtle and internalized I would never have recognized them without students' help. But anyone who is a reader knows how words and ideas from reading reverberate in our memories long after a book is shelved. When we are also writers, the retrieval of words and ideas is an integral part of the process of making our own meanings.

I think it's important to understand that in retrieving and borrowing, Lance isn't imitating or plagiarizing. Everyone who writes anything is a borrower because everything we've ever read comes into play when we write. We can't write without appropriating ideas, frameworks, rhythms, traditions, concepts, and formulas from our literary heritage. The nature of this heritage is the real issue for teachers and students. The wider the range of resources and models, the richer the heritage. And the greater students' sense of ownership of their reading, the more apt they are to tap into the heritage. Students who seldom read for pleasure, seldom choose their own books, or seldom encounter texts that capture their imaginations or satisfy their needs, will not become literary borrowers. Elementary school students who read only the voiceless committee prose of basals don't borrow, nor do secondary school students who read only the prescribed canon of anthologized "classics." It is what captivates students as readers that inspires writing.

At the local high school, freshmen write occasional book reports. One English teacher tells them they may choose to report on any book they would like to read "just as long as it's not by that S. E. Hinton." The teacher knows that students love Hinton and that many would choose Hinton if they could. She does not consider Hinton to be Literature. The poet X. J. Kennedy recently said, "I would define literature generously, as memorable writing of any sort" (1984). For many of Boothbay's adolescents, S. E. Hinton is as memorable as they come. It's easy and safe for teachers to scoff at Hinton's novels and her fans, but she is important to adolescent readers because they love her writing. Kids who otherwise might never know they like to read, like Hinton. She is just as important to adolescent writers; they too love her writing. Hinton is the most influential of all the authors my kids read in eighth grade. Part of it is the identification they feel with her: she wrote *The Outsiders* when she was fifteen years old to protest the unhappy social situation in her home town. Part of it is Hinton's style: the narrative voice of *The Outsiders* is honest and compelling. The rest of it is her characters. My students empathize with the boys from the wrong side of the tracks and the themes they embody. They are captivated as readers and inspired as writers. The richness and diversity of their inspirations should dispel any teacher's qualms about "that S. E. Hinton."

Earlier in this chapter I shared the way B.J. borrowed Hinton's identical lead and conclusion device for his short story "A New Beginning." Many eighth graders tried the same effect in many different kinds of writing — essays, poetry, other kinds of narratives. For some writers it was their first satisfying finish to a piece of their writing, the first time a piece concluded rather than simply stopping when the writer ran out of things to say. And from there they were able to go after other kinds of concluding effects. Because of Hinton they recognized how readers respond to good endings and began to create their own.

Hinton also inspired eighth graders' topics. After reading *The Outsiders* Damon wrote a short story decrying urban violence. Daniel wrote a series of personal experience narratives about his adventures with his friends Tyler and Gary, Hintonesque stories about boys on their own without adults, loyal to each other, told with humor and lyricism. Rhonda wrote an essay about the dangers of stereotyping kids because of where they live and what they wear. Rachel wrote her poem "The Big Crash" from the perspective of Dally Winston, the character in *The Outsiders* most on the outside of society. Rachel remembered from a mini-lesson discussion how logic prevents a narra-

tor from describing his own death; she switches to a third-person epilogue in
the nick of time.

The Big Crash

Walking into the store,
I knew I was gonna blow.
I just couldn't take it anymore.
Everything was going slow.

The time hadn't changed.
The town hadn't changed.
Nothing had changed.

The salesman made me angry —
I just couldn't take it.
He asked me if I was going to buy anything —
I just couldn't fake it.

The time hadn't changed.
The town hadn't changed.
Nothing had changed.

"Give me the money," I yelled.
"Give me the money!" I yelled with all my might.
The heater wasn't loaded,
But the man, that guy felt fright.

I headed for the door,
His money in my hand.
The salesman shot three shots.
I felt a sharp pain . . . but I ran.

I dropped a coin in the phone and dialed.
"Can you meet me in the park?"
The voice on the other end said, "Sure — just a while."
Then everyone ran through the dark.

Epilogue

The cops were behind him —
Chasing him, following him.
He ran to the streetlight
And hauled his heater from his belt.

"You'll never get me alive!" he yelled.
And then six shots were fired.
All was quiet except for the cries
Of the boys – his friends.

He was ready for the big crash.

RACHEL BARTER

Tara's experience with *The Outsiders* was like my own with *A Wrinkle in Time* back in the sixth grade. When she read Hinton, Tara became aware of literary theme for the first time in her career as a reader, and she started to look for and consider ideas in all of her reading. She said, "I just realized I'm starting to like books with points, books that make me think, that have meaning." In her writing, Tara began to try to capture ideas, "to not just tell the facts but to make other people stop and think about things when they read my stories like I did when I read S. E. Hinton." Tara's personal experience narrative "Beautiful Mountains," written just after she finished *The Outsiders*, was the first of her themed compositions and the first piece of her own writing she considered a success.

Beautiful Mountains

"This is so fun, and it's beautiful!" was all I could think as Justine and I skied down Lower Winter's Way. We were at Sugarloaf, and this was our first run down. Justine was a little ways ahead of me, but I was too involved in making sure I didn't fall to watch her. This entire slope was covered with moguls so I had to pay attention. Every so often we would stop to look around, It really was beautiful! There were mountains all around. and the trees were so weighted down with snow most were bent over. The mountains were bluish with lots of white patches. There were clouds covering the peaks. I had never seen anything that looked like this, so as we skied down, my mind was filled with beautiful pictures.

All of a sudden, Justine's voice interrupted my thoughts. "Tara!" she yelled in a horrified voice. "Look!" My eyes focused on where she was pointing. Two ski patrolmen were dragging a rescue sled about fifteen feet away from us. The only part of the person that we could see was the face. It was a woman; she reminded me of a mannequin. Her eyes were closed, and even though I've never seen a dead person, that is what I think one would look like. She had fair skin, but underneath it was very dark. She looked so cold. She also looked like she was in pain — tensed up, I guess . . . dead; that's the best word to describe how she looked.

The sled passed by in a matter of seconds, but it was long enough to get a picture of her fixed in my mind. I looked again at the once-beautiful mountains. All I could see was her. I'll never know if she was dead, but beautiful mountains will never look the same.

TARA KELLER

As I've noted earlier, Hinton's *The Outsiders* includes the Frost poem "Nothing Gold Can Stay." The poem, via the book, is the beginning of many kids' love affair with Frost. They understand it in the context of the novel (see Jane and Arelitsa's correspondence, Chapter 8) and take off from it to create their own meditations on innocence, maturity, and change.

Autumn Tears

Bony fingers reach for blue sky
Where once stood pine trees, dark and green,
Their wisdom vanished with the leaves.
The clock ticks on, or so it seems.

The ground is warmed now by a blanket of leaves,
And the birds have stopped their song.
Darkness covers where once buds bloomed.
Days grow short and faces long.

Sitting alone by my window to the world
Thinking of days gone past
I dream of the future and the coming of spring,
And wish that everything could last.

ALICE GILCHRIST

Dawn

The lake sparkled
in the light of the moon.
Dawn was near —
it would be soon.
The clouds gave off a goldish light
And broke the silence of the night.

Now the dawn has come to be noon,
just like life — all too soon.

BILL SNOW

Beyond the Light

The sunset is so lovely,
    with its warm colors and bright glow.
I could sit and stare for hours
    at the elegant sight.
Then I shiver
    as a cold breeze blows —
to warn me of the darkness
    and to warn me of the night.

DEDE REED

Finally, "Nothing Gold Can Stay," via S. E. Hinton, inspired B.J., too, but as a parodist. His version is faithful to the rhythms of the original but shows off B.J.'s smart-aleck, adolescent wit.

Nothing Dull Can Stay (I Hope)

School's first day is dull.
Teachers' talk rings in your skull.
Homework makes you sour,
But only so an hour.
Then class subsides to class.
You know you'll never pass.
The bell rings down the day.
Nothing dull can stay.

B.J. SHERMAN

Another major topic borrowed by eighth graders was sports, especially poems about basketball. At the start of basketball season, I read a series of poems about athletes and athletics. Kids were floored. "Can you do this?" Scott asked. "Can you write poems about sports?" They didn't know poets wrote about things important in kids' lives. Immediately there was a flurry of basketball poems. Jenny borrowed from Edwin Hooey's "Foul Shot," about a one-pointer that eventually, dramatically makes it. In her poem she described one of her own recent trips to the foul line.

The Game Point

She stands silently behind the line.
The referee hands her the ball and says,
"You've got one shot, shooter,"
then stands behind her
waiting patiently for her to shoot.
She dribbles once,
then twice.
She stands there praying silently
that she will make this shot.
She hears the other team's fans' screams
but pays no attention.
She lifts the ball
and places it in line with the basket
and shoots with all her strength.
The ball hits the rim,
and just when she thinks
it's going in . . .
it wobbles out.

JENNY GILES

The next year I added Jenny's poem and a few others by students to the sports poems I shared in mini-lessons. This time around Luanne borrowed basketball as a topic from Edwin Hooey, John Updike, and Jenny Giles. She also picked up on the way Jenny had grounded the piece in an incident from her own experience — Lu was on vacation and in the middle of a basketball tournament, and the first draft of her poem arrived at my house in the mail. She had borrowed from Updike a simile from his description of the "Ex-Basketball Player" whose hands were "like wild birds."

The Turnover

I was going for a lay-up
as I remember it;

the brown leathered ball
under my hands,
through half-court
and down toward the middle.

When suddenly the rhythm

stopped.

A hand came down
in place of mine —
like a bird doing
a wild dive:

Just empty space
between my hands
and the floor.

I stood there
wondering where I'd gone wrong.

when I looked up to see
two more points
added to the other side's score.

LUANNE BRADLEY

From the sports poems I learned another lesson about the kind of writing that captivates readers and inspires writing. It's necessary to expose kids to good writing: that is understood. But if they're to be touched, to become borrowers, it's crucial that the good writing be about topics important to them. One of the ways we can facilitate students' learning from other writers is by introducing well-crafted pieces they will care enough about to internalize as models.

Luanne's inducement to borrow from Pete Seeger was motivated by a different impulse: need. One morning after the mini-lesson she called me over to her desk. "Are there any writing contests going on right now that you know about?" she wanted to know. "I need some money wicked bad."

"What's up?" I asked.

"There are these Calvin Klein jeans I want that my mother won't buy for me. They are so excellent. I need, like, thirty dollars. I thought maybe I could enter some writing contests."

"Well," I answered, "there's a land preservation group that's sponsoring an essay contest. I just got the announcement the other day. First prize is fifty dollars. Are you interested?"

"Sure," Luanne said. The contest rubric asked students to explain why it is important for humans to maintain the balance between our needs and those of nature. Luanne hadn't given this subject a lot of thought prior to her obsession with Calvin Klein. Now she began to read essays like a demon since she had never before written one, to brainstorm arguments, and to talk with others about environmental issues. One of the others was Anne Blaney, an assistant in the school's reading lab. She gave Luanne the lyrics of the Pete Seeger song, "My Rainbow Race," and Luanne had her theme, borrowed from Seeger. A few weeks later she also had her Calvin Klein's.

> One blue sky above us,
> One ocean lapping at our shore.
> One earth so great and round,
> Who could ask for anything more?
> And because I love you,
> I'll give you one more try —
> To show my rainbow race
> That it's too soon to die.
>
> PETE SEEGER

We and Our Earth

It is too soon to die. If we humans fail to keep a balance between our needs and the needs of the natural world, our great, round Earth will no longer be fit to live on.

I can think of many reasons for maintaining this balance.

For one, if we continue to over-fish the seas, certain species will disappear. The kinds of fish that we humans catch feed on smaller ones, and if all these predators disappear, the smaller fish will overwhelm the seas. Edible fish — as well as many fishermen's livelihoods — will disappear.

And if we continue to clear land, cutting down trees at the rate we are now, there will someday be no lumber left to heat people's homes or to build new ones.

The animals will suffer from a disturbance of this balance, too. They use the trees as a food source and for shelter. If we don't maintain this natural resource, they will die and eventually become extinct.

Since we Mainers love the beauty and grace of deer and moose running in our woods, protection against over-hunting is also a must. If hunters break our laws and kill animals when it is not time, then these species won't be there anymore — for beauty or hunting.

Finally, if man keeps polluting and littering the waters — fresh and salt — nonbiodegradable substances will build up and make the water unfit to support marine life. Again, many people who make their living from the sea will no longer be able to.

Reservoirs would become clogged with so many scientifically named diseases that we would not have access to clear, fresh, drinking water. No longer would the beaches be crowded with children in the summers. No parent would want his or her children to catch something dreadfully harmful from the water, and one of our pleasures of coastal living would be gone.

Most of all, we need this balance to maintain the beauty of our world for ourselves and for our children and grandchildren. For if that beauty vanishes, everything man can hope to accomplish will be lost forever.

LUANNE BRADLEY

Ideas regularly spread like wildfire through the classroom, as students borrow topics and themes from each other. One winter Claire and Arelitsa began writing stories about things they did as little children. When they shared their memories in group meetings they opened a floodgate of associations among their classmates. Tom remembered driving his mother's car in the driveway and the resulting maternal panic. Julie heard Tom's piece and wrote about a time when she was five and she and a friend had almost been hit by a car. Luanne heard Julie's piece and wrote about a time her mother had left her to wait in their car with its engine idling and Lu had sat paralyzed with fear, convinced the car was going to blow up. Carol responded to Luanne's story one day after school when they were sitting around in Lu's bedroom, and they got to talking about other early memories. This was the genesis of Carol's "Remembering When."

Remembering When

"Remember how dumb we used to be when we were little?" I said to Luanne, deep in thought. And my mind left Luanne's bedroom and drifted back in time as I began to remember one of my childhood memories . . .

*   *   *   *   *

"Mommy, where did they go?" I asked, nearly in tears as I sat in front of the dead-looking television screen.

"Where did what go?" my mom asked, bending down to see what the problem was.

"You know what I'm talking about!" I said, beginning to get angry.

"Carol, please tell me what you're yelling about!"

I began walking around the T.V., peering into the grids in the back, and putting my ear up to them, listening.

"Is there something wrong with the T.V.?" my mom asked. "We can get it fixed so that you can watch 'Sesame Street,'" she said in a know-it-all tone.

"No, no, no! Where are the television people, mommy?" I yelled. "Did they die?"

"The television people?" my mom asked, totally confused.

"The people that do 'Sesame Street' and 'Mr. Rogers!'" I said, glaring at her. "Did you sweep them up?" I asked anxiously.

"Carol," my mom said laughing, "there are no television people."

"Yes, there are! I know it!" I replied, pulling myself to the fullest height my body would allow. Inside I was hurt that she was laughing at me.

"We get those people on the screen from the television station," my mom said, resuming her know-it-all tone — but also explaining as best as she could to a three-year-old daughter who thought actors and actresses lived in the television set.

"Open it up," I said, pointing to the casing of the T.V.

"All right, all right. If this is the only way to convince you." My mom got a screwdriver and began prying off the back of the television. When it was entirely open I looked in and, to my great disappointment, there was only a mass of wires — no little people running around getting ready for their next show or just sitting around talking.

*   *   *   *   *

"You really believed people lived in the T.V.?" Luanne asked in amazement, pulling me back to the present.

"Yeah, I did," I said, startled to discover I'd been talking out loud.

"You sure were dumb!" Luanne said, starting to laugh.

"Well, not as dumb as you were!" I replied. "I remember when you thought that a car would blow up if you left the engine running!"

At this point Luanne had stopped laughing and turned bright red.

"Well, I remember when you . . ."

CAROL CREASER

The memories these writers captured were already so tenuous they might have been lost if they hadn't been written down; this wouldn't have happened without the chain of recollections that began with Claire and Arelitsa — with writers borrowing ideas from each other because they were aware of each other's ideas. Conferences and group share meetings set off the chain reaction. There is no more important source of inspiration for writers in the workshop than other writers' pieces, no single more important kind of reading. When the context is right — when kids can choose their own topics and share what they've written — other students respond to the authentic voices and information by borrowing what captivates them to create voice and information of their own.

Borrowing Technique

When the context is right, eighth graders make all kinds of amazing discoveries. Kelli discovered . . . asterisks. During one morning's reading workshop she brought me a novel, opened it, pointed, and asked, "What are these? What are they supposed to do?" They were three asterisks side by side, showing a shift in time and place. I explained, and Kelli nodded and crawled back under her desk to continue reading.

The next week in writing workshop she submitted a piece to me to edit about accidentally breaking Heather's nose while playing raquetball at the Y. Five times in the course of the narrative, correctly albeit heavy-handedly, Kelli had inserted three asterisks side by side — just as she later learned how to use a double dash and a colon, not from me but from the authors whose novels and poetry she read.

Mike took a similar lesson to the extreme. He is a good editor, one of those eighth graders who had already conquered most issues of usage, punctuation, and transcription. He submitted a narrative for me to edit that contained some arresting peculiarities. Every line of dialogue was enclosed in single quote marks instead of doubles, and there were all these peculiar misspellings. Words that should have begun with an *f* started in *ph. Horror* and *sailor* ended in *-our.* Then I remembered what Mike was reading: the *Dr. Who* series by Terrence Dicks, published in England. Much of the print he had seen in the previous month was spelled and punctuated in the British fashion.

Kelli and Mike taught me another facet of the experience Frank Smith calls "reading like a writer" (1983). Because they write they notice the techniques of other writers and try them out for themselves. Sometimes when I'm reading I find myself stopping in the middle of a line to note the spelling of a word I'd drafted that day. And then I shift right back into reading like a reader, becoming caught up in the story again. I didn't learn everything I know about writing mechanics or techniques through the osmosis of reading, and neither do students. But an interesting and important range of skills and devices becomes apparent to readers who write. Kids demonstrated the range in their evaluation conference comments.

Robbie learned from *Ask for Love and They Give You Rice Pudding* by Bradford Angiera and Barbara Corcoran. He borrowed from them for a short story: "I'm using the same format. It's like a journal, written right as it's happening, present tense instead of past." Rachel learned from Susan Beth Pfeffer. She said, "I'm trying to put more descriptions of thoughts and feelings into my pieces. I notice Pfeffer doing this all the time, especially with Lynn in *About David.* And I'm trying to give personalities to all the characters in my stories." Scott learned from me. "In my poetry," he remarked, "I've noticed how I'm not just putting in any word that will rhyme. I'm putting in rhyming words that make sense like you do and using that trick you taught me of brainstorming through the alphabet all the words that'll rhyme with the one I want." Suzy learned from the dialogue in Wilson Rawl's *Where the Red Fern Grows.* She told me, "It sounds so natural, his dialogue. I'm trying to imitate the way people talk in his books, with all the pauses and rhythms." Bean learned from the poetry of Richard Sparks, trying in his own pieces "to stick little jokes in here and there, even in serious pieces, and to exaggerate just enough to make real life even funnier."

Mike learned words. All through eighth grade he borrowed single words from other writers. He was one of the kids who borrowed "defunct" from E. E. Cummings. He also borrowed Cummings' use of negative prefixes and running together of words. "Starunlight" and "undeath" were two of Mike's creations. From Robert Frost and "Dust of Snow" he cadged a verb. Mike's "Snow" poem concluded with the couplet:

Snow is a precipitation that is sometimes rued
But it always puts me in a better mood.

And Hilary learned enjambment, the running over of a sentence from one verse into another. In his poem "Double-Play" Robert Wallace shows the seamless grace of a baseball double-play by using enjambment to straddle the verses. Hilary liked the effect so much she borrowed it to show the seamless cycle of the seasons.

Changes

Leaves on a tree,
blowing endlessly.
As I watch, they blow away
turning into winter day,
turning all the water into

frost on the windowsill;
I take it in my head to fill,
making designs
to mix my mind,
until

it starts to melt after hours and hours
of sun bringing springtime flowers.
Birds are singing their springtime songs.
The apple trees blossom but not for long,
as

soon the blossoms blow away,
turning into summer day.
The beaches fill up fast;
my heart knows this will never last
when

temperatures quickly go down;
green turns into brown.
Leaves on a tree,
blowing endlessly.
As I watch they blow away
turning into winter day.

HILARY SMITH

There is one other kind of borrowing, beyond genre, topic, and technique, that I haven't touched on. It's more nebulous, but I catch glimmers. It is the way literature permeates the lives of kids who write and read. They borrow from their reading not just for their writing; the ways they walk, talk, and look at the world are subtly altered. Literature seeps into their waking hours — and their sleeping hours, too. I laughed when I read Jane's latest letter to me. She began by telling me about her book, then went on to describe the dream she'd had the night before:

I had just got to a weird part in my book, about a weird house. Suddenly, that night I dreamt I was in this house.
The house was big and creepy. It looked just the way I'd pictured it in reading class. So I started to go up the stairs. I looked up and saw my friend Hilary Smith. She was a ghost. I was really scared now.

So I ran into a room that had candles all around it. It was a strangely shaped room. Over in the corner was a rocking chair. The chair was the very one Mrs. Tomgallon's ancestor died in. (In the book, Mrs. Tomgallon is the woman who owns the house.)

It started to give me the creeps because I was going to have to sleep in that room. I put on my nightgown and got in the cold bed. As I blew the candles out the windows were rattling, the bed was shaking, and . . .

"Jane! Get up! Time to go to school!" It was my mother.

Ms. Atwell, I walked into my book.

Jane walked into her book because their classroom and their lives are filled with literature; in Don Graves's phrase, these eighth graders are surrounded. The interactions between kids and all this literature take a very particular shape, one formed by Mary Ellen Giacobbe's three-part formulation. Students adopt other writers' ways because they write and read in a classroom where they have plenty of *time* to do both, where they can *choose* what they'll write and read, and where they give, receive, and hear plenty of *response* to printed texts. Every genre, topic, theme, and technique becomes fair game, both to read and to write, because I finally dismantled two sets of barriers, those separating reading and writing and those separating literature and kids. We lost "the mystique of authorship" — not a great loss — and gained its joys. When kids write in a genre, address a theme, or try a technique, they own it.

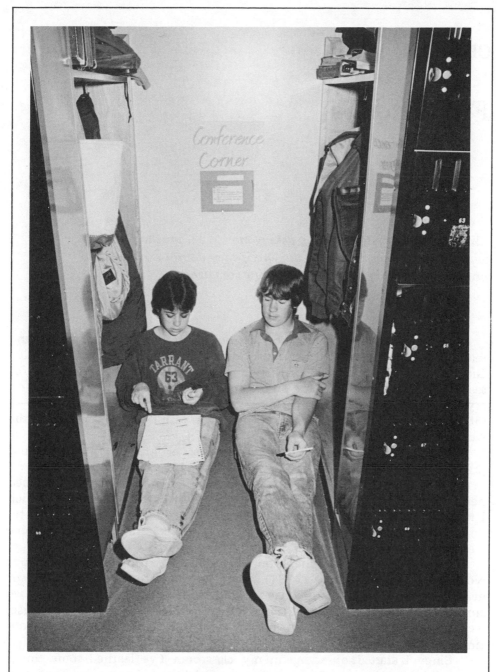

In a conference corner, Kelli tells Allan her story.

CHAPTER 11

Five Stories

*"What do you want, they keep asking me . . . I want them to do
what I do not expect them to do, and if they do not do what I do
not expect them to do I must be failing somewhere."*
Donald Murray

In the middle two sections of this book I defined in detail writing and
reading workshops: what I do, what kids do, and why. I quoted Mary Ellen
Giacobbe's formula of time, ownership, and response as my maxims for
teaching, stressed the need for predictability and routine, and elaborated on
my hard-earned dictums for teaching writing and reading. In short, the evolution to which I referred in the opening pages wasn't always apparent in the
workshop chapters.

In the Middle is about one moment in my evolution — my beliefs and
practices based on what I know now about teaching and learning. What I do
in my classroom next year will not look exactly like the classroom I described
here. New observations and insights will amend theory; the process by which
I translate theory into action will change. The agents for change are my students. The classroom itself becomes an evolving text — a communal scribble
we revise together.

In one of his best articles Don Graves warns writing teachers that our
worst enemy is orthodoxy (1984). When we teach to someone else's — or
even our own — rules about what we and students can and cannot do, we
surrender authority and abrogate our responsibilities as professionals. Worse,
we stop learning. Graves says orthodoxy is a fate we avoid as long as we continue to write and to observe and learn from students' learning.

Since I started observing in my classroom I've learned some things
about eighth graders, chief among them that eighth graders are not a separate
species I can characterize through the tunnel of orthodoxy. My students approach written language expecting the same sense and satisfactions as I do, as
all literate humans do. Harste, Woodward, and Burke recently wrote that
there are "no developmental stages to literacy but rather, only experience,
and with it fine-tuning and continued orchestration" (1984, p. x). Eighth
graders continually fine-tune and orchestrate their uses and views of written
language, and so do we all, ages three to ninety-three. As a teacher of eighth

graders I'll continue to give students the conditions they need to fine-tune and orchestrate: lots of time to write and read, freedom to make choices, and chances to talk with others about the choices they make. This is the bedrock on which my beliefs about literacy learning and teaching are founded. Beyond it, I'm not sure what any of us will do next. And this is the sheer joy of it. I will be surprised every day I teach.

As a final word about orthodoxies Graves wrote, "Orthodoxies make us tell *old stories* about children at the expense of the new stories that children are telling us today" (1984, p. 193). As my final word about eighth graders I have five stories to tell, stories of wonderful surprises of the last year when kids did not do what I expected. Each celebrates empowered and literate eighth graders. I hope each points the way for you to listen to the stories your students are telling you today.

$$* \quad * \quad * \quad * \quad *$$

Tom's mother warned me in August that Tom wasn't going to be an enthusiastic writer or reader, and she was right. But he was wildly enthusiastic about the out-of-doors. Just as soon as I knew his interests I started feeding Tom books about the natural world. It didn't take long for him to begin finding books of his own. One was *Cache Lake Country* by John Rowlands. Tom and I wrote back and forth about the book in his reading journal.

11/22

Dear Ms. Atwell,

I finished *Cache Lake Country* last night and I think its the best book I've ever read. It tells every little detail about the wilderness. Its so descriptive, it tells about every little sight, sound or smell. For instance how a squirrel turns a mushroom around while its eating it. I saw a squirrel do it Saturday. Its wonderful!

Tom

11/23

Dear Tom,

My hunch is *Cache Lake Country* is a book you'll remember for years and come back to. It's such a great feeling when a book has this effect — when an author speaks to us so clearly and informatively about something we love. This happens to me a lot with Donald Murray's writing. He describes the experience of writing — all the pains and pleasures. Sometimes I have the squirrel-mushroom sensation with Murray's stuff. I'll suddenly see exactly what he was describing in my real world, in kids' writing or friends' or my own . . .

Ms. A.

11/24

Dear Ms. Atwell,

Your absolutely right about everything. A matter-of-fact my father liked the book so much he gave it to me for Christmas! And I have tried to make some "baking powder" can lanterns that are in *Cache Lake Country*. They look kind of sloppy but I got the idea . . .

Tom

Rowlands' descriptions of his wilderness experiences caused Tom to see things in his real world he never would have seen except through the prism of the book. Tom's world and Rowlands' had intersected. The ring of connections circled wider when Tom wrote another letter about *Cache Lake Country*, this one in writing workshop to John Rowlands, and received a response that placed him squarely at the center of the whole community of writers and readers. The boy who disliked writing and reading discovered that writers and readers are people like him, people who write and read *about something*. Tom had something to say of interest to others; they had something of interest to say to him.

19 Chester Avenue
Boothbay Harbor, Maine 04538
November 29, 1984

John J. Rowlands
c/o W. W. Norton & Company, Inc.
New York, New York 10010

Dear Mr. Rowlands:

I'm a thirteen-year-old boy and live in a rural, shore-line town in Maine.

I have just finished reading your *Cache Lake Country* book. I think it's wonderful.

A lot of information is always helpful, but when you know what the information is talking about, it's even more helpful! I liked the way you used yourself and your experiences. I also liked the different methods you showed, like how to catch mice or your "cellar refrigerator."

A couple of weeks ago, while I was out hunting, I saw a red squirrel sitting on a log eating a mushroom, just the way you described it, twirling it around. It was really fascinating.

I also made some "candle lanterns" out of baking soda cans. They don't look too good, but they work.

I'm wondering one thing: where is Cache Lake and its country?

Sincerely,
Tom Apollonio

Mr. Tom Apollonio
19 Chester Avenue
Boothbay Harbor, Maine 04538

Dear Tom Apollonio:

Your fine letter addressed to John J. Rowlands has just come to my attention. You did not receive an answer from him because, sadly for us all, he died in 1972. I do know that he would have liked your letter enormously — perhaps especially your story of seeing the red squirrel eating the mushroom.

As to where Cache Lake country is, that is an open question. I suspect he made it up out of all his wilderness experience, but there are those who think it is in Ontario, north of Georgian Bay. I have enclosed a copy of the map of the area near a town called Cache Bay. Perhaps it is there. Others say they think it is in northern Minnesota. If you want to make sure, you can write his daughter as follows: Mrs. Hope R. Brackett, 365 Atlantic Avenue, Cohasset, Mass. 02025. If anyone knows, she will.

I want to add also that you write very well yourself and I urge you to keep reading and writing (reading makes writers) and some time, in the not very distant future, when you are a little older, perhaps you will try a book and send us the manuscript. We are always eager for good books about the outdoors, life in the woods, life on the seacoast, or anything you may want to try.

Sincerely,

Eric Swenson
Eric P. Swenson
Vice Chairman
Executive Editor

EPS:ec
enc.

* * * * *

One day in May we were sitting around reading in readers' workshop. Everyone, as usual, was reading something different. I was reading Eudora Welty's *One Writer's Beginnings* and was struck by this passage:

Ever since I was first read to, then started reading to myself, there has never been a line read that I didn't hear. As my eyes followed the sentence, a voice was saying it silently to me . . . It is to me the voice of the story or poem itself. The feeling that resides in the printed word reaches me through the reader voice. I have supposed, but never found out, that this is the case with all readers — to read as listeners — and all writers, to write as listeners. By now I don't know whether I could do either one, reading or writing, without the other (1984, p. 11).

I read the passage once, twice, and again, listening and pondering. When I don't like what I'm reading — or what I have written — it's usually because I don't hear a voice in the piece. That's when I put down the book, or push my drafts aside and try it again. I marked the section in *One Writer's Beginnings* and moved on.

That afternoon David wrote to me in his reading journal. Echoes of Welty's voice, of "the feeling that resides in the printed word," reverberated anew. Eudora Welty, David and I were in on something together: we all three were members of the same club (Smith, 1983). David had written:

> During in-school suspension [his second suspension of the school year] I read two books, both by Jim Kjelgaard, one *Lion Hound*, the other *Big Red*. I liked *Big Red* best because the writing got me really into the book. Like sometimes I read a book and just see pages. But when I read a *good* book I see right through the pages and into the story. You know what I mean? I feel it. I can hear the voice.

*   *   *   *   *

In seventh grade, when Trevor could choose his own books he chose Tolkien and only Tolkien. In the first months of eighth grade he chose . . . Tolkien. In our letters in his reading journal Trevor talked about plot and I talked about how Tolkien had written *The Lord of the Rings*, helping Trevor discover that the trilogy was *authored* — that there was a man behind the books making choices as authors do. In letters to me and to his cousin Allan, also an eighth grader, Trevor took his discovery one step further, to the realization that Tolkien was fallible. All of us who write, write well sometimes and other times not so well. Even J. R. R. Tolkien.

11/14/85

Allan,

Sorry I haven't written to you in a while but I have been reading as much as I can when ever I got the chance and it didn't leave me much time to write.

I finished *The Two Towers* Sunday. Near the end of the book I was quite confused because it told in one paragraph that Frodo was fighting a giant spider and then in the next paragraph it would seem to me that a person who had fought the spider before and failed was telling the story. It kept jumping back and forth like that and was very confusing. I would have written like the person who had fought the spider describing the spider at the beginning of the chapter. Then towards the end tell what happened to Frodo.

The end of the book was very suspenseful. And I think it made up for the carelessness in the last two chapters.

On Sunday I also started *The Return of the King*. The beginning of the book was not as good as *The Two Towers* because it didn't continue the ending of *T. T. T.* as well as *T. T. T.* did for *The Fellowship of the Ring* and that is because there is a change of scenes between the book

I just finished and the one I started. And that is what I call starting off on the wrong foot.

Sincerely,
Trevor

11/20/85

Dear Ms. Atwell,

I have finished *The Return of the King*. As you know in a way I was happy to end the series because I could picture Tolkien sitting in his study writing and he is very tired and wants to finish the series. I get that through the way he writes the last book. It doesn't have the same style or flow as the two before.

I think I am going to read a mystery.

Sincerely,
Trevor

*   *   *   *   *

In November 1985, my students participated in Maine's first annual assessment of the educational progress of all fourth, eighth, and eleventh graders in the state. For the language arts section of the test students produced two writing samples, one narrative and the other persuasive, in response to assigned topics. The samples were read by trained cadres of Maine teachers and scored according to six criteria: topic development, organization, supporting details, correct and varied sentence structure and syntax, vocabulary and usage, and mechanics (spelling, punctuation, capitalization, paragraphing, and form). In short, content and mechanics were given equal weight.

I was finishing the last chapter of *In the Middle*, then called "Four Stories," when the test results came back from Augusta. Our eighth graders, in this small school isolated at the end of the Boothbay peninsula, achieved Maine's second highest scores in writing. We were beaten out only by Great Salt Bay, a district where Don Graves, Mary Ellen Giacobbe, and Boothbay Writing Project teachers provided training — so much as far as I'm concerned for George Hillocks' recent "findings" concerning the relative efficacy of writing workshop methods (1986).

Results were reported as percentiles, and fully a fifth of Boothbay's eighth graders scored at the ninety-ninth percentile. This means that twenty percent of our kids did better than virtually every other eighth grader in the state. Almost half of our students scored above the ninetieth percentile; their mean score was at the eighty-seventh percentile. And the results included all the eighth graders — special education, Chapter I, everyone.

Perhaps this is the happiest story of *In the Middle* — not because of the test scores but because of the preparation for the test, all five years of it. Most of my students were third graders in 1980, the first year of the Boothbay Writing Project. Coming up through the grades they had many writing teachers, teachers who learned about writing by writing, reading research, and conducting their own; teachers who came together one by one to finally stand together and say, "This is how we believe writing is learned and should be taught." Students don't become exemplary writers overnight or because of the efforts of one teacher. One teacher at a school can make a difference. Five or eleven or eighteen teachers at one school can move mountains.

*   *   *   *   *

Students who write every day, year in and out, become writers. Something else happens, as well. They become experts at teaching writing. Donald Graves wonders how many Boothbay kids will grow up to become English teachers. I wonder, too. They know things I never learned in methods courses or student teaching. They know exactly how and why a writing workshop works. It can get unnerving — some are already such good writing teachers they could put me out of business in a minute.

In December I received a letter from a teacher who heard a speech I made, returned to his school, and re-formed his language arts program as a writing workshop. Now, he was having problems. He sent me a list of questions and a copy of a checklist he devised for his kids. Students checked off steps as they progressed through each piece of their writing. Over sixty steps were described. I didn't know where to begin by way of response, so I referred the matter to my in-house consultants. I shared the teacher's letter and his concerns in writing workshop, and Alice, Kim, and Michelle volunteered to write a reply:

> Ms. Atwell's 8th Grade Writing Class
> Boothbay Region Elementary School
> Boothbay Harbor, Maine 04538

Dear Mr. _____:

A while ago you wrote to Nancie Atwell and enclosed a copy of the check sheet you use with your writing class. Ms. Atwell is our eighth grade English teacher and she asked us to answer your letter because she didn't know where to begin.

We understand that it is hard for you to go directly from "textbook" English to an attempt at "writing" English. That is probably why your checksheet was so much like a textbook. It tells students what to do, rather than letting them think for themselves.

With your checksheet there is little room for choices. The entire reason we do "writing" English is so we can make our own choices and use our own ideas. Besides, there are few rules about writing a piece. Mostly it is just common sense.

When the writing program was started in our school we were in the third grade and from then on we have always made our own choices as writers. The outline is in our heads. All your students need to remember is: first draft, conference (if needed), second draft, and so on until you are ready to edit. Then — a final. It is that simple.

Judging from your checklist we thought we should explain what a first draft and conferences consist of because you seem to have a lot of steps that are not necessary.

The best way to describe a first draft is as jotting down your ideas as they come. There is no plan. It's just "I think I'd like to write about our camping trip," and then writing down what comes to mind. Pre-writing won't work too well because it doesn't leave much room for choice. Later, in other drafts, you may want to change parts around, etc., using the cut and paste method, which saves extra drafts.

Now a conference. A conference is like a conversation. It's natural. The readers read their pieces and the responders listen and ask questions about parts they can't understand. There are no set questions to ask.

What we do learn of textbook essentials is taught during mini-lessons. Mini-lessons start off the class every day. Ms. Atwell has a new topic all the time. The mini-lesson usually takes about ten minutes. At this time Ms. Atwell explains something to us that will help us to write better. For example, she may teach us some keys to writing good fiction, what homonyms are, spelling demons, etc.

Lastly, if you are unsure as to how to keep each student working at his or her own pace, try this: at the beginning of every class ask each student what he or she will be doing that day. Record what the student tells you. (See the attached example of a status-of-the-class conference record.) If you feel a certain student is behind, work together to set a deadline.

We hope our letter has helped you. Enclosed are some papers which may assist you. Explanations are also included.

Sincerely,

Michelle Murphy
Alice Gilchrist
Kim Soler

The girls made the essential point, one that didn't occur to me when I read through the checklist. The teacher had the very best of intentions. He wanted his students to function as writers in a workshop — to know and do what my eighth grade writers know and do. But he did not have a grasp of the principles underlying the practice. In trying to move away from mastery learning — from what the girls called "textbook English" — without a theory to buttress his movement, his wholehearted and level best was simply another version of mastery teaching.

When a classroom becomes theory in action, more than the outward appearance of the room changes. A cumulation of first-hand experiences — reading, writing, talking, listening, observing, speculating, and tinkering —

changes our perspectives. Because of what we know we can never again look at literacy learning in the old way, as one small step upon another. Instead, in all the ways we teach we acknowledge the varied, rich, and purposeful processes of writing and reading, and the equally various and rewarding ways our students will learn them. We give them the workshop, that predictable environment that is itself an invitation to openendedness and change. And then we dispel the easy, received truths of orthodoxies, welcome students' diverse processes and intentions, and embrace revision as a way of life.

Appendixes

Appendix A

MATERIALS FOR WRITING AND PUBLISHING

I. Paper of different sizes, weights, colors and textures:
   Lined papers (of various sizes, colors, and types)
   Construction paper
   Ditto paper
   Colored bond
   Drawing paper
   Stationery and envelopes (an assortment)
   Graph paper
   Index cards
   Scratch paper
   Poster board and oak tag
   Other (e.g., Post It notes, butcher paper, blank labels, etc.)

II. Writing implements of various sizes, colors, and styles:
    Regular pencils
    Colored pencils
    Ball point pens
    Crayons
    Markers (broad-tipped, fine-tipped, italic, etc.)
    Manuscript and brush pens
    Watercolors, poster paints, and brushes

III. General supplies and equipment:
     Erasers (ink and pencil)
     White-out liquid
     Postage stamps
     Staplers
     Staple removers
     Paper clips and brass fasteners
     Scissors

Transparent and masking tapes
White glue and paste
Rubber cement
Rulers and yardsticks
Paper punches
Rubber bands and thumbtacks
Clipboards
Rubber date stamp and pad
Book display stands or racks
Tape recorder and blank tapes
Overhead projector, transparencies, and markers

IV. Materials for school-based publishing:

Cardboard
Wallpaper
White glue or rubber cement
Vinyl adhesive letters
Lettering stencils
Sewing supplies (needles and dental floss if a sewing machine is unavailable)
Bookbinding tape (cloth or ropestock)
Typewriter
Ditto masters (lined and unlined)
Bulletin boards
Photocopier
Offset printing press
Word processor and printer

V. Resource and reference materials:

Dictionaries and Spellex Spellers (Curriculum Associates, Inc.)
Usage handbooks
Models of standard formats for business and friendly letters
Classroom libraries of encyclopedias and other reference books; literature in a variety of modes (e.g., fiction and non-fiction narratives, poetry, plays, etc.); magazines; etc.
Classroom libraries and displays of student authors' publications
Address file (supplemented by NCTE's *All About Letters* and *P.S. Write Soon*)
A card file of professional publications that feature children's writing

VI. Materials for organizing writing:

File folders or portfolios (at least two per student: daily and permanent)
Within each student's daily folder:
1. A list of topics already written about
2. A list of potential topics
3. A list of editing skills the writer had been taught
Within each student's permanent folder:
1. All drafts of all pieces of that year, filed chronologically
2. Notes from quarterly evaluation conferences

A file cabinet, plastic milk crates, or some other sturdy and permanent
means for storing students' folders

For the teacher's records:

1. A status-of-the-class checksheet (weekly)
2. A conference log (daily or as appropriate)

Trays or boxes for writing ready for editing, publishing, or photo-
copying

A rug for students to sit on together during group sharing times

Appendix B

WAYS BOOTHBAY ELEMENTARY SCHOOL WRITERS
HAVE GONE PUBLIC

A sense of audience — the knowledge that someone will read what they
have written — is crucial to young writers. Kids write better when they know
that people they care about will read their texts. More importantly, through
using their writing to reach out to the world students can learn what writing
is good for. Writing workshop is much more than a method for filling up
writing folders with "pieces." Instead, the workshop is a daily occasion for
students to discover what is significant, what is appropriate for sharing, and
how it might best be shared.

In this context, "publication" takes on many meanings. It includes all the
ways a writer acquires readers beyond the writer and teacher. The following
is a list of ways Boothbay students have acquired readers, ways developed by
writers or teachers in response to occasions that arose in our classrooms. In
some cases the idea for the writing came first: the writer or teacher recognized a publication possibility for a piece-in-progress and said, "Hey — this
could be *a poetry poster for the bulletin board* or *a special letter for grandmother* or *a petition to the principal* or *written on a ditto master and run off
for friends.*" In some cases the idea of the publication came first — the writer
or teacher knew of an option and said, "Why not try writing something for
the new class magazine about family ties or *our school paper* or *the Humane
Society essay contest*?" One of the writing teacher's roles is to help writers
discover how to go public — how to recognize a potential audience for a
given piece — and to share and create new publication options. And another
of our roles is to remember that not everything needs to go public, that there
will be pieces written solely for the expressive purposes of the writer.

In all of this it's especially important that going public is a given. Publication should be frequent and on-going. It should not be an award bestowed
on what we decide is "good" writing. If our class and school magazines are
juried, with selections made by the teacher or the writer's peers, the students
who most need response to finished pieces will never be published, and the
same "good" writers will be published time and again.

1. Individual bound books (personal experience, short stories, content area research, poetry, lyrics, etc.). Mary Ellen Giacobbe's simple book-binding technique, described in Graves (1983, p. 59), requires only cardboard, wallpaper, glue, and dental floss, and the results are sturdy and attractive. Students can easily make their own.
2. Individual pieces handwritten or typed on ditto masters, duplicated, and distributed by the author. Students can write their finals directly on masters and achieve instant publication.
3. Individual pieces photocopied and shared with friends and families. Again, the result is instant publication. It helps to provide a tray or box labelled "To Be Photocopied" so students may submit writing on an as-needed basis.
4. Class magazines — collaborations and collections — typed or written on masters and collated. My monthly class magazines are either themed (e.g., people who taught us but weren't "teachers") or require a specific mode (e.g., poetry or idea writing). Everyone who meets the guidelines of my call-for-manuscripts is published in that magazine.
5. Submissions to the school's paper. *The BRES Reporter*, started in 1980 by two of Susan Stires's resource room students, appears six times each year. It features all kinds of writing from students in grades K–8. *The Reporter* is published on newsprint by a firm that handles high school newspapers; ads from local businesses pay for the costs and every student in the school receives a free copy.
6. Submissions to the eighth grade yearbook. During the past seven springs junior high students have produced and paid for (through sponsors) their own yearbook which includes feature articles, reminiscences, and poetry.
7. Submissions to the local newspaper, including a school news column, feature articles about school events, and poetry.
8. Submissions to trade magazines which publish student writing. (See Appendix *C* for a list of junior high possibilities.)
9. Submissions to writing contests — local, regional, state, and national. Boothbay student writers have won books, plaques, subscriptions, scholarships, a computer, and hundreds of dollars.
10. Intercom communications: notices, poems, songs, and stories shared by students or the principal with the school community.
11. Posters — poetry, announcements, jokes and riddles, and advertisements — for classroom bulletin boards and school corridors.
12. Classroom bulletin board and school corridor displays, *changed frequently*.
13. Displays at public events (e.g., projects featuring writing presented at local fairs and festivals and at the school's annual open house).
14. Enactments or recitations of scripts, speeches, and awards. These include tape-recorded radio plays, videotaped scenes and commercials, short plays, puppet shows, and assembly presentations.
15. Petitions — to the principal, the school board, the local board of selectmen, etc.

16. Correspondence — pen pal letters, letters of inquiry, complaints, greeting cards, postcards, fan letters, messages in bottles, time capsule lists, letters to the editor, etc.
17. Pieces shared in readings in other classrooms (e.g., eighth graders and first graders in pairs reading aloud their favorite pieces of their writing).
18. Pieces shared with classmates in writing conferences and during group share meetings: when all is said and done, the easiest and most essential form of going public.

Appendix C

STUDENT WRITING CONTESTS AND PUBLICATIONS THAT ACCEPT STUDENT WORK

Co-Ed Magazine. Your Space, *Co-Ed* Magazine, 50 West 44th Street, New York, New York 10036. Poetry page. No poem published without a written statement from the author as well as his/her English teacher attesting to its originality. Teacher's statement must be on school stationery. Poets must include their name, address, home phone number, age, grade, and school. No poems are returned.

Cricket. Box 100, LaSalle, Illinois 61301. Ages 6–13. Accepts poetry, stories, and drawings according to contest guidelines provided in the back of each month's issue. Submissions must be accompanied by a statement signed by a teacher or parent assuring originality and that no help was given.

English Journal. 1111 Kenyon Road, Urbana, Illinois 61801. Annual "Spring Poetry Festival" for students and teachers. Rules for submission are published in an autumn issue of *English Journal.*

Kids Magazine. P.O. Box 3041, Grand Central Station, New York, New York 10017. Ages 5–15. Accepts all kinds of student work (short stories, poetry, nonfiction, black-and-white art, puzzles, games). 400-word length limit. Entries should be typed or neatly printed and accompanied by a SASE. Small honorary payments awarded for published work.

Merlyn's Pen. P.O. Box 716, East Greenwich, Rhode Island 02818. Grades 7–10. A new magazine devoted to student writing and drawing. Accepts all types of writing (short stories, poems, sci fi, reviews, essays, scripts, interviews, even novels). Submissions must state on title page the author's name, grade, and age; home and school address and phone numbers; county; and name of supervising teacher. Include a SASE. Typed work is preferred: 2″ margins and double spaced.

National Council of Teachers of English Promising Young Writers Program. NCTE, 1111 Kenyon Road, Urbana, Illinois 61801. Open to eighth graders; number of nominees per school based on student population. Students must be nominated by February. Each nominee submits a sample of his/her best writing and an impromptu theme written under teacher supervision. Applications can be obtained by writing to NCTE. May 1 is the deadline for submitting the two pieces of writing. A maximum of 438 awards are made each year based on state population.

Read Magazine. Xerox Education Publications, 245 Long Hill Road, Middletown, Connecticut 06457. Grades 7–9. Once a year features a special student issue devoted to students' poetry, short stories, plays, and feature articles. Regularly includes students' jokes and poetry.

Reflections. Dean Harper, Editor, Box 368, Duncan Falls, Ohio 43734. Attractive poetry magazine published by Duncan Falls Junior High students. Accepts poems by students from nursery school to high school. Manuscripts may be handwritten, if legible. Authors include name, age, school, address, and teacher's name in upper right-hand corner of ms. Include a SASE and a statement signed by author and teacher or parent attesting to the originality of the poetry. Acceptance is normally made within 10 days. Payment is a copy of *Reflections.*

Scholastic Writing Awards Program. 50 West 44th Street, New York, New York 10036. Junior Division (Grades 7, 8, 9) contest features essays, poetry, short stories, and dramatic scripts. Entries must be prepared in accordance with current rules and accompanied by an official entry blank. Deadline for submissions is January of each year. Cash awards.

Scholastic Scope Magazine. 50 West 44th Street, New York, New York 10036. Grades 7–12. Regularly publishes students' poems, stories, plays, "mini-mysteries." Entries should be typed or neatly printed and accompanied by a note certifying originality and signed by the student and teacher or parent. Send entries in care of "Student Writing" or "Mini-Mysteries." (Written for adolescents who read at fourth–sixth grade level.)

Scholastic Voice Magazine. 50 West 44th Street, New York, New York 10036. Grades 7–12, with an emphasis on materials written for grades 8–10. Publishes students' poems and stories of under 500 words and features frequent writing contests on specific themes. Entries should be typed or neatly printed and accompanied by a note certifying originality and signed by the student and teacher or parent. Send entries in care of "Your Turn."

Stone Soup. Box 83, Santa Cruz, California 95063. Ages up to 15. The entire magazine is devoted to student work: stories, poetry, personal essays, art work, and photographs.

Young Miss Magazine. "Through Your Eyes . . ." 685 Third Avenue, New York, New York 10017. Poetry page. Authors accompany submissions with a statement attesting to originality. Also "Youth Beat," where readers speak their own minds.

Teachers should also alert principals, superintendents, and language arts coordinators to pass on all notices of writing competitions and student publishing opportunities (notices that are often tossed out), and should keep an eye out for local and state writing contests (e.g., competitions sponsored by local newspapers, civic organizations, teachers' organizations, NCTE affiliates, etc.).

Appendix D

KINDS OF WRITING THAT HAVE EMERGED IN
BOOTHBAY'S WRITING WORKSHOPS

The following is a list of the kinds of writing that have turned up in Boothbay Elementary classrooms since teachers began allowing students to choose their own topics and modes. The list goes well beyond the ubiquitous personal experience narrative. When students have chances to read different kinds of writing and when teachers introduce new genres in conferences and mini-lessons, writers begin to identify and explore many purposes for their writing. Writing becomes a sensible activity appropriate to a wide range of real-life situations, and teaching and learning about genre take on new significance as we help writers begin to make sophisticated decisions about the requirements of particular genres as well as the appropriateness of particular genres for particular concepts.

Personal Experience Narratives
Fictional Narratives
  Short Stories and Novellas
  (tall tales, sci-fi, historical,
  romance, fairy tales, contem-
  porary realism, etc.)
Autobiographies
Biographies
Essays
Research Reports
Textbooks
Reviews of Books, Records, Plays,
  Movies and TV Shows
News Stories
Reports of Current Events and
  Features
Children's Books
Jokes and Riddles
Games and Puzzles
Captions and Labels
Coloring Books with Text
Cartoons
Annotated Calendars
Advertisements
Poetry
  Ballads
  Limericks
  Rhymed Couplets
  Acrostics
  Counted-Syllable Formats
  Free Verse
  Other Formats

Editorials and Opinions
Parodies
Song Lyrics
Diaries and Journals
Field Journals and Learning Logs
Petitions
Scripts
  Skits
  Plays
  Radio Plays
  Puppet Shows
  TV Commercials
  Speeches
Public Notices
  Posters
  Dittoed Announcements
  Intercom Announcements
Last Will and Testaments
Eulogies
Recipes
Memoranda and Messages
Interviews
Oral Histories
Instructions and Advice
Rules and Regulations
Lists and Notes
Mottoes and Slogans
Scrapbooks (and Accompanying
  Texts)
Yearbook Blurbs
Contest Entries
Time Capsule Lists

Correspondence
  Friendly Letters (to pen pals,
  teachers, friends and relatives)
  Invitations
  To the Editor
  Celebrating Holidays
  Marking Special Occasions
  Requesting Permission
  Letters of Thanks,
  Complaint, Love,
  Application, Sympathy,
  Inquiry, Farewell, Protest,
  Advice, Apology,
  Congratulation

Awards and Inscriptions
Forms (for others to complete)
Computer Programs
Resumés and Cover Letters

Appendix E

WRITING SURVEY

YOUR NAME _____ DATE _____

1.   Are you a writer? _____
     (If your answer is YES, answer question 2a. If your answer is NO,
     answer 2b.)

2a. How did you learn to write? _____

_____

_____

_____

2b. How do people learn to write? _____

_____

_____

_____

3.   Why do people write? _____

_____

_____

_____

4. What do you think a good writer needs to do in order to write well? ____

_____

_____

_____

_____

5. How does your teacher decide which pieces of writing are the good ones?

_____

_____

_____

_____

6. In general, how do you feel about what you write? _____

_____

_____

Appendix F

READING SURVEY

NAME _____ DATE _____

1. If you had to guess . . .
   How many books would you say you owned? _____
   How many books would you say there are in your house? _____
   How many novels would you say you've read in the last 12 months?

   _____

2. How did you learn to read? _____

_____

_____

3. Why do people read? _____

_____

4. What does someone have to do in order to be a good reader? _____

_____

_____

5. How does a teacher decide which students are good readers? _____
_____
_____

6. What kinds of books do you like to read? _____
_____
_____

7. How do you decide which books you'll read? _____
_____
_____

8. Have you ever re-read a book? _____ If so, can you name it/them
here? _____
_____
_____

9. Do you ever read novels at home for pleasure? _____ If so, how
often do you read at home (for pleasure)? _____
_____

10. Who are your favorite authors? (List as many as you'd like.) _____
_____
_____

11. Do you like to have your teacher read to you? _____ If so, is
there anything special you'd like to hear? _____
_____

12. In general, how do you feel about reading? _____
_____
_____

Appendix G

FAVORITE ADOLESCENT FICTION

Each June my students look back over the novels they read during their eighth grade year — an average of around thirty — and rate them for me. The scale runs 1–10. I use their ratings as the basis for my shopping list when I restock the classroom library over the summer. The following is a list of the two hundred or so novels that received high ratings (a nine or a ten) from at least three eighth graders. If I were setting up a classroom paperback library, I'd start with these titles.

Douglas Adams	*The Hitchhiker's Guide to the Galaxy* Series
Louis L'Amour	*The Daybreakers; The Sackets; Shadow Riders*
Fran Arrick	*Steffie Can't Come Out to Play; Tunnel Vision*
Jean M. Auel	*Clan of the Cave Bear*
Natalie Babbitt	*Tuck Everlasting*
Alice Bach	*The Meat in the Sandwich*
Betty Bates	*Love Is like Peanuts; Picking Up the Pieces*
Peter S. Beagle	*The Last Unicorn*
Jay Bennett	*The Birthday Murderer; The Dangling Witness; The Executioner; The Long Black Coat; The Pigeon; Say Hello to the Hitman*
Judy Blume	*Deenie; It's Not the End of the World; Then Again, Maybe I Won't; Tiger Eyes*
Lori Boatright	*Out of Bounds*
Frank Bonham	*Cool Cat; Durango Street; The Nitty Gritty*
Mari Brady	*Please Remember Me*
Sue Ellen Bridgers	*Home Before Dark; Notes for Another Life*
Terry Brooks	*Sword of Shannara; Elfstones of Shannara; Wishsong of Shannara*
William Buchanan	*A Shining Season*
Patricia Clapp	*Jane Emily*
Beverly Cleary	*Jean and Johnny; Fifteen; The Luckiest Girl; Sister of the Bride*
Hila Colman	*Accident; Boy Meets Girl; Claudia, Where Are You?; Diary of a Frantic Kid Sister*
Ellen Conford	*Hail, Hail Camp Timberwood*
Barbara Conklin	*P.S., I Love You; Falling in Love Again*
Robert Cormier	*After the First Death; I Am the Cheese; The Chocolate War*
Maureen Daly	*Seventeenth Summer*
Milton Dank	*Game's End*
Paula Danziger	*Can You Sue Your Parents for Malpractice?; The Cat Ate My Gymsuit; Divorce Express; The Pistachio Prescription; There's a Bat in Bunk Five*
Lew Dietz	The *Jeff White* Series
Lois Duncan	*A Gift of Magic; Down a Dark Hall; Chapters; Killing Mr. Griffin; Ransom; Stranger with My Face; Summer of Fear; They Never Came Home; The Third Eye*
David Eddings	*Pawn of Prophecy; Queen of Sorcery; Magician's Gambit; Castle of Wizardry; Enchanter's End Game*
June Foley	*Love by Any Other Name*
Anne Frank	*Diary of a Young Girl*
The Freedmans	*Mrs. Mike*
Paul Gallico	*The Snow Goose*
Jean George	*My Side of the Mountain*

William Goldman	*The Princess Bride*
Bette Greene	*The Summer of My German Soldier*
Shep Greene	*The Boy Who Drank Too Much*
Bruce and Carol Hart	*Sooner or Later; Waiting Games*
Deborah Hautzig	*Second Star to the Right*
Ann Head	*Mr. and Mrs. Bo Jo Jones*
Nat Hentoff	*Does This School Have Capital Punishment?; Jazz Country; This School Is Driving Me Crazy*
John Hersey	*Hiroshima*
S. E. Hinton	*The Outsiders; Rumble Fish; Tex; That Was Then, This Is Now*
Isabelle Holland	*Hitchhike*
Irene Hunt	*The Lottery Rose; No Promises in the Wind; William*
M. E. Kerr	*Gentlehands*
Stephen King	*Christine; Cujo; Pet Sematary*
Jim Kjelgaard	*Lion Hound; Savage Sam; Big Red; Irish Red; Outlaw Red; A Nose for Trouble*
Harper Lee	*To Kill a Mockingbird*
Madeleine L'Engle	*The Arm of the Starfish; Meet the Austins; The Moon by Night; A Ring of Endless Light; A Swiftly Tilting Planet; The Young Unicorns; A Wind at the Door; A Wrinkle in Time*
Ursula K. LeGuin	*A Wizard of Earth Sea; The Tombs of Atvan; The Farthest Shore*
Robert Lipsyte	*The Contender; One Fat Summer; Summer Rules; Summer Boy*
Jack London	*Call of the Wild; White Fang; Sea-Wolf and Other Stories*
Lois Lowry	*Autumn Street; Find a Stranger, Say Good-bye; A Summer to Die*
Doris Lund	*Eric*
Mary MacCracken	*Lovey; A Circle of Children*
Kevin Major	*Hold Fast*
Harry Mazer and Norma Fox Mazer	*The Last Mission; The Island Keeper; Snowbound; The Solid Gold Kid; Taking Terri Mueller*
Farley Mowat	*Never Cry Wolf; The Dog Who Wouldn't Be*
Barbara Murphy and Judie Wolkoff	*Ace Hits the Big Time*
Walter Dean Myers	*Fat Sam, Cool Clyde, and Stuff; Hoops; Won't Know Till I Get There*
Robert Nathan	*Portrait of Jenny*
Joan Lowery Nixon	*The Kidnapping of Christina Lattimore; The Séance*
Sterling North	*Rascal; The Wolfling*
Robert C. O'Brien	*Z for Zachariah*
Scott O'Dell	*Kathleen, Please Come Home; Zia*
Zibby Oneal	*The Language of Goldfish*
Francine Pascal	*Hanging Out with CiCi; My First Love and Other Disasters*

Katherine Paterson	*Bridge to Terabithia*
Ira Peck	*Midway*
Richard Peck	*Close Enough to Touch*
Stella Pevsner	*And You Give Me A Pain, Elaine*
Susan Beth Pfeffer	*About David; The Beauty Queen; Marly the Kid; A Matter of Principle; Starring Peter and Leigh*
Wilson Rawls	*Summer of the Monkeys; Where the Red Fern Grows*
Willo Davis Roberts	*Don't Hurt Laurie!*
Arthur Roth	*Against Incredible Odds; The Castaways; The Iceberg Hermit; Trapped; Two for Survival*
Marilyn Sachs	*Class Pictures; A Summer's Lease; Fourteen; The Bus Ride*
J. D. Salinger	*The Catcher in the Rye*
Judith St. George	*Haunted*
William Sleator	*Blackbriar; House of Stairs; Into the Dream*
Robert Specht	*Tisha*
Todd Strasser	*Friends Till the End; Rock 'n' Roll Nights*
J. R. R. Tolkien	*The Hobbit; The Lord of the Rings; The Silmarrilion*
Mark Twain	*Huckleberry Finn; A Connecticut Yankee in King Arthur's Court; Tom Sawyer*
Anne Tyler	*Dinner at the Homesick Restaurant; Searching for Caleb*
Cynthia Voigt	*Building Blocks; Dicey's Song; Homecoming; Tell Me if the Lovers Are Losers; Solitary Blue*
Jean Webster	*Daddy-Long-Legs; Dear Enemy*
Barbara Werbsa	*Tunes for a Small Harmonica*
Rob White	*Deathwatch; Frogmen; The Survivor*
Paul Zindel	*Pardon Me, You're Stepping on My Eyeball; The Pigman; The Pigman's Legacy; The Undertaker's Gone Bananas*

Appendix H

DIALOGUE JOURNALS ABOUT READING

When my eighth graders recently read through their dialogue journals — sets of correspondence between me and each reading student — over 150 kinds of talk emerged. All of the talk of our letters is personal and contextual. In other words, what I say in my half of the dialogue journal comes from my knowledge of how a student reads and thinks, of what the student knows. My responses grow from what I've learned about a reader and how I hope to move the reader's thinking. In general my comments do three things, to *affirm*, *challenge*, or *extend* the reader's thinking. These comments take various forms: gossip, questions, recommendations, jokes, restatements, arguments, suggestions, anecdotes, instruction, and "nudges."

I'm still learning how to authoritatively and helpfully respond to my students' letters about their reading. So far I've learned some crucial lessons. In brief:

1. As Toby Fulwiler reminds teachers, the subject of an academic journal is not "I," as in a diary, but "I-it," the relationship between the student and the subject at hand. In this case the subject is books, authors, reading, and writing. The purpose of the letters is not to invite kids' personal problems or offer counsel.

2. Readers' most perfunctory letters to me were responses to letters that read like a teacher's manual. When I bombarded kids with teacher questions, I turned the dialogue journals into a test. One good, thoughtful question is more than enough.

3. I received students' most interesting letters when I responded as a curious human being, asking about something I really wanted to know, but also when I leveled with readers about my own experiences, tastes, and opinions, sharing freely and frankly, agreeing and disagreeing.

4. The letters were conceived as first-draft chat, not polished pieces of writing. I make no corrections on students' letters, but I do comment if I'm having trouble reading them.

5. Everyone keeps a dialogue journal and everyone writes in his or her own log at least once a week as the bare minimum for passing the course.

6. Grades are based on fulfillment of this requirement as well as depth of response, use of classroom independent reading time, and progress made toward a few, individual goals set at the beginning of each quarter.

Kinds of Talk About Books

I. How the Author Wrote

- Topic: What was the book about?
- Description and Detail: Could we see it happening? Feel it? Hear it? Too little description? Too many details?
- Dialogue: Is the talk realistic, full of voice? Could we hear the characters' voices? Too much dialogue? Too little?
- Lead: How did the author bring readers into the story?
- Conclusion: How did the author leave readers? Was the ending satisfying?
- Flashbacks and Foreshadows: How the author used shifts in time and why.
- Humor/Sadness: Did you laugh? Cry? Why?
- Setting: Where and when did the story take place?
- Specific Information: what the reader learned about the world through the narrative.
- Character Development: How were the characters' actions, thoughts, and feelings depicted? Were they believable? Could the reader enter the characters' hearts and minds and see through their eyes?
- Main Characters: Who are they? What makes a main character a main character?

- Titles: Was it appropriate? Was it a grabber?
- Realism: Could the reader believe in this plot? In these characters? Did it matter?
- Suspense: Did the reader wonder what would happen next?
- Action: Was there enough happening to hold a reader's interest? Too much action and not enough character development?
- Theme: What was the author showing about life and living through the story?
- Formula: Could the reader tell too easily what was going to happen in this book?
- Conventions: Ex: Did the reader notice all the extremely short paragraphs in *Sooner or Later*? Why did the Harts write this way?
- Information: Were there enough specifics about character, action and setting in this book? Too many?
- Brevity/Length: Was this book too long? Too short?
- Narration: Who told the story? Was it first person? Third person? Why this point of view? Did the author switch between narrators? To what effect?
- Grace of Language: Did the sentences flow? Were they choppy? Did the reader notice him- or herself thinking about how well particular lines were written? Metaphors? Imagery?
- Plot: Did the story hold together? Ring true? Go on and on? Come to a point?
- Epigraphs and Epilogues: How were these special introductions and conclusions used, and to what effect?
- Prefaces and Introductions: How used, and to what effect?
- In-Jokes: Did the reader pick up on X?

II. The Author

- Speculations on or accounts of the author's process
- Titles of other books by a particular author, including sequels
- Comparisons with other books by this particular author
- Drawing on biographical information on the author or the author's published comments on his/her work to open up the text
- Idle gossip about the author
- Ways authors use elements of their own knowledge and lives in their fictions
- Other ways authors might have researched their subjects (for example, reading a particular kind of fiction)
- Finding authors' addresses and initiating correspondence
- Reviews of an author's works
- New releases by particular authors
- Similar books (in terms of topic or theme) by other authors

III. Concepts of Genre and Mode

- Novels (What makes a novel a novel?)
- Short stories (What makes a short story a short story?)

- Poetry (What makes a poem a poem? In what ways does poetry differ from prose?)
- Fiction and Non-Fiction (How do we classify?)
- Autobiography
- Biography
- History
- Science Fiction/Fantasy
- Adventure
- Animals and Wildlife
- Kids' Lives and Problems
- Love Stories and Romances
- Humor
- Westerns
- Sports
- Urban Life
- Horror/Gothic/Supernatural
- Historical Fiction
- Movie/TV/Book Tie-Ins
- Death and Dying
- Mystery/Suspense
- War and Espionage
- Other kinds of writing one might try to read

IV. The Reader's Process

- Skimming and skipping: How to and to what effect
- Abandoning: How and when a reader makes this decision
- Re-reading particular parts of a book
- Re-reading whole texts: Reasons for; differences noted a second time through
- Planning ahead: Anticipating reading a particular book
- Predicting: Imagining what will happen next
- Revising: Considering other ways the author might have written
- Length of time it took to read a particular book
- Reading "easy" books, and why
- Strategies when a book is difficult (and too difficult)
- Where a book was read
- When a book was read
- How the reader is learning about himself/herself as a reader; about writing, about reading, about books
- How the reader learned to read
- How the reader decides what to read
- Whether the reader buys/owns/collects books
- Problems a reader is encountering and possible solutions

V. The Reader's Affect

- How the book made the reader feel
- What the book made the reader think
- Connections between a book and the reader's own life

- What the reader thinks that he/she didn't think before
- The reader's degree of involvement with the characters and their actions
- Comments about other readers' reactions
- What the reader learned/learned about through the story
- What the reader liked/didn't like about the book
- Best and worst aspects of a book
- Readers' various rating scales and how the rating systems work

VI. The Reader's Own Writing

- What the reader is writing and how it's coming
- Ideas for current and future pieces of writing
- Ways the reader might use (or has used) elements of others' writing in his/her own
- Connections and comparisons between an author's style or subjects and the reader's

VII. Recommendations

- Whether a book is worth recommending
- Others who might enjoy a particular book
- Reactions of other readers to a particular book
- Titles of other good books by this author or dealing with a similar subject or theme
- Names of good authors
- Titles of good books
- Arranging to borrow, lend, and return books
- Where to find a particular book
    other classrooms
    other students
    the town library
    the school library } where to find appropriate titles within
    good bookstores   } these collections

VIII. Book Publishing

- How a book is published
- What editors do
- What agents do
- Advances and royalties
- Remaindering
- First editions
- How and when hardcovers become paperbacks

IX. The Letter Writer's Style

- When necessary, comments on conventions:
    legibility
    punctuation   } all elements that affect the
    spelling   } readability of the letters
    spacing of words and letters }

how to indicate titles of books (caps and an underline) and titles of
stories and poems (caps and quotes)
● When necessary, comments on content:
too "book-reportish"; too much recounting of plot (boring if the
teacher has read the book in question; maddening if it's a book
the teacher anticipated reading)
too brief (postcards rather than letters)
unclear as to the reader's meaning

X.   Miscellaneous Residue

● Format
appropriateness of jacket copy
appropriateness and effectiveness of cover and other illustrations
about-the-author information
copyright date
size of type
length of chapters
index
table of contents
● Books vs. movies, plays, and television programs based on books
● Anecdotes about readers' own lives and experiences, and jokes, cartoons,
and drawings

Appendix I

STRATEGIES FOR INTRODUCING WRITING PROCESS
IN YOUR SCHOOL

In the summer of 1985, Mary Ellen Giacobbe and I were joined on
Martha's Vineyard by forty teachers, veterans of graduate courses we had
taught in other summers. All the returnees had successfully implemented
writing process in their classrooms. Many had helped implement writing
process in their schools and districts. One afternoon they talked about what
they had done to introduce process instruction to skeptical colleagues, administrators, and local parents. This is an elaboration of the list they created.
Writing teachers interested in recruiting others may want to consider these
strategies. The advice is grounded in successful — and sometimes not-so-
successful — firsthand experience. The measures make sense, and they work.

1. To be at all credible, before trying to convert anyone else you must put
writing to work in your own classroom — so you can speak from your
experience, and so you can show others what a writing workshop looks
like. Close your door and begin. Then open the door to visitors — colleagues, parents, administrators.

2. Write a concise description of your classroom program, one that outlines what you do, what kids do, and why. This plan is for you, to clarify your thinking. It's also a document you can show others.

3. Begin to gather evidence that will lend authority to your program: quotes from writers, researchers, and theorists; research findings; accounts of successful practices; samples of students' writing. Be prepared to demonstrate or articulate your evidence.

4. Talk with other teachers about what's going on in your classroom. Share pieces of your kids' writing and anecdotes that demonstrate kids' abilities. Keep the focus on students' fascinating behaviors and accomplishments, not yours as their teacher. Educators are usually intrigued by stories of student achievement. They are rarely intrigued by colleagues' accounts of their own great practices. You also might comment favorably on good things other teachers are already doing with writing as a way to open up the topic for discussion.

5. Begin to organize a group of teachers willing to try a writing workshop approach. Start slowly with a few interested colleagues. Even one interested colleague is enough. Then you might:

- loan one good book or article that helped you and then *arrange a time to talk* about the reading. It's more likely material will be read if it's kept to a minimum and if something is going to happen afterward.

- make access to writing process books and articles easy. Set up a display or file box in the teachers' room.

- form a study group of teachers that meets regularly after school to talk about current research and practice. Select one or two articles or a chapter from a book and distribute copies a week in advance of the study group meeting. Base discussion on the text and its application to your students and classrooms. When talk digresses, gently steer it back to the text.

- form a writing workshop for teachers that meets regularly after school to write and to share writing. Set it up as you do your classroom, with open topic choice and peer conferences. After group share time, discuss teachers' reactions to the workshop itself: questions, concerns, insights, etc. Whichever kind of group you decide to try, plan if at all possible to meet outside of school, away from beckoning intercoms, ditto machines, piles of student papers, and lesson plan books. Definitely plan to meet for no longer than an hour, and be sure to end the session at the appointed time. Otherwise others will be reluctant to attend the next time around, knowing the group will take a commitment of time most teachers don't have.

- join professional organizations (International Reading Association, National Council of Teachers of English, and their state and local affiliates) so you may receive their journals and keep apprised of professional meetings. Attend professional meetings and take your colleagues with you when conference presenters include someone whose work you know is credible and helpful. By example, I would not want to miss such speakers as Phyllis Arata-Meyers, Carol Avery,

David Bartholomae, Glenda Bissex, Garth Boomer, James Britton, Denise David, Peter Elbow, Janet Emig, Cora Five, Toby Fulwiler, Yetta and Ken Goodman, Dixie Goswami, Jerry Harste, Shirley Brice Heath, Charlotte Huck, Angela Jagger, Nancy Martin, Donna Maxim, James Moffett, Rudine Sims, Susan Sowers, Susan Stires, Stephen and Susan Tchudi, or Art Young; from the University of New Hampshire program, Ellen Blackburn, Mary Ellen Giacobbe, Donald Graves, Jane Hansen, Ruth Hubbard, Jane Kearns, Donald Murray, Tom Newkirk, Linda Rief, Tom Romano, and Tim Rynkofs; from Teachers College of Columbia University, Lucy Calkins, Joanne Curtis, Shelley Harwayne, Martha Horne, and Hindy List.

- tap an outside consultant — again, someone whose work you know is credible and helpful — and use this person as a catalyst who can start the ball rolling. Don't depend on a consultant to "give" your school a writing program. Such attempts rarely work. If you encounter a problem you can't solve once the ball is rolling, tap a consultant who can help you with your specific concern.
- organize your teachers' group as an in-service course. Inquire to your state department of education or local university about participating teachers receiving recertification or graduate credit for their study.
- encourage a group of colleagues to enroll together in a summer school course in writing process. On the East Coast there are excellent programs at the University of New Hampshire, Teachers College of Columbia University, the Bread Loaf School of English of Middlebury College, and Northeastern's Martha's Vineyard Workshops.

6. Begin to convince your administration. Talk to the principal, curriculum coordinator, or department head about what you are doing in your classroom and why. Give him or her one good article at a time and *arrange a time to talk* about each reading. Try to involve administrators in your study group or teachers' writing workshop. Or conduct a demonstration writing workshop for administrators and members of your local school board.

7. Send a letter to your students' parents providing concise, specific information about what their children will be doing and why. Ease their minds that you haven't abandoned skills or rigor. Present your program at the school's open house, using overhead transparencies of students' writing to demonstrate writing process. If possible, present to parents with other teachers from your school so parents see a unified team of committed professionals. During parent-teacher conferences show and discuss students' writing folders and your records of individuals' growth.

8. Keep records, and have students keep records, that will show their growth. Keep track of the concepts and skills you teach in individual conferences. Focus evaluation on individual writers' growth over time.

Appendix J

WHEN A WRITING PROGRAM WORKS

I am leery of listing components of a successful writing program — of reducing the richness and complexity of writing workshop to a handful of "ingredients." Effective teaching is always more than the sum of its parts. But in my own classroom and in the classrooms of successful writing teachers with whom I have worked, I have consistently observed certain principles at work. At all grade levels, K–12, teachers took on similar roles, assuming a new kind of authority as writers, readers, and scholars so their students might become authorities too. Conversely, when writing workshop wasn't going well in a particular classroom it was because something was not happening — students had few opportunities to publish their writing, or the teacher was not able to keep conferences short and see many students, or there were not clearly delineated areas within the classroom for writing and for conferring with peers.

The following are the circumstances I encounter in classrooms where students and teachers are becoming expert writers and helpers. In brief, this is what *is* happening in the best writing workshops.

1. Teachers write and share their writing, processes and products, with their students. They personally experience what they ask of student writers, from finding a topic through going public. Teachers do not require student writers to do anything they don't do themselves as writers. They draw on their personal knowledge of writing when conferring with students. And they read, so they may learn from and help their students learn from the voices and choices of professional authors.

2. Teachers know that students' desire to write comes not from the teacher's techniques for motivating writers (e.g., whole-group "pre-writing activities"), but from teachers' establishment of an environment that encourages writers to discover and act upon their own intentions and interests. Teachers expect all students will write and take responsibility for their writing but offer help when help is needed.

3. Teachers carefully plan the writing environment so students know what to expect and what is expected of them. They establish a regular schedule for writing (Donald Graves recommends allotting at least three hours each week), create predictable procedures for writing time, organize the classroom so it allows for any and all of the activities in which student writers engage (places to confer, select materials, work quietly, etc.) and monitor writers' activity so individual students know their agenda for any given day, and their teacher knows too.

4. Teachers talk to their students about their writing just as they would like their students to talk to each other. In conferences, teachers let their students lead. They listen to the writer and the writing and keep conferences short and to the point. They ask the kinds of questions that will enable writers to consider what they have done and want to do next. In mini-lessons, teachers identify information of potential use or interest to their students and present it authoritatively and succinctly.

5. Teachers put editorial concerns in their proper place. Only after the writer has decided that the content of the writing is set does editing

begin. The first editor of any piece is always the writer, who edits using a pen or pencil different in color from the text. Then the teacher edits and in conference with the writer explains one or two high-priority editorial issues as to their function in the piece at hand.

6. Teachers document. They keep track of what happens in conferences and in pieces of students' writing, noting skills used correctly, skills introduced, changes made between drafts, and other observations. They maintain permanent folders of individual students' writing, dating, collecting, and filing all of each writer's drafts.

7. Teachers evaluate writing for growth over time, basing their judgments on the writing collected in the student's permanent folder. Teachers establish criteria for evaluation and explore and explain areas of success, progress, and concern in conference with the writer.

8. Teachers know that much of the satisfaction in writing comes from others' responses to finished pieces, and they provide writers with options for sharing their writing: as published books or via other modes of class-based publication, with classmates during sharing times, in school newspapers or magazines, on posters or bulletin boards, through correspondence, etc.

9. Teachers know that writers use a wide variety of utensils, materials, and equipment and they provide as large an assortment as possible: different kinds of pens, pencils, and markers; different weights, formats, sizes and colors of paper; stationery and envelopes; lined and unlined ditto masters; staplers, staples, and staple removers; tape and glue; scissors; erasers and white-out liquid; etc.

10. Teachers make use of resources. When something "isn't working," they ask *why*. They consult with their students and with other teachers, and they refer to the mass of published articles and texts currently available on writing process.

References

Alexander, K. L., Cook, M., & McDill, E. L. (1978). Curriculum tracking and educational stratification: Some further evidence. *American Sociological Review, 43,* 47–66.

Applebee, A. (1978). *The child's concept of story.* Chicago: University of Chicago Press.

Atwell, N. (1982). Class-based writing research: Teachers learn from students. *English Journal, 70,* 84–87.

Atwell, N. (1985, March). How *we* learned to write. *Learning,* pp. 51–53.

Atwell, N. (1985). Everyone sits at a big desk: Discovering topics for writing. *English Journal, 74,* 35–39.

Bissex, G. (1980). *GNYS AT WRK: A child learns to write and read.* Cambridge, MA: Harvard University Press.

Blackburn, E. (1984). Common ground: Developing relationships between reading and writing. *Language Arts, 61,* 367–375.

Borg, W. R. (1966). *Ability grouping in public schools.* Madison, WI: Dembar Educational Research Services.

Borg, W. R., Findley, & Bryan, M. (1970). *Ability Grouping.* ERIC Document No. ED 048382.

Britton, J., Burgess, T., Martin, N., McLeod, A., & Rosen, H. (1975). *The development of writing abilities (11-18).* London: Macmillan. (Available through NCTE.)

Calkins, L. M. (1981, November). Presentation at the National Council of Teachers of English annual convention, Boston.

Calkins, L. M. (1983). *Lessons from a child: On the teaching and learning of writing.* Portsmouth, NH: Heinemann.

Calkins, L. M. (1986). *The art of teaching writing.* Portsmouth, NH: Heinemann.

Chute, C. (1985). Interview in *Bittersweet, 8, No. 5.*

Cooper, C. R. (1984). The contributions of writing to thinking and learning. *English Record, 34, No. 1.*

Donaldson, M. (1978). *Children's minds.* New York: Norton.

Emig, J. (1983). *The web of meaning: Essays on writing, teaching, learning, and thinking.* Upper Montclair, NJ: Boynton/Cook.

Fiske, E. B. (1983, September 8). Americans in electronic era are reading as much as ever. *New York Times,* p. 1.

Fry, D. (1985). *Children talk about books: Seeing themselves as readers.* Philadelphia: Milton Keynes.

Fulwiler, T. (1980). Journals across the disciplines. *English Journal, 69.*

Giacobbe, M. E. (1983, July). Presentation at Northeastern University Writing Workshops, Martha's Vineyard, MA.

Giacobbe, M. E. (1984, October). Helping children become more responsible for their writing. *Live Wire.*

Goodlad, J. (1984). *A place called school.* New York: McGraw-Hill.

Graves, D. H. (1975). The child, the writing process, and the role of the professional. In W. Petty (Ed.), *The writing processes of students.* Buffalo: State University of New York.

Graves, D. H. (1978). *Balance the basics: Let them write.* New York: Ford Foundation.

Graves, D. H. (1981, November). Presentation at the National Council of Teachers of English annual convention, Boston.

Graves, D. H. (1983). *Writing: Teachers and children at work.* Portsmouth, NH: Heinemann.

Graves, D. H. (1984). *A researcher learns to write.* Portsmouth, NH: Heinemann.

Halberstam, D. (1984, October 14). Teachers with class. Special to *The Boston Globe*, p. 83.

Halley, H. K. (1982). The bundle. In T. Newkirk & N. Atwell (Eds.), *Understanding writing: Ways of observing, learning and teaching.* Portsmouth, NH: Heinemann.

Harste, J., Woodward, V., & Burke, C. (1984). *Language stories and literary lessons.* Portsmouth, NH: Heinemann.

Harwayne, S. (1984, November). Presentation at the National Council of Teachers of English annual convention, Detroit.

Hillocks, G. (1986). *Research on written composition.* Urbana, IL: ERIC Clearinghouse on Reading and Communication Skills, and the National Conference on Research in English.

Huck, C. (1986, September). Presentation at the Maine Reading Association, Bangor, ME.

Kennedy, X. J. (1984, November). Presentation at the National Council of Teachers of English annual convention, Detroit.

Kozol, J. (1985). *Illiterate America.* New York: Anchor/Doubleday.

Maxim, D. (1986, April). Presentation at the Wiscasset Primary School, Wiscasset, ME.

McQuade, D. (1984, July). Presentation at the Northeastern University Writing Workshops, Martha's Vineyard, MA.

Moffett, J., & Wagner, B. J. (1976). *Student-centered language arts and reading, k–13* (2nd ed.). Boston: Houghton Mifflin.

Murray, D. M. (1980). Questions to produce writing topics. *English Journal, 69*, 69.

Murray, D. M. (1982). *Learning by teaching.* Upper Montclair, NJ: Boynton/Cook.

Murray, D. M. (1983). First silence, then paper. In P. Stock (Ed.), *Fforum: Essays on theory and practice in the teaching of writing.* Upper Montclair, NJ: Boynton/Cook.

Murray, D. M. (1984). *Write to learn*. New York: Holt, Rinehart & Winston.

Murray, D. M. (1985). *A writer teaches writing* (2nd ed.). Boston: Houghton Mifflin.

Newkirk, T. (1982). Young writers as critical readers. In T. Newkirk & N. Atwell (Eds.), *Understanding writing: Ways of observing, learning, and teaching* (pp. 106–113). Portsmouth, NH: Heinemann.

Newkirk, T. (1985). On the inside where it counts. In J. Hansen, T. Newkirk, & D. M. Graves (Eds.), *Breaking ground: Teachers relate reading and writing in the elementary school* (pp. 111–119). Portsmouth, NH: Heinemann.

Paterson, K. (1981). *FLB newsletter, 3, No. 3*. Chicago: Follett Library Book Co.

Plimpton, G. (Ed.). (1965). *Writers at work: The Paris Review interviews* (second series). New York: Viking Press.

Purves, A. (1972). *Literature and the reader: Research in response to literature, reading interests, and the teaching of literature*. Urbana, IL: NCTE.

Rodriguez, R. (1983). *Hunger of memory*. New York: Bantam.

Rosen, H. (1983, September). Speech to the Ontario Council of Teachers of English.

Rosenbaum, J. (1976). *Making inequality: The hidden curriculum of high school tracking*. New York: Wiley.

Rowe, M. B. (1974). Wait — time and rewards as instructional variables, their influence on language, logic, and fate control. *Journal of Research in Science Teaching, 11*, 81–94.

Simmons, J. (1982). The writer's chart to discovery. In T. Newkirk & N. Atwell (Eds.), *Understanding writing: Ways of observing, learning, and teaching*. Portsmouth, NH: Heinemann.

Smith, F. (1971). *Understanding reading*. New York: Holt, Rinehart & Winston.

Smith, F. (1982). *Writing and the writer*. Portsmouth, NH: Heinemann.

Smith, F. (1983, October). The club of readers and writers. Speech to the Maine Reading Association, Bangor, ME.

Smith, F. (1984). *Reading without nonsense*. New York: Teachers College Press.

Sowers, S. (1982). Reflect, expand, select: Three responses in the writing conference. In T. Newkirk & N. Atwell (Eds.), *Understanding writing: Ways of observing, learning, and teaching*. Portsmouth, NH: Heinemann.

Staton, J. (1980). Writing and counseling: Using a dialogue journal. *Language Arts, 57*, 514–518.

Staton, J. Shuy, R., Kreeft, J., & Reed, L. (1982). *Analysis of dialogue journal writing as a communicative event*. NIE-G-80-0122. Washington, D.C.: Center for Applied Linguistics.

Vonnegut, K. *Palm Sunday*. New York: Dell.

Vygotsky, L. (1962). *Thought and language*. Cambridge, MA: MIT Press.

Welty, E. (1984). *One writer's beginnings*. Cambridge, MA: Harvard University Press.

Whitehead, F. (1977). *Children and their books*. London: Macmillan.

Zinsser, W. (1985). *On writing well* (2nd ed.). New York: Harper & Row.

Index